SHAKESPEARE'S
RELIGIOUS BACKGROUND

Shakespeare's
Religious Background

PETER MILWARD

INDIANA UNIVERSITY PRESS

BLOOMINGTON AND LONDON

SECOND PRINTING 1974

Library of Congress catalog card number: LC: 73-77854

ISBN: 0-253-35200-2

MANUFACTURED IN THE UNITED STATES OF AMERICA

Contents

Introduction

It is not uncommon for literary critics to examine masterpieces of literature as works of art existing in themselves, without reference to their historical background, and to regard them – in Jonson's words – as being 'not of an age, but for all time'. Up to a point such an approach is quite justifiable. Masterpieces have a right to be read and enjoyed in themselves, apart from all the apparatus of learning. Precisely because they are masterpieces their literary value remains undiminished by the passing of time, and may even gain added lustre from the varied interpretations of age after age. But they are also human, and composed of human words; and with the passing of time words and meanings, as T. S. Eliot laments in *Four Quartets*, also pass away or become altered beyond recognition. Masterpieces are, moreover, not only 'monuments more lasting than bronze', but also 'abstracts and brief chronicles of the time'. They are as it were eternal moments that pass with time, bound by many threads to the age that gave them existence, and leaving behind them as they pass precious 'intimations of immortality'. Their general meaning may remain intelligible to later generations, so long as their language survives in the world. But the historical associations implicit in their words and phrases are gradually forgotten, until ignorance of their background begets ignorance of their original meaning. What remains may be no more than a husk of this meaning – though the husk itself retains the old power of fascinating new readers. But the kernel of truth within, which derives its life from the temporal flavour of the words, tends to wither and even to disappear.

For this reason the literary critic of past literature needs the assistance of the scholar to explore the full meaning of a masterpiece – in the light of its historical, social, economic, intellectual and religious background. On both sides there is need of humility to recognize human limitations. The critic has to admit that the meaning of past literature is not so obvious as it may seem to a twentieth-century reader. The scholar has to admit that he is ignorant of many factors in a historical situation, without which he cannot give a balanced interpretation of a masterpiece. For critics it is all too easy to judge past literature by present fashion or personal prejudice. Limitations, whether of an individual or of an age, have to be overcome by wide acquaintance with the writings of the past and by the assistance of historical scholarship. But scholarship, too, has its limitations. The further we go back into the past, the scantier become the relevant documents; and even when they exist and are to hand, they are not always accurate or reliable. Even with all the relevant documents, scholars will not always agree in their interpretations of them; and the value of what they say will depend on their sympathy with the age they wish to interpret. The most objective scholar remains a man, subject to personal feelings and preferences; and it is only by perfecting his humanity that he will attain to such objectivity as is possible to a man.

These general considerations have special reference to the study of Shakespeare's plays, which are separated from the present by a gap of four centuries. During this period of time the history of England has been disturbed by a succession of upheavals, such as change the minds of men and the meaning of the words they use. The religious controversies of the Elizabethan and Jacobean ages which overflowed into the Civil War; the political struggles which came to a head in the Revolution of 1688; the social and economic troubles which were comprehended in the agrarian and industrial revolutions of the eighteenth century; the Napoleonic wars at the beginning of the nineteenth century, followed by the prosperity of the Victorian Age; and then the two world wars that have devastated the population and the land in our own century –

all these things have served to cut us off from the age of Shakespeare and from the true understanding of his plays. From the viewpoint of vocabulary alone, many of Shakespeare's words have simply disappeared from the English language. Others have undergone a 'sea-change' into meanings which are the dull opposite of 'rich and strange'. Yet others, while retaining their dictionary meanings, have lost that richness of association which would have been familiar to Shakespeare and his contemporaries. In order to reconstruct their lost meanings and associations, it is not enough to make a study of historical philology, or even to compare the plays with one another and with the literature of the time. It is also necessary to consider the Elizabethan background as a whole, and especially the prevalent conception of man and human life.

Needless to say, this is a task which has by no means been neglected by Shakespearian scholars, past or present. Indeed, the flourishing condition of Shakespearian studies today is largely due to the combined work of Elizabethan historians and literary scholars in devoting their attention to the various aspects of sixteenth-century literature – culminating in the drama of Shakespeare. Their studies reveal not only the universality of his genius, but also the extent to which he is representative of his age and nation; so that it seems there is hardly an aspect of Elizabethan or medieval culture which is unreflected in his plays or poems.

Nevertheless, with all these studies of Shakespeare's background, there is one aspect, by no means the least important, which has been left by scholars in comparative neglect: I mean, the religious aspect, as related to the plays and poems. Many reasons may be given for this neglect. The plays and poems of Shakespeare are of a secular rather than religious nature, and they refer only occasionally to the religious background of his age. In any case, this background is an exceedingly complicated one: it easily deceives the unwary student, while intimidating the more wary with the consideration that 'fools step in where angels fear to tread'. In modern criticism, moreover, there is a prevalent – and no doubt, healthy – tendency to avoid discussing religious issues in literary matters, unless they are explicitly raised by a work of literature. Emphasis is rightly laid, by theologians no less than by literary critics, on the so-called 'autonomy' of literature; and consequently the religious background is often, wrongly, thought to be irrelevant to the literature of the time. But if literature is indeed the record of human thoughts and feelings, and if religion has a deep influence on these thoughts and feelings, one cannot afford to overlook the connection between literature and religion, not only when it appears on the surface, as in Milton's *Paradise Lost*, but also when for some reason it goes underground. It has even been maintained by serious thinkers that individual inspiration, no less than national culture, is religious in origin, and that the character, if not the quality, of a literary work depends in large measure on the religious beliefs of the author.

Whatever may be thought of this general theory, there is no doubt that religion forms an important, if not the most important, part of the Elizabethan background. During the Middle Ages, when religious unity prevailed in the West, the fundamentals of religious faith could be taken for granted; and increasing emphasis was laid on the practice of faith in terms of morality and worship. But as a result of the Reformation, these fundamentals were brought again into the consciousness of men amid the conflicting tenets of Catholics and Protestants concerning the nature of the true Church and the way to eternal salvation. Nowadays many are disposed to shrug off these disputes as narrow-minded and of minimal importance; but in so doing they only reveal their own narrow-mindedness and lack of sympathy with the outlook of the Elizabethans, which was to some extent shared by Shakespeare himself. The power of his tragedies, for instance, depends in large measure on the conviction he shared with his contemporaries that the eternal salvation of one's soul is a matter of utmost concern to everyone. Even today, of course, there are many who retain this deep conviction. But they all too often assume that the difference between Catholics and Protestants in the Elizabethan Age was much the same, at least in matters of doctrine and worship, as it is today – only feelings were then much higher. Thus they fall into the common mistake of 'hindsight', interpreting the past in terms of the present. They forget that in Elizabethan England the Anglican Church, though established by the laws of the realm, was still a novelty, not yet established in the hearts of the majority of the nation, nor possessed as yet of any long tradition. By few it was welcomed as a reformed Church; by others it was accepted either as a necessary means of preferment, or merely to avoid the penalty of the law for non-attendance; by yet others it was strongly opposed, either because it was not sufficiently reformed to the model of Geneva, or because it was reformed in a manner contrary to Catholic tradition.

Older people, like Shakespeare's parents, could look back to a time when the Catholic religion was everywhere observed, when the Latin Mass was celebrated in the churches and the Divine Office chanted in the monasteries, when the spiritual authority of the Pope was recognized no less in England than in France, Spain, and Italy. They could remember the Act of Parliament by which Henry VIII had asserted his novel claim to be 'supreme head' of the Church in England, and the steps he had subsequently taken to strengthen his position by dissolving some 900 religious houses throughout his realm. They could also see the continuing effects of these and other religious changes, which had been initiated by Henry and successively extended by Edward VI and Elizabeth, as contrasted with the condition of England they had known before the changes and during the short-lived restoration of the old order under Mary.

These events are all narrated with more or less detail in histories of sixteenth-century England and in biographies of sixteenth-century personalities. But when it comes to Shakespeare, the representative poet and dramatist of the Elizabethan Age, there descends a strange silence, partly because the poet is himself strangely silent on this matter, partly because it is assumed that he dutifully conformed to the official religion, or else that he was loftily unconcerned with the topic of most concern to the majority of his contemporaries. He is hailed as the national poet of the Golden Age of Queen Elizabeth, riding upon the tide of England's victory over the Spanish Armada. He thus takes his place in that Elizabethan myth which emphasizes the superficial glitter of the period, while overlooking its sordidness, cruelty and misery. Such a romantic view of Shakespeare is a gross distortion of the truth, and is based on mere wishful thinking. However well it may seem to apply to his contemporary, Edmund Spenser, who

magnified the glory of Elizabeth as his Faerie Queene in contrast with the gloom of his Irish exile, it is quite inapplicable to
Shakespeare, who was 'nothing if not critical' of his own age,
and who could see the reality of life at Elizabeth's court
through the disillusioned eyes of courtiers like Essex and
Southampton.

What is needed is a careful analysis of Shakespeare's plays
and poems in precise relation to their religious background in
all its various aspects – Catholic and Protestant, Anglican and
Puritan, religious and anti-religious. In such an analysis it is
not enough to limit one's attention to established facts and
allusions, though on these it is necessary to take a firm stand.
Beyond them lies a penumbra of innumerable hints and
possibilities, of which account has to be taken according to the
extent of the evidence for and against them. They must all be
carefully considered and weighed with one another and with
ascertainable actualities, remembering that certain conclusions can be drawn from a convergence of probabilities. Such
an approach is particularly admissible in the case of one who
is generally recognized as the most enigmatic of poets, who
lived in an age widely regarded as most baffling to historians,
and who wrote in a literary and dramatic style characterized
by ambiguity and simultaneous layers of meaning.

For this reason, it may seem safer to restrict one's attention
to what is certain in the text and background of the plays and
poems, without venturing into the treacherous territory of
conjecture and reconstruction. But such a policy of 'safety
first' is not perhaps the most enlightened or even the most
faithful to the dramatist himself – at least, when it is elevated
into a reason for refusing all but what is absolutely certain.
Particularly in this matter of Shakespeare's religious background, which of its nature exercises a deep, but hidden influence on the human mind, it is hardly wise, or even safe, to
keep resolutely to the superficial level. Rather, in approaching
the deeper, religious levels of the dramatist's meaning, it is all
the more necessary to bear in mind every relevant fact, and
even every probability, both in his dramatic work and in the
religious situation of his time. Different aspects of this situation have indeed been taken up by different scholars in the
past – such as the Catholic or Puritan connections of Shake-

speare, his knowledge of the Bible and the Homilies, his ethical viewpoint, his medieval inheritance; but in such piecemeal studies there dwells a certain danger of disproportion or lack of balance. What is still needed is a general survey of this religious situation in relation to the writings of Shakespeare; with the intention of throwing light not so much on the personal opinions of the dramatist, as on the deeper levels of meaning in his drama.

In recent years two books have been published whose titles seem to promise the fulfilment of this need: *Shakespeare and Christian Doctrine*, by R. M. Frye (Princeton, 1963), and *Shakespeare and Religion*, by G. Wilson Knight (London, 1967). Neither of these books, however, does justice to its title. The aim of the former book is largely negative: to reject the theologizing tendencies of a group of writers referred to as 'the School of Knight', and to reaffirm the predominantly secular meaning of Shakespearian drama. The latter book, by Knight himself, is a collection of scattered essays, rather than an exhaustive study of the subject in question. In any case, the author approaches Shakespeare from a modern rather than an Elizabethan viewpoint. The need, therefore, as I have stated it, still remains unsatisfied: namely, to ascertain precisely how far Shakespeare is influenced by Christian doctrine and in what ways his dramatic and other work reflects the religious currents of his time. In the present volume I have endeavoured to meet this need, by examining one by one the influences of Catholic tradition, of Protestant reform, both moderate Anglican and extreme Puritan, and of the 'atheism' which developed out of the religious disputes of the time, and by going on to outline what may be said of Shakespeare's own ethical and theological viewpoint. There still remains the larger endeavour to correlate all this material on his religious background and the inner meaning of his plays one by one.

In conclusion I must express my indebtedness, first of all to the innumerable scholars and critics, living and dead, whose writings on Shakespeare have assisted me in my work on the present volume. The precise points of my indebtedness I have tried to indicate, so far as possible, in the form of notes – reserving my main text for the discussion of primary material. Secondly, I have a personal debt of gratitude to Professor

T. J. B. Spencer, for having provided me with the opportunity of gathering much valuable material for this study during a sojourn of six months at the Shakespeare Institute, Birmingham, in 1965–6; also to the trustees, the librarians and the staff of the Huntington Library, San Marino, for enabling me to make considerable additions to this material during the summers of 1968 and 1971. Thirdly, I am grateful to all who have encouraged me in various ways and at various stages in the preparation of this volume: to Professor G. Wilson Knight, Dr M. C. Bradbrook, and Mr John Vyvyan in England; to Professor Irving Ribner, Professor Virgil Whitaker, Dr Leland Carlson, and Dr Richard Stensgaard in America; and to my friend and colleague in Japan, Mr Tetsuo Anzai. 'For all, our thanks.'

Sophia University, Tokyo   Peter Milward, S.J.
5 April 1972

I

Family Background

QUEEN ELIZABETH succeeded to the throne of England in November 1558, less than six years before the birth of William Shakespeare in Stratford-upon-Avon. The following January she summoned her first Parliament to meet at Westminster; and it proceeded to reverse the Catholic policy of her half-sister, Mary, in favour of the religious changes brought about during the previous reign of her half-brother, Edward VI. From this time onwards the movement of religion in England was, in fact, though it did not seem so at the time, set in the direction of Protestantism.

During this critical year for the future of England, the authority of the sovereign in ecclesiastical matters was re-affirmed in a new Act of Supremacy, which ratified the breach with Rome made by Henry VIII in 1534. Protestant doctrine and worship were reimposed on the people by a new Act of Uniformity, which recalled the similar Act of Edward VI. Henceforth the English Prayer Book of 1552, with some emendations, replaced the Latin Missal in all churches; and attendance at the new services was made obligatory, under penalty of a fine. Royal Injunctions were added for the removal of altar furniture and vestments, and for the destruction of sacred shrines and images. The official doctrine of the reformed Church of England was later codified in the Thirty-Nine Articles at a meeting of Convocation in 1563 under the supervision of the new Archbishop of Canterbury, Matthew Parker. It was further expounded in two volumes of *Homilies* –

to the first volume, which had been published by Cranmer in 1547, was now added a second in 1563; and these were assigned to be read every Sunday in all churches of the realm, as few priests in the early years had licence to preach.

By these statutes and regulations the traditional religion of England was effectively outlawed, and, as time went on, increasingly suppressed. On the other hand, a new form of religion was introduced, adapted from the teachings of the continental reformers, according to the convenience of the Queen and her government. The Church in England was no longer independent of the State, as it had been up to 1534: it was now a function of the State, under the Queen as its 'supreme governor'. But the mere fact of statutes being passed in Parliament did not mean that they immediately won general acceptance from the people. Religious beliefs and customs are not changed overnight by decrees of Parliament; and this Parliament, which was in fact more Protestant than the Queen herself wished, can hardly be said to have represented the majority of the people. Protestant ideas had already spread through many counties of England, at first surreptitiously under Henry VIII, and later openly with official encouragement under Edward VI. They had gained most ground in those districts which were nearest London and most exposed to continental influence. But Protestantism was as yet by no means the religion of the majority of Englishmen; and the early Elizabethan bishops, who had replaced the Catholic bishops of Queen Mary, were loud in their lamentation over this fact. Typical of many is the complaint voiced by Bishop Sandys of Worcester in 1569: 'I have here long laboured to gain good will: the fruits of my travail are counterfeited countenances and hollow hearts. . . . Hard it is to find one faithful . . . Religion is liked as it may serve their own turn.'[1]

The diocese of Bishop Sandys lay, it is true, in those 'wilder' regions of the country which remained more attached to the 'old faith'. It extended as far as the western district of Warwickshire, which included Stratford-upon-Avon. It is interesting to note that, according to the bishop's report to the Privy Council in 1564, the majority of the gentry were opposed to the religious changes.[2] Around Stratford, in particular, many of the leading families – the Ardens of Parkhall, the Catesbys

of Lapworth, the Cloptons of Stratford, the Middlemores of
Edgbaston, the Sheldons of Beoley, the Throckmortons of
Coughton, the Underhills of Idlicote – were solidly Catholic.
On the other hand, the eastern district of Warwickshire came
under the diocese of Coventry and Lichfield, which showed
less opposition from the gentry to the religious changes.
Coventry was itself a centre for the spread of Protestant ideas.
Here had taken place the only burnings for heresy in the whole
county during the reign of Mary; and the city now became a
centre for the Puritan apostolate of Thomas Lever. To the
south of Coventry were situated the imposing castles of the
Dudley brothers, Ambrose, Earl of Warwick, and Robert,
Earl of Leicester, both of them stout champions of Protestantism. Between their castles and Stratford were the country
houses of two other important Protestant families, the Lucys
and the Grevilles, who wielded influence not only in the
county, but also at court and in Parliament.

As for Stratford itself, the religious situation is not very
clear. It may be doubted whether the religious changes were
welcomed by the townspeople, seeing that here – unlike
London – they were put into effect only after much delay. The
Marian vicar of Holy Trinity Church was replaced in 1560 by
John Bretchgirdle, whose library (as detailed in his will)
affords evidence of Protestant leanings.[3] It was he who baptized William Shakespeare on 27 April 1564. It was, no doubt,
under his supervision that the church was brought into conformity with the new regulations; but after four years he died
of the plague. His successor, William Butcher, formerly Presi-
dent of Corpus Christi College, Oxford, was Catholic in
sympathy. After the rising of the Northern Earls in 1569, he
was replaced by a more 'reliable' vicar, Henry Heycroft,
whose Protestantism is attested by his receipt of a preacher's
licence from the Bishop of Worcester in 1571. In addition to
the Church of the Holy Trinity, there was a Guild Chapel in
Stratford, under the care of the town corporation; and for this
fuller records have survived than for the church. It was not
until 1564 that its images were defaced and its rood screen
pulled down, probably on the insistence of the Bishop of
Worcester during his first visitation of his new diocese. It was
in that year John Bretchgirdle died, and there is no further

record of Protestantizing activity until the time of Henry Heycroft, who may well have insisted on the eventual disposal of the copes and other vestments belonging to the chapel which took place in 1571.

In Stratford, as in other country towns, it is probable that the people adopted a temporizing policy with regard to the religious changes. Even the Catholics for the most part complied outwardly for the sake of peace and the avoidance of legal penalties, while at the same time looking forward to the expected restoration of the old order (as the next heir to the English throne, Mary Stuart, was a Catholic). Thus there were few disturbances of a religious nature during the first decade of Elizabeth's reign. But with the failure of the rising of 1569 and the subsequent excommunication of the Queen by Pope Pius V in 1570, the division between Catholics and Protestants gradually became clearer. On the one hand, the Protestant policy of Elizabeth's government grew more determined and even ruthless, reinforced by increasingly stringent laws against the Catholics. On the other hand, many Catholics, now for the first time called 'recusants' for their refusal to attend services in the Church of England, resolved to follow their consciences, at whatever cost. Their state of mind is poignantly expressed in a contemporary poem by a Lancashire gentleman, Thomas Houghton, whose newly built mansion, Houghton Tower, may have been visited several years later by the young William Shakespeare.[4]

> At Houghton High, which is a bower
> Of sports and lordly pleasure,
> I wept and left that lofty tower
> Which was my chiefest treasure.
> To save my soul and lose the rest
> It was my true pretence;
> Like frighted bird I left my nest
> To keep my conscience.

During this decade of uncertainty, Shakespeare's father, John Shakespeare, rose to a position of prominence in the town corporation of Stratford. Appointed chamberlain in 1561, he continued to act in this capacity until 1565. It was towards the end of this term that the Guild Chapel was reformed in accordance with the Queen's Injunctions; and he appended his signature to the account of expenses incurred on that occasion. This fact has been interpreted as a sign of Protestant sympathy; but it must be remembered that he was merely acting in his official capacity, and from an official document of expenses signed by him no legitimate conclusion can be drawn as to his personal feelings about the matter. This long-delayed step was more probably forced upon the unwilling town corporation (as suggested above) by the combined insistence of the Protestant vicar and the visiting Bishop of Worcester. Subsequently, John Shakespeare was promoted to the dignity of bailiff in 1568. As such, he was required by law to take the anti-Catholic oath of supremacy, rejecting the spiritual authority of the Pope and acknowledging the Queen as supreme governor of the Church in England. If he were a Catholic, he clearly could not take this oath with a good conscience. But it is unlikely that the issue was ever presented to him; since at that time the Sheriff of Warwickshire, who was charged with tendering the oath, was himself a Catholic, Robert Middlemore.

The following decade saw a significant decline in the fortunes of John Shakespeare. From 1577 onwards he began to absent himself from meetings of the town corporation, though he was treated by them with considerable indulgence. During the same time he placed much of his property under mortgage, as though he were in serious financial difficulties. In 1580 he was mysteriously summoned to appear before the Court of the Queen's Bench; and he was heavily fined for not doing so. Finally, his name was twice recorded on the recusancy returns for Warwickshire in 1592, with the reason given that he came not to church 'for fear of process for debt'. The validity of this excuse has, however, been called in doubt. In 1580 he was still accounted one of the principal freeholders in Stratford; and in 1586–7 he twice stood surety for friends, to the amounts of £22 and £10 respectively, considerable sums of money at that time. It may also be observed that the excuse of debt was a not uncommon subterfuge of recusants who wished to avoid the penalties for refusing to attend church and who could, like John Shakespeare, count upon the connivance of the town officials.

These facts have been interpreted as pointing to a Puritan recusancy, when taken together with John Shakespeare's nominal association with the defacing of the Guild Chapel and the disposing of its copes and vestments.[5] It is conjectured that his presumed Puritan sympathies were further confirmed by the preaching of the Puritan leader, Thomas Cartwright, who came to Warwick in 1585 under the patronage of the Earl of Leicester. It is further pointed out that in the recusancy returns of 1592 the name of John Shakespeare is not linked with the names of any known Catholics. On the other hand, the same facts may be seen to point with no less plausibility to a Catholic recusancy.[6] The change in John Shakespeare's fortunes occurred long before Cartwright settled in Warwick, and is significantly contemporaneous with the coming of the first Seminary priests to the Midlands about 1575. They did much to encourage the wavering Catholics in their faith and to dissuade them from a temporizing attitude concerning church services. They may also have suggested practical means of securing property against the continual danger of fines and confiscation. The custom of mortgaging property in such a way that it could hardly be confiscated from its real owner became increasingly common among Elizabethan Catholics, who were well represented in the legal profession. Further, the summons before the Queen's Bench in 1580 coincided with an outburst of severity against the Catholics, which the government was unwilling to present as a form of religious persecution. Lastly, the recusancy returns of 1592 were compiled in response to a Royal Proclamation of the previous year, which was aimed specifically against the Catholics. Thus far the balance of evidence seems to point towards a Catholic rather than a Puritan recusancy. This is confirmed by a further item of information which places the matter beyond reasonable doubt.[7] The coming of the Seminary priests was followed in 1580 by that of two Jesuit priests, Edmund Campion and Robert Persons, both of whom passed through the Midlands on their separate journeys that year. They stayed at the houses of the Catholic gentry; and one of their hosts was Sir William Catesby at Lapworth, not far to the north of Stratford. For the shelter he gave Campion he was later arrested in August 1581. In the course of their journeys they distributed copies of a Spiritual Testament, or profession of adherence to the Catholic faith, composed by St Charles Borromeo, who was then Archbishop of Milan. These testaments seem to have proved quite popular among the English Catholics, as Persons wrote for three or four thousand more of them. Very few copies have survived; but in 1784 one of them, drawn up in the name of John Shakespeare, was discovered by a bricklayer while working on the house of Shakespeare's birthplace in Henley Street, Stratford. It was submitted to the Shakespeare scholar, Edmund Malone, who first thought it to be genuine, but later changed his mind. For a long time it was regarded by scholars as one of the many Shakespeare forgeries of the period. Only in the past fifty years have other copies of the Spiritual Testament come to light, thereby establishing the authenticity of this particular one. It may, therefore, be conjectured that John Shakespeare received his copy from Campion at the house of Sir William Catesby, who was related to his wife; and at the time of the Somerville affair in 1583 he would have hidden it among the rafters of his house to avoid its detection. Through his wife he was also related to John Somerville; and on the occasion of that affair, and the persecution of Catholics it provoked, the Clerk of the Council, Thomas Wilkes, reported to Sir Francis Walsingham that 'the papists in this country [i.e. Warwickshire] do greatly work upon the advantage of clearing their houses of all shows of suspicion'.[8]

Additional confirmation of John Shakespeare's recusancy is provided by the religious background of his wife, Mary Arden. Her father, Robert Arden, who died in the reign of Mary, was evidently a devout Catholic – to judge from the wording of his will: 'First, I bequeath my soul to Almighty God and to Our Blessed Lady, Saint Mary, and to all the holy company of heaven, and my body to be buried in the churchyard of Saint John the Baptist in Aston ...'

Some doubt has been expressed as to her connection with the Ardens of Warwickshire, who were strongly Catholic, on account of the description of the coat of arms for which Shakespeare applied in 1596; but the connection is at least a probable one.[9] At the time of the above-mentioned Somerville affair, when a mentally unbalanced cousin, John Somerville, was convicted of an attempt to assassinate the Queen, the head of the family, Edward Arden of Parkhall, was unjustly implicated and put to death (it was said) through the envy of the Earl of Leicester. This was also the occasion for renewed persecution of the Catholics in the area; and particular instructions were given to apprehend 'such as shall be in any way akin to all touched, and to search their houses'. It is quite possible that these instructions were interpreted as extending to Shakespeare's family through his mother. The active prosecution was entrusted for the most part to the local magistrate, Sir Thomas Lucy of Charlecote, who had received a Puritan education from his former tutor, John Foxe. He is the magistrate who is said – by Richard Davies and Nicholas Rowe – to have prosecuted the young William Shakespeare for deer-poaching.[10] The antipathy suggested by this tradition may have been connected with Lucy's prosecution of Shakespeare's relatives at this very time.

On his father's side, Shakespeare may have had other Catholic connections. The forbears of John Shakespeare seem to have come from the neighbourhood of Wroxhall, to the north of Stratford, where there was a large convent of nuns up to the time of its dissolution under Henry VIII.[11] In the early years of the sixteenth century the prioress was an Isabella Shakespeare, whose name strangely tallies with that of the novice-heroine in *Measure for Measure*. It is significant that both the name of the heroine and the fact that she is a novice in the sisterhood of St Clare are deliberate departures of the dramatist from his source. Later on, at the time of dissolution, the sub-prioress was a Joan Shakespeare, who lived on till 1576. It has been conjectured, though on insufficient evidence, that she was an aunt of William Shakespeare.[12] That there may have been some kinship, however, is suggested by the favourable portrayals of nuns in some of the plays: as, for example, those of the Abbess Æmilia in *The Comedy of Errors* (v. 1) and of Sister Francisca in *Measure for Measure* (i. 4). As for Isabella herself, though she is understandably immature as a novice in the early part of the play, she comes to stand in its subsequent development for the high ideal of mercy. Not only the nuns themselves, but also their religious calling is respected, in *The Comedy of Errors*, for its 'charitable duty' and 'holiness' (v. 1). And in *A Midsummer Night's*

Dream, while emphasizing the difficulty of a life 'in shady cloister mew'd', Duke Theseus has praise for the religious ideal :

> *Thrice blessed they that master so their blood,*
> *To undergo such maiden pilgrimage . . .* (i. 1)

II

Religious Formation

GIVEN THE likelihood, as stated in the previous chapter, that Shakespeare's parents adhered to the 'old faith', they would naturally have been concerned about the religious education of their eldest son. There is, indeed, a tradition that this task was entrusted to an old Benedictine monk, Dom Thomas Combe, who was related to the Combes of Stratford.[1] In any case, the plays themselves yield a considerable body of evidence. In them the beliefs and customs of Catholics are mentioned with astonishing frequency, and with a familiarity and reverence quite exceptional among Elizabethan dramatists. There are no signs of awkwardness or misunderstanding, still less of hostility or prejudice.

In the first place, it is interesting to remark the many occasions on which the adjective 'holy' is applied to material objects in the sacramental sense used by Catholics and often ridiculed by Protestants. Thus things and persons connected with the church or church services, whether in a Christian or a pagan context, are regularly designated as 'holy'. The building itself is a 'holy edifice of stone' (*The Merchant of Venice* i. 1). Outside is the 'holy churchyard' (*Coriolanus* iii. 3); within are 'holy altars' (*Troilus and Cressida* iii. 3), the 'holy bell' (*As You Like It* ii. 7), and perhaps a 'holy shrine' (*Henry VI Part II* ii. 1). At 'holy rites' (*The Tempest* iv. 1) 'holy priests' (*Antony and Cleopatra* ii. 2), wearing 'holy vestments' (*Timon of Athens* iv. 3), use 'holy bread' (*As You Like It* iii. 4), 'holy oil' (*Henry VIII* iv. 1) and 'holy water' (*Titus*

Andronicus i. 1). Mention is made of 'holy crosses' by the wayside in country districts (*The Merchant of Venice* v. 1), of the 'holy fields' in Palestine trod by the 'blessed feet' of Christ (*Henry IV* Part I i. 1), and of the 'holy rood' on which he hung for our salvation (*Richard III* iii. 2, iv. 4). The adjective is also regularly used of the traditional ranks and orders in the hierarchical Church – papal legates and bishops, clergymen and churchmen, monks and friars, hermits and nuns, pilgrims and palmers – some of which had been retained, and many others abolished by the Elizabethan Church. Much of this is, naturally, for the sake of 'local colour'; but it seems to come more spontaneously from Shakespeare than from any other dramatist of his age.

In particular, there are several significant references to 'holy water' in plays which have a pagan setting but an underlying Christian meaning. In *King Lear* Cordelia's tears for her suffering father are described as 'holy water from her heavenly eyes' (iv. 3). Similarly, in *Cymbeline* the old king says to his kneeling daughter, Imogen : 'My tears that fall prove holy water on thee!' (v. 5). In other words it is mentioned in *The Tempest*, in connection with the ceremony of marriage, as the 'sweet aspersion of the heavens' (iv. 1). This connection is also emphasized in the final scene of *A Midsummer Night's Dream*, when the fairies led by Oberon bless the best bride-bed and consecrate the chamber with 'this field-dew' – in allusion (it has been pointed out) to the ceremony of '*benedictio thalami*' in the Old Sarum Rite.[2]

Moreover, the Catholic custom of blessing oneself with the sign of the cross, which was abandoned by the Protestants, is occasionally mentioned, often with a pun on 'blessing' and 'crossing'. The pun is used, for example, in a comic sense by Dromio of Ephesus in *The Comedy of Errors*, protesting to his mistress :

> *He will bless that cross with other beatings:*
> *Between you I shall have a holy head.* (ii. 1)

and in a melodramatic sense by Don John, the villain in *Much Ado About Nothing*, while framing his plot against Claudio :

> *If I can cross him in any way, I bless myself every way.*

(i. 3)

Other old Catholic customs, such as praying at wayside crosses 'for happy wedlock hours' (*The Merchant of Venice* v. 1), 'creeping' to the cross on Good Friday (*Troilus and Cressida* iii. 3), and hallowing 'trinkets' with the sign of the cross (*The Winter's Tale* iv. 3), seem to come spontaneously to the dramatist's mind without any necessary link with their context.

Devotional practices to the Blessed Virgin and the saints, such as abounded in medieval England, are recalled time after time. The 'beads' of Our Lady's Rosary are frequently mentioned in the history plays. The devotion of the pious King Henry VI is signalized by his bent 'to number Ave-Maries on his beads' (*Henry VI* Part II i. 3, and Part III ii. 1). On the other hand, when Richard of Gloucester simulates piety for his ambitious end, he adopts the pose of a 'holy and devout religious man' at his beads (*Richard III* iii. 7). In his hour of deposition Richard II declares his resolution to 'give my jewels for a set of beads' (iii. 3). The same connection of jewels with beads is seen in the 'crystal beads' of tears with which Arthur bribes heaven in *King John* (ii. 1). The other devotion of the Angelus, recited thrice a day, at morning, noon and night, in honour of the Blessed Virgin, is recalled in *Cymbeline*, when Imogen sends her parting message to Posthumus : desiring him

> *At the sixth hour of morn, at noon, at midnight,*
> *To encounter me with orisons, for then*
> *I am in heaven for him.* (i. 3)[3]

Prayer through the intercession of Our Lady is, moreover, hinted at in connection with Helena in *All's Well That Ends Well* (iii. 4) and with Miranda in *The Tempest* (v. 1) – where the heroines may be seen as types of the Virgin (see Chapter 5, pp. 93–4). The custom of kneeling before her statue is implied in Perdita's impulse, in the miraculous conclusion of *The Winter's Tale*, to kneel before her mother's statue and so 'implore her blessing' (v. 3).

Devotion to the saints is mentioned in the cases of Henry VI, with his 'brazen images of canonized saints' (*Henry VI* Part II i. 3), and of Richard II, with his 'pair of carved saints' (iii. 3). The custom of going on pilgrimage to famous shrines of saints, such as that of St James at Compostella, serves to enrich the theme of romantic love in several plays. It forms the main imagery of the love-duet between Romeo and Juliet during the mask at Capulet's house (i. 5). It verbalizes the ideal of Bassanio at the outset of *The Merchant of Venice*, as he goes on 'a secret pilgrimage' (i. 1) in order (as Morocco later declares) 'to kiss this shrine, this mortal-breathing saint' (ii. 7). It provides Helena in *All's Well That Ends Well* with the means of achieving her heart's desire, disguised as 'Saint Jaques' pilgrim . . . with sainted vow' (iii. 4).

Prayer for the souls of the faithful departed, though rejected by the Protestants on account of its implications of the Catholic doctrine of Purgatory, also receives honourable mention. In *Romeo and Juliet* the Nurse, after naming Juliet's deceased sister Susan, adds the pious ejaculation : 'God rest all Christian souls!' (i. 3). In *Hamlet* Ophelia prays for the soul of her father and for 'all Christian souls' (iv. 5); and she is in turn the object of a similar prayer on the lips of the grave-digger (v. 1). This is also the instinctive prayer of Old Gobbo in *The Merchant of Venice*, when he asks Lancelot in a somewhat confused manner : 'I pray you, tell me, is my boy – God rest his soul! – alive or dead?' It is perhaps significant that such expressions come most naturally to the lips of simple and unsophisticated characters in the plays. On a larger and more dignified scale, Henry V undertakes to have two chantries built, 'where the sad and solemn priests sing still for Richard's soul', by way of penance for his father's crime (iv. 1).

The connection between prayer and fasting for a special intention, though not unknown among Elizabethan Puritans, was usually regarded as a practice of 'monkish' times'. It appears in two of the final plays, whose setting is pagan, while the meaning is often transparently Christian. In *Cymbeline* the soothsayer tells how he 'fasted and prayed' to obtain intelligence from the gods (iv. 2). In *The Winter's Tale* Paulina speaks of praying and fasting 'upon a barren mountain' as a means to 'move the gods' (iii. 2).

There are also occasional echoes of prayers and hymns of the old Catholic liturgy, which had fallen into disuse with the general adoption of the *Book of Common Prayer*. In *Love's Labour's Lost* the wording of the King's sonnet, 'No thought can think, nor tongue of mortal tell' (iv. 3), seems to echo St Bernard's famous hymn on the Name of Jesus:

> *Nil canitur suavius,*
> *Nil auditur jucundius,*
> *Nil cogitatur dulcius.*

In *Hamlet* Horatio's reference to the cock, 'that is the trumpet of the morn', and at whose warning 'the extravagant and erring spirit hies to his confine' (i. 1), may well have been suggested by two hymns for Lauds – that for Tuesday:

> *Ales diei nuntius*
> *Lucem propinquam praecinit.*

and that for Sunday:

> *Praeco diei iam sonat,*
> *Jubarque solis evocat;*
> *Hoc excitatus Lucifer*
> *Solvit polum caligine,*
> *Hoc omnis erronum cohors*
> *Viam nocendi deserit.*[4]

The same Horatio's concluding prayer for Hamlet's soul, 'And flights of angels sing thee to thy rest!' (v. 2) – while it may also echo the dying prayer of Essex: 'Send thy blessed angels which may receive my soul and convey it to thy joys in heaven' – looks back to the antiphon regularly chanted at the Catholic burial service: '*In paradisum deducant te angeli: in tuo adventu suscipiant te Martyres, et perducant te in civitatem sanctam Jerusalem. Chorus angelorum te suscipiat, et cum Lazaro quondam paupere aeternam habeus requiem.*'[5]

In *Cymbeline* the night prayer of Imogen, 'To your protection I commend me, gods . . .' (ii. 6), is remarkably similar to the hymn of Compline:

> *Te lucis ante terminum,*
> *Rerum Creator, poscimus*
> *Ut pro tua clementia*
> *Sis praesul et custodia.*
> *Procul recedant somnia*
> *Et noctium phantasmata.*[6]

In *Romeo and Juliet* the hero's delighted exclamation in the famous love-scene, 'O blessed, blessed night!' (ii. 2), recalls the solemn chant of Holy Saturday, the *Exultet*, with its repeated '*O vere beata nox*'. In *The Tempest*, too, Gonzalo's concluding speech, 'O, rejoice beyond a common joy, and set it down with gold on lasting pillars!' (v. 1), recalls other passages in the same chant :

> *Gaudeat et tellus tantis irradiata fulgoribus . . .*
> *O felix culpa, quae talem ac tantum meruit habere*
> *Redemptorem . . .*
> *Columnae hujus praeconia novimus, quam in honorem*
> *Dei rutilans ignis accendit.*

The sacrifice of the Mass is, however, mentioned very rarely. In all the plays there is only one open reference to it, where the medieval Italian custom of 'evening Mass' is mentioned in *Romeo and Juliet* (iv. 1).[7] But there is a possible allusion to the Mass at the turning-point of *The Winter's Tale*, where the pagan sacrifice to Apollo at Delphos is enthusiastically described by Dion and Cleomenes. The former speaks of 'the celestial habits' and 'the reverence' of the priests, and expresses his admiration of the 'ceremonious, solemn and unearthly' manner of the sacrifice (iii. 1). In the setting of the play, of course, the reference is to pagan worship; but in its underlying Christian meaning – which runs through the whole play – the parallel at this point would be to the Catholic Mass, as offered up at St Peter's in Rome.

Communion is generally spoken of as 'the sacrament', especially in connection with taking some solemn oath (*cf. Richard II* iv. 1). The Catholic rule that all mortal sins must be confessed before receiving communion is implied by Mowbray in *Richard II*, when he acknowledges his trespass against John of Gaunt :

> *But ere I last received the sacrament,*
> *I did confess it.* (i. 1)

The archaic word for communion, 'housel', particularly as given to the dying in the form of '*viaticum*', occurs in the bitter complaint of the ghost in *Hamlet* :

> *Cut off even in the blossoms of my sin,*
> *Unhousel'd, disappointed, unaneal'd,*
> *No reckoning made, but sent to my account*
> *With all my imperfections on my head:*
> *O, horrible! O, horrible! most horrible!* (i. 5)

What is particularly horrible for the ghost is precisely that he was murdered at a moment when he could not receive the Catholic sacraments for the dying – the 'housel' of communion, the 'appointment' of confession, and the 'anealing' of extreme unction.

More prominent in the plays is the part played by the sacrament of penance, or confession. It provides the setting for romantic meetings between Valentine and Silvia in *Two Gentlemen of Verona*, between Romeo and Juliet, and between Claudio and Hero in *Much Ado About Nothing*. It emphasizes a significant contrast in *Macbeth* between the original Thane of Cawdor, who dies confessing his treasons and setting forth 'a deep repentance' (i. 4), and Macbeth himself and his Queen, whose troubles need more 'the divine than the physician' (v. 1) and who remain impenitent to the end. It is, above all, a recurrent theme in *Hamlet* and *Measure for Measure*, where the importance of contrition and confession is underlined as the only means of forgiveness. In these plays the reference to confession does not remain merely on a general level; but precise mention is made of its several elements, as distinguished in Catholic theology.

In *Measure for Measure* the preliminary examination of conscience is mentioned by the Duke when, disguised as a friar, he comes to Juliet in prison and teaches her 'how you shall arraign your conscience' (ii. 3). He also glances at the theological distinction between contrition ('as we love' heaven) and attrition ('as we stand in fear'). A similar distinction occurs in *Richard II*, when York declares of his offending son : 'Fear, and not love, begets his penitence' (v. 3). In *Hamlet* we find the three conditions for forgiveness conjoined in the hero's advice to his mother : 'Confess yourself to heaven; repent what's past; avoid what is to come' (iii. 4) – or, in technical terms, confession, contrition, and a firm purpose of amendment. In *Romeo and Juliet* there is frequent mention of the confession of sins to a priest, with consequent 'shrift' or absolution, as in the words of Friar Laurence to Romeo: 'Riddling confession finds but riddling shrift' (ii. 3). In *All's Well That Ends Well* the traditional formula used in confession (recalling the parable of the Prodigal Son) is echoed in Helena's words to the Countess: 'Then I confess, here on my knee, before high heaven and you' (i. 3). In *Much Ado About Nothing* the imposition, or 'enjoining', of a penance in satisfaction for sin is alluded to by Claudio in his request of Leonato:

> *Impose me to what penance your invention*
> *Can lay upon my sin.* (v. 1)

The same theme of penance interestingly recurs in the pagan settings of *Cymbeline* (v. 4) and *The Winter's Tale* (v. 1). In the latter play, moreover, where an underlying Christian meaning has already been remarked upon, Camillo is presented as a 'ghostly confessor' who 'priest-like' cleanses the bosom of Leontes from sin (i. 2.)

Of special significance is the emphasis Shakespeare frequently lays – in accordance with Catholic tradition – on the need of right preparation for death by means of the 'last sacraments'. In *Measure for Measure* it seems that the main preoccupation of the Duke in his disguise as a friar, is not so much what he originally plans, to find out 'what our seemers be' (i. 3), as to 'visit the afflicted spirits' of those in prison (ii. 3) and to encourage them to 'be absolute for death' (iii. 1). In *Hamlet*, too, there is a structural contrast between the unprepared state of the father, 'cut off even in the blossoms of my sin' (i. 5), and the readiness of the son (v. 2) – though the latter refuses to take his revenge on Claudius 'in the purging of his soul' (iii. 3) and sends Rosencrantz and Guildenstern 'to sudden death, not shriving time allowed' (v. 2). The whole play is remarkably full of allusions to Catholic beliefs and practices with regard to the dying and the dead, from the apparition in the first Act as of the ghost of England's Catholic past, to the circumstances of the twin deaths of Ophelia and Hamlet.[8] The ghost introduces himself as coming from a place where he is condemned 'for a certain term' to suffer the pain of fire till his sins 'are burnt and purg'd away' (i. 5) – a precise description of the Catholic purgatory. The subsequent exclamation of Hamlet, 'by Saint Patrick', is prompted by this description on account of the Irish legend of St Patrick's Purgatory as told in Campion's *History of Ireland* and later incorporated in Holinshed's *Chronicles*.[9] Mention has already been made of the prayers for the dead uttered by Ophelia and the grave-digger, and of the antiphon in the burial service echoed in Horatio's parting prayer for Hamlet. As for the 'maimed rites' for Ophelia (v. 1), they accord with the prescriptions in Canon Law for the treatment of suicides; but the priest who performs them is referred to in the second Quarto as 'Doctor' – which seems to mean an Anglican clergyman.[10] This interpretation (which is probable, but not certain) would emphasize the contrast between the old Catholic order, represented by the ghost, and the new Protestant order, represented by Claudius; for the burial takes place under the new order.

In addition to these various references to Catholic beliefs and customs, there are many allusions in the plays to the religious drama of the Middle Ages which managed to survive, in spite of Protestant disfavour, until well on into the reign of Elizabeth. One of the principal centres of this drama was the nearby city of Coventry, where as a boy Shakespeare could have witnessed the last performances of the cycle of 'mystery' plays, which ranged in subject-matter through the whole history of salvation from the creation of the world to the final judgement.[11] The influence of these plays on his own later drama is difficult to trace with any degree of accuracy, as it overlaps with the direct influence of the printed Bible; but it was evidently profound.

Overt references to the 'mystery' plays are not so frequent. The ranting of Herod in the Nativity play is mentioned twice: in Hamlet's 'It out-Herods Herod' (iii. 1), and in Mistress Page's exclamation at Falstaff's letter, 'What a Herod of Jewry is this!' (*Merry Wives of Windsor* ii. 1). The stage-property of Hell-mouth common to many of the plays (such as the Fall of Man, the Harrowing of Hell, and the Last Judgement) is implied in the grotesque Porter scene of *Macbeth* (ii. 3) and in the Bastard's description of the mouth of Death in *King John*:

O, now doth Death line his dead chaps with steel;
The swords of soldiers are his teeth, his fangs;
And now he feasts, mousing the flesh of men,
In undetermin'd differences of kings. (ii. 1)

It is also perhaps alluded to by Othello in his despairing words, 'Whip me, ye devils, from the possession of this heavenly sight!' (v. 2).[12] The frequent use of the Biblical stories of Adam and Eve, Cain and Abel, Noah's flood and the Exodus from Egypt, may indeed be explained by the direct influence of the Bible; but the vivid and popular manner of their phrasing seems to point rather to the medieval drama as their source. A popular rather than a literary origin is suggested by such phrases as 'that Adam that kept the Paradise' (*The Comedy of Errors* iv. 3), 'Adam was a gardener' (*Henry VI Part II* iv. 2), 'all that Adam had left him before he transgressed' (*Much Ado About Nothing* ii. 1), 'God saw him when he was hid in the garden' (*ibid.* v. 1), 'thou old Adam's likeness set to dress this garden' (*Richard II* iii. 4), and 'the old days of goodman Adam' (*Henry IV Part I* ii. 4). No less deeply does the story of Cain and Abel, involving the 'primal eldest curse' (*Hamlet* iii. 3), enter into the imaginative structure of the histories and tragedies, with visual implications. In particular, Hamlet's casual reference to 'Cain's jawbone, that did the first murder' (v. 1), is a clear pointer to popular British tradition (from an etymological confusion between *cinban*, or 'chin-bone', and *Cain-bana*, or Cain as his brother's bane); and the use of a jaw-bone by Cain is specifically required in the old stage directions of the Cornish Creation play.[13]

As for the New Testament, the scenes of Judas betraying his Master with a kiss and of Pilate washing his hands at the trial of Jesus seem to have made a particularly deep impression on the imagination of Shakespeare. An interesting example of their impact by way of the medieval drama occurs in the form of Judas's greeting, 'All hail!', as given both in *Henry VI Part III* (v. 7) and in *Richard II* (iv. 1). The use of this form by Shakespeare has been cited as an instance of his defective knowledge of the Bible, seeing that it is found in none of the existing versions of his time.[14] But it is precisely the form used in the Chester play of the Betrayal; and it may well have been used also in the Coventry play, which has unfortunately not survived. The popular play of the *Woman Taken in Adultery* (from John viii) is recalled in the general situation of *Measure for Measure*, though there is perhaps no clear indication of medieval influence. But the particular theme of conflict between the respective claims of justice and mercy in that play has a clear connection with the medieval debate between the four Daughters of God, Truth and Justice, Mercy and Peace, which is featured both in the *Ludus Coventriae* and in the 'morality' play *The Castle of Perseverance*.[15] In a more general way, the comic representation of 'low life' in Shakespeare's comedies is, not without justice, related to the earthy realism and humour of the Wakefield Master, as shown in his portrayal of Noah's wife and the three shepherds – though it is difficult to assess the precise extent of kinship or influence.[16]

The impact of the 'morality' plays on Shakespeare is somewhat easier to trace. In the first place, there are many obvious, though relatively superficial, allusions to such stock 'morality' characters as 'the formal Vice, Iniquity' (*Richard III* iii. 1; *cf. Twelfth Night* iv. 1); 'the evil angel' or 'the Devil' (*Twelfth Night* iv. 1; *The Comedy of Errors* iv. 3; *King John* ii. 1); 'unsubstantial Death, the lean, abhorred monster' (*Romeo and Juliet* v. 3; *cf. Richard II* iii. 2), who, as God's serjeant, is 'strict in his arrest' (*Hamlet* v. 2; *Sonnet* 74); and the 'better angel' who is in conflict with the 'worser spirit' (*Sonnet* 144; *cf. Henry V* i. 1, *Othello* v. 2). The Seven Deadly Sins, which receive general mention as 'the deadly seven' in *Measure for Measure* (iii. 1), also appear one by one in personified form : 'lean-fac'd Envy in her loathsome cave' (*Henry VI* Part II iii. 2); 'Revenge sent from th' infernal kingdom' and escorted by 'Rape and Murder' (*Titus Andronicus* v. 2); 'Lechery at the gate', as Viola is imagined by Sir Toby (*Twelfth Night* i. 5); 'the devil Luxury' (*Troilus and Cressida* v. 2); 'the devil Wrath' and 'the devil Drunkenness' (*Othello* ii. 3). Other allegorical personages introduced by Shakespeare into his plays are : Vanity (*Henry IV* Part I ii. 4; *King Lear*), Fear (*Troilus and Cressida* iii. 2; *Antony and Cleopatra* ii. 3), Rumour (*Henry IV* Part II Ind.), Remorse (*Henry IV* Part

I i. 2), Time (*The Winter's Tale* iv. Chor.), Consideration (*Henry V* i. 1), Expectation (*ibid.* ii. Chor.) and Peace (*ibid.* v. 2).

Of greater significance than such lists is the pervasive presence of the 'morality' pattern in the later histories and the great tragedies. In the two Parts of *Henry IV* Shakespeare gives dramatic treatment to the subject, so often discussed in the Tudor period, of the moral education of a Prince. He does so in terms of a contrast between Prince Hal and his boon companions, among whom the character of Sir John Falstaff stands out as 'that reverend Vice, that grey Iniquity, that Father Ruffian, that Vanity in years' (Part I ii. 4).[17] During the time of his youth the Prince is shown in association with them; but when he succeeds to his father's throne he symbolically turns away from his companions, as if from his 'former self', and declares to Falstaff: 'I know thee not, old man' (Part II v. 5). His reformation is subsequently described by the Archbishop of Canterbury in the language of a 'morality' play:

> *Consideration, like an Angel, came*
> *And whipp'd the offending Adam out of him,*
> *Leaving his body as a Paradise*
> *To envelop and contain celestial spirits.*
>
> *(Henry V i. 1)*

It is not only Prince Hal who is conceived in terms of Everyman, but Brutus, Othello and Lear variously represent the same general character. In each case, though in different degrees, they are shown as turning aside from their 'better angel', represented by the heroines, Portia, Desdemona, and Cordelia, and following the suggestion of their 'worser spirit', represented by the villains, Cassius, Iago, Goneril, and Regan – to their ruin. In particular, *Macbeth* is often compared with Marlowe's *Doctor Faustus*, as a 'morality' play of damnation, in which the hero progressively forfeits the good will of the audience when he yields to the temptation of the witches, plunges into a succession of horrible murders for the sake of his ambition, and ends with his bloody death.

A third type of medieval drama, the 'miracle' play in the strict sense of the word, has an important bearing on the last plays of Shakespeare. This was a dramatic representation of one or other of the '*legenda Sanctorum*' that were so popular in the Middle Ages, and in particular of the miracles attributed to the intercession of the Blessed Virgin./ Few English texts have survived of these plays; but a number of interesting similarities have been noticed between one such play, that of Mary Magdalene in the Digby MS, and Shakespeare's *Pericles* – such as the birth of a baby daughter on board ship in the midst of a tempest, the mother's apparent death and miraculous preservation.[18] Among the more abundant French texts, there is a miracle play of the Blessed Virgin, *Ostes Roy d'Espaigne*, which affords an interesting parallel to *Cymbeline* and supplements the generally accepted source in Boccaccio's *Decameron*. Another French 'miracle' play of the Virgin, the *Miracle de l'Emperis*, whose plot is related to Chaucer's *Man of Law's Tale* of Dame Custance, may well lie behind *The Winter's Tale*.[19] Finally, the general pattern of these 'miracle' plays of the Virgin is discernible in *All's Well That Ends Well*, which is usually numbered among the problem plays, though it is rather to be regarded as a forerunner of the romances. The very name of the heroine, Helena, is that of one of the most popular saints in medieval legend, St Helen, the British mother of the Roman emperor Constantine. She is described by the Countess as one whose prayers 'heaven delights to hear and loves to grant' (iii. 4) – in terms traditionally used of Our Lady's intercession. Similar terms are also applied to Miranda in *The Tempest*, when Prospero mildly rebukes Alonso in the concluding scene :

> *I rather think*
> *You have not sought her help, of whose soft grace*
> *For the like loss I have her sovereign aid*
> *And rest myself content.* (v. 1)

Lastly, in connection with St Helen, it is possible that the idea for an earlier play, *The Merchant of Venice*, was suggested to the dramatist by an incident in her legend, which featured in the wall-paintings that once adorned the walls of the Guild Chapel in Stratford.[20]

Another important element in Shakespeare's religious formation was, no doubt, the language of the new Anglican service-books, the English Bible, and the two volumes of *Homilies*, which will be examined at length in later chapters. Even if his family background was Catholic, there is every likelihood – as has been pointed out – that his parents would have temporized with the law and attended the Anglican services, at least up to the time of the arrival of the Seminary priests and the Jesuits in the Midlands. There is, of course, no direct proof that this was so; but indirectly the plays provide sufficient evidence of familiarity with the *Book of Common Prayer*, the Bishops' and the Geneva Bibles, and the *Homilies* – more than could have been derived from hearsay, or even from a literary study of the books in question. In particular, it is significant that Shakespeare's echoes of the Psalms bear closer relation to the version used in services, from Cranmer's Great Bible, than to either the Bishops' or the Geneva version. There is also, in *As You Like It*, a picture of the interior of an Anglican church during the reading of a homily – in Rosalind's amused remark on finding the Forest of Arden strewn with Orlando's interminable love-poems:

> *O most gentle pulpiter! what tedious homily of love have you wearied your parishioners withal, and never cried, 'Have patience, good people'!* (iii. 2)

It may be noted that one of the homilies is, in fact, entitled 'Of Christian Love', and that the congregation is addressed from time to time as 'good people' or 'good Christian people'.

At the same time, the influence of a Protestant vicar like Henry Heycroft would be offset by that of 'old religious men' like those mentioned in *As You Like It* (v. 4), namely, Marian priests and old monks now living in retirement. Mention has already been made of a Dom Thomas Combe, an old Benedictine monk, who may perhaps be glimpsed in Antonio's shadowy brother 'in the cloister' in *Two Gentlemen of Verona* (i. 3). Then there was old John Frith, a Marian priest, who was allowed to remain at the little church of Temple Grafton in spite of his 'unsound doctrine', partly in view of his old age and partly as his position was relatively insignificant. He was still living in 1586, when his name is recorded in the Puritan *Survey of the Ministry* for Warwickshire, with the description: An old priest and unsound in religion, he can neither

preach nor read well, his chiefest trade is to cure hawks that
are hurt or diseased, for which purpose many do usually
repair to him.[21]

There is something about him that recalls the character of
Friar Laurence. Interestingly enough, it was precisely at
Temple Grafton that Shakespeare's bride was living at the
time of their marriage – at least, if we are to accept the usual
identification of Anne Whateley with Anne Hathwey in the
marriage register of the Bishop of Worcester.[22] It may therefore be conjectured that here also the marriage ceremony took
place, according to the Catholic rite, with Father Frith
officiating – like another Friar Laurence, incorporating two in
one. For there is no record of Shakespeare's marriage in the
parish church of Stratford. In this case, it is possible that the
Catholic ceremony preceded the official registration by several
months, allowing for Shakespeare's eldest daughter, Susanna,
to have been conceived in wedlock; for whereas the registration was made towards the end of November 1582, Susanna
was born in May 1583. Thus the marital situation of Shakespeare would show an interesting parallel with that of Claudio
in *Measure for Measure*; since it was 'upon a true contract'
that the latter 'got possession of Julietta's bed' – only he
lacked 'the denunciation of outward order' (i. 2).

At school the young Shakespeare would have received
instruction in the elements of Christian faith as outlined in the
standard *ABC with Catechism*. This was the 'shorter catechism, identical with that contained in the *Book of Common
Prayer* under the heading of 'Confirmation'. That Shakespeare was familiar with its contents is indicated by his many
echoes of its phraseology, particularly its wording of the Ten
Commandments. On several occasions he also refers to the
Catechism and catechizing in general. There is a notable
example of this in *Much Ado About Nothing*, where Hero
asks: 'What kind of catechizing call you this?', and Claudio
answers with a punning allusion to the first question of the
catechism: 'To make you answer truly to your name' (iv. 1).
Other references to the catechism itself are to be found in *As
You Like It* iii. 2, *Twelfth Night* i. 5, *Henry IV* Part I v. 1,
and *Othello* iii. 4. It has been suggested that Shakespeare also
had to learn the larger Latin Catechism of Dean Nowell – at

least, in its English translation by Thomas Norton; but the
parallels adduced in evidence for this suggestion are too
general and few in number to be convincing.[23] Another
doubtful suggestion is that he would have learnt the Bible at
school; doubtful since there is as yet no sufficient proof that the
Bible was generally taught in country schools at that time.[24]

The religious influence Shakespeare would have received
during his studies at Stratford Grammar School must have
been more Catholic than Protestant – to judge by the known
sympathies of his schoolmasters. In theory, of course, they
were obliged to take the Oath of Supremacy; but during the
early years of Elizabeth's reign this Oath was not so widely
insisted upon. What is certain is that of the three masters at
Stratford between 1571 and 1582 no less than two were shown
in the light of subsequent events to have been Catholics.
Simon Hunt, who was schoolmaster from 1571 to 1575, left
Stratford and England in the latter year to join the Seminary
at Douai; and from there he journeyed on to Rome, where he
entered the noviciate of the Society of Jesus.[25] With him went
one of his pupils, Robert Dibdale, who remained at Douai,
was ordained priest, and returned to England, where he
eventually died as a martyr (in Catholic eyes) or a traitor (in
Protestant eyes) in 1586. John Cottam, who was schoolmaster
from 1579 to 1582, came from a strongly Catholic area in
Lancashire, not far from the above-mentioned Houghton
Tower.[26] His brother Thomas was a Jesuit priest, who was put
on trial with Edmund Campion in 1581 and received the
death sentence in the following year. Perhaps it was the execution of Thomas which prompted John to relinquish his position as schoolmaster, amid increasing pressure on the Catholics, and to retire to Essex, where his name subsequently
appears on the recusant lists for that county. On the other
hand, Thomas Jenkins, who was schoolmaster in the inter-
vening period, must have been a Protestant, for he later took
orders in the Church of England. On account of his Welsh
name, he has been suggested as the prototype of Sir Hugh
Evans, the irascible schoolmaster-parson in *The Merry Wives
of Windsor*, who questions little William 'in his accidence'
(iv. 1) and is derided as 'one that makes fritters of English'
(v. 5).[27]

During the early eighties, partly because of the enterprise of the Seminary priests and the Jesuits, partly also in connection with the Somerville affair, the pressure of the penal laws against Catholic recusants became much heavier than before. Shakespeare was now in his teens, and the problem of his future must have presented itself acutely to his parents. All we know concerning this period in his life are the events of his marriage with Anne Hathwey in 1582, and the birth of his eldest daughter, Susanna, in 1583. In addition, there is the tradition of his poaching in Sir Thomas Lucy's deer park, which may be interpreted as his way of taking reprisals against the magistrate for his unjust prosecution of the Ardens after the Somerville affair. Finally, there is another tradition, recorded by William Beeston, son of Shakespeare's fellow-actor Christopher Beeston, that the dramatist 'had been in his younger years a schoolmaster in the country'.[28]

The gap presented by these 'hidden years' in Shakespeare's life is filled by an interesting theory which argues a sojourn of several years in Lancashire, notoriously one of the most Catholic counties in England. The evidence for this theory, which has won the support of many eminent scholars, is the will of a Catholic gentleman, Alexander Houghton, brother of the above-mentioned Thomas Houghton, of Lea Hall near Preston, who died in 1581.[29] In this will he commends a certain William Shakeshafte, presumably a young man and a player, to the special care and protection of Sir Thomas Hesketh, of Rufford Hall not far away, who, like Houghton, maintained a small company of players and musicians. Besides being a firm Catholic, Sir Thomas was a frequent visitor at Knowsley House, the Lancashire residence of the Earl of Derby, whose son and heir, Lord Strange, patronized the company of players known as Strange's Men. Sir Thomas died in 1588. Subsequently, in the spring of 1592 the repertory of Strange's Men on the London stage included two plays entitled *Harey the VI* and *Titus and Vespasian*, which have been identified by scholars as possibly Shakespeare's *Henry VI* Part I and *Titus Andronicus*. This company also included the nucleus of the future Chamberlain's Men, the company to which Shakespeare belonged from the time of its formation in 1594 – after the tragic death of Lord Strange shortly after his succession to the earldom. It is, therefore, tempting to identify William Shakeshafte with William Shakespeare, and to trace his footsteps from Stratford to London by way of Lancashire.

Before this identification can be made with any probability, however, there are two questions which have to be answered satisfactorily. For one thing, there is the noticeable difference of surname: why should the young Shakespeare have decided to change his name, with his change of county? Secondly, there is the distance between the two counties: what could have brought the young Shakespeare so far afield as to Lancashire? In the first place, the difference of surname presents less of a problem than it may first appear, considering the variety of forms and spellings in the sixteenth century. The name of Shakespeare seems to have been particularly fluid even by sixteenth-century standards; and among the diversity of forms used by the poet's own family, that of 'Shakeschaft' was employed on occasion by his grandfather, Richard. It may be that Robert Greene was glancing at this variability of name when, in his famous diatribe against Shakespeare in *A Groatsworth of Wit* (1592), he dubbed him 'the only Shakescene in a country'. It has been pointed out that the name Shakeshafte was not unknown in Lancashire at that time; but this very fact, which seems to weaken the case for identification, provides a possible reason why – if it was indeed he – Shakespeare should have changed his name, or perhaps have had his name changed for him, in that northern county.

With regard to the second question, recent investigations have disclosed a remarkable number of connections between Stratford and the part of Lancashire round Preston. They may ultimately be derived from no less a person than William Allen, founder of the Seminary at Douai, who was possibly related to the great tragic actor, Edward Allen. There is evidence that Allen, who was a native of this very part of Lancashire, spent some time between 1562 and 1565 in the neighbourhood partly of Oxford, and partly of Stratford. In 1564–5 an assistant teacher named Allen received the sum of £3 for 'teaching the children' by John Shakespeare – at a time when it is known that William Allen himself was in the district.[30] During the next twenty years it is interesting that of the five schoolmasters at Stratford three were from Lancashire, Walter Roche, John Cottam and Alexander Aspinall. Of the three John Cottam, in particular, had been a neighbour of Alexander Houghton at Lea Hall; and it was during his brief tenure of office that Derby's players were twice entertained at Stratford for the festivities after Christmas.[31] It may therefore have been in company with these players that the young Shakespeare was first sent north by his father, bearing a letter of introduction from the schoolmaster to Alexander Houghton. His subsequent sojourn at Rufford is said to be attested by a local tradition in the village, and confirmed by his later connection with Thomas Savage, a native of Rufford, who became one of the trustees for the Globe Theatre in 1599.[32]

Thus the county where Shakespeare spent his younger years as a schoolmaster – according to the Beeston tradition – may have been Lancashire. This might account for the interest he shows in his early histories in the wars between the Houses of York and Lancaster. His first employment could well have been that of tutor in the Houghton family, with his studies at Stratford Grammar School behind him; and as such he would have had the opportunity to widen his reading and improve his education along self-chosen lines. Next, it was not infrequent for the tutor in a gentleman's family to undertake the role of actor-composer on special occasions, such as Christmas-time. Of course, this is only conjecture; but a further piece of solid evidence connects Shakespeare with these very parts of the country, and with the family of Stanley (the surname of the Earls of Derby). At the church of Tong in Shropshire, there are two epitaphs in honour of the brothers, Sir Thomas (d. 1576) and Sir Edward Stanley (d. 1609), and attributed to Shakespeare. In each, and especially in the latter, there are echoes of the *Sonnets*, particularly of *Sonnet* 55, which seem to make the attribution authentic.[33] But in spite of all proofs, the theory still remains a theory – though perhaps the best substantiated of all the suggestions about the 'hidden years'.

III

English Jesuits

IN THE forefront of the Catholic Counter-Reformation was the Society of Jesus, which had been approved as a new religious order by Pope Paul III in 1540. It was through the insistence of William Allen that the General of the Society, Fr Everard Mercurian, decided to send Jesuits to England in order to assist the Seminary priests in their task of bringing spiritual comfort to the persecuted Catholics. In the first group to be sent over were two former Oxford graduates, Robert Persons and Edmund Campion, both of whom were to leave an indelible imprint on the religious history of their time. Their sojourn in the country was, indeed, all too short. Within two years of their arrival in June 1580, Campion had been arrested and executed for high treason, and Persons obliged to take refuge on the continent. But their brief stay had been intensely active, and had given new impetus to the Catholic cause in England. Its outcome may be discerned in a rich variety of ways in the life and drama of Shakespeare.

Even before their arrival, Shakespeare must have been familiar with the name of this new Society from the time of his boyhood. It is surprising how many of his schoolmasters at Stratford had links of one kind or another with the Society of Jesus. Simon Hunt, who left Stratford in 1575 for the Seminary at Douai, ultimately made his way to Rome, where he entered the Jesuit noviciate. Thomas Jenkins, who succeeded him at Stratford, had known Edmund Campion as a fellow-member of St John's College, Oxford. John Cottam, who was schoolmaster from 1579 to 1582, was the brother of Thomas Cottam, who was not only a Jesuit, but also stood trial with Edmund Campion in November 1581 and was executed like him for high treason in the following year.[1]

There is also the possibility of an even closer connection between Shakespeare and the two Jesuits, in the course of their journeys through England in 1580. The Spiritual Testament of St Charles Borromeo, of which mention has already been made, must have come into the hands of Shakespeare's father when Persons or Campion passed through the Midlands at that time. The latter certainly stayed at the house of Sir William Catesby at Lapworth, a few miles to the north of Stratford; and both are reported to have stayed with Edward Arden at Parkhall.[2] Moreover, if the identification of William Shakeshafte with William Shakespeare is correct, the future dramatist could have listened to the preaching of the future martyr at Houghton Tower, a residence of the Houghton family (mentioned in Thomas Houghton's poem quoted above) which Campion visited in the winter of 1580.[3]

The trial of Campion and his friends at Westminster Hall in 1581 attracted much public attention, and detailed accounts of it were later published on both sides. It has even been conjectured that Campion's speech in defence of himself is echoed in Hermione's words on a somewhat similar occasion in *The Winter's Tale* :[4]

> *Since what I am to say must be but that*
> *Which contradicts my accusation and*
> *The testimony on my part no other*
> *But what comes from myself, it shall scarce boot me*
> *To say 'Not guilty'.* (iii. 2)

A more certain trace of Campion's literary influence is to be found in *Henry VIII*, where Shakespeare's characterization of Cardinal Wolsey – in the speeches of Queen Katharine and Griffith (iv. 2) – is derived from Campion's *History of Ireland*, as incorporated into Holinshed's *Chronicles*. There is another probable echo of this work in Hamlet's passing reference to St Patrick's Purgatory (i. 5).

Of greater interest is the question to what extent Shakespeare may have been influenced by the subsequent literary output of Robert Persons, which was very considerable both in amount and in contemporary importance.[5] After withdrawing to the continent on Campion's arrest, he devoted his talents to the organization of the Jesuit mission in England and to the composition of devotional and controversial writings. The most widely read of all his works was that generally referred to as *The Resolution*, or *A Book of the Christian Exercise, appertaining to Resolution*, which came out in 1582. In Protestant England it owed its popularity to a pirated edition which was soon brought out, with various expurgations and additions, by a clergyman named Edmund Bunny.[6] As such, it soon became a best-seller, and was declared by its printers to be 'the most vendible copy' they had received 'these many years'. Persons himself, however, was less pleased; and three years later he reissued the book in an expanded form under the altered title of *The Christian Directory*. Its influence on Shakespeare's literary contemporaries is amply witnessed by Robert Greene and Thomas Nash. In *The Repentance of Robert Greene*, which was published in 1592 together with *A Groatsworth of Wit*, the former attributes his death-bed conversion to having taken 'the Book of Resolution in my hand'; and in the following year the latter strongly recommended its perusal in his book, *Christ's Tears over Jerusalem* – especially for its skilful refutation of atheism.[7]

The vivid phraseology of Persons, no less than his religious subject-matter, may well have appealed to the mind of Shakespeare. Time and again one comes across words and sentences that seem to be taken up in the plays, especially in *Hamlet*. Taken separately, they may appear to be commonplaces of the age; but seen together, they are precisely the commonplaces that recur in the plays of Shakespeare concerning the 'four last things' of human life. To give a few examples of ideas that recur in *Hamlet*, Persons has much to say about 'the day of our death' and reflects – in words that strongly recall Hamlet's opening soliloquy – how

that body, which was before so delicately entertained . . . whereupon the wind might not be suffered to blow, nor the sun to shine . . . is left for a prey to be devoured of worms.

In his exposition of the traditional proofs for God's existence, he considers – again like Hamlet, in his better frame of mind – how this earth is

> enriched with inestimable and endless treasures, and yet itself standing, or hanging rather, with all this weight and poise, in the midst of the air, as a little ball without prop or pillar.

Yet he goes on to persuade his readers 'against the love of the world' and to give reasons why 'man delights not me' in the present order of things; for in this world a discerning man

> shall see justice sold, verity wrested, shame lost, and equity disguised. He shall see the innocent condemned, the guilty delivered, the wicked advanced, the virtuous oppressed.

In contrast, he recommends frequent meditation on death, almost in the manner of Hamlet in the graveyard; for death it is, he remarks, which

> layeth truly before us, what a man is, how frail and miserable a creature, how fond and vain in the haughtiness of his cogitations while he is in health and prosperity. It is the true glass that representeth a man as he is indeed : other glasses are false and counterfeit.

In this connection he develops the traditional motif of *'Ubi sunt?'* in a manner that points forward even verbally to Hamlet's reflections on the skull of Yorick. On that 'great and last accompting day', he asks with rhetorical insistence,

> Where will all your delights, recreations and vanities be? all your pleasant pastimes? all your pride and bravery in apparel? your glistering in gold? your wanton dalliances and pleasant entertainments?

Not only in *Hamlet*, but in the other great tragedies as well, there are many interesting echoes of the thought and language of Persons' *Christian Directory*. There is, for instance, the same imaginative contrast between calm and tempest as in the second Act of *Othello* (with further echoes in *Othello* iv. 2):

A calm is more pleasant unto passengers after a trouble-some tempest.

This is the only rest set up in the heart of a virtuous man . . . come never so violent seas and waves of temptation.

There is also a detailed characterization of a sinner, which may be seen dramatized in the character of Othello:

He loseth the quiet, joy and tranquillity of a good conscience, and all the favours, cherishments and consolations, and other comforts where with the Holy Ghost is wont to visit the minds of the just . . . He maketh himself guilty of eternal punishment, and enrolleth his name in the book of perdition . . . an inheritor of hell and damnation.

Other remarks on the psychology of the sinner have a closer application to Macbeth: first, his readiness before the deed to 'jump the life to come' –

Let every sinner examine the bottom of his conscience in this point, whether he could not be content there were no immortality of the soul, no reckoning after this life, no judge, no punishment, no hell, and consequently no God at all, to the end he might the more securely enjoy his pleasure.

and then his troubled conscience after the deed, as presented in a long quotation from St John Chrysostom:

Such is the custom of sinners that they suspect all things, in so much as they doubt their own shadows; they are afraid at every little noise, and they think every man that cometh towards them to come against them. Such a thing is sin as it betrayeth itself though no man accuse it . . . For that he hath within his own conscience an accuser, that doth pursue him, the which accuser he always carrieth about with him. And as he cannot fly from himself, so can he not fly from this accuser, that resteth within his conscience.

A further echo, or illustration, of Macbeth's despairing realization that he has given his 'eternal jewel' to 'the common enemy of man' (iii. 1) may be found in Persons' statement that 'a most lively hope or confidence of eternal salvation is one of the greatest treasures and richest jewels that Christian men have left them in this life.'

King Lear, too, is abundantly illustrated in the pages of this book, whose very title sounds in the words of Gloucester to Edmund : 'I would unstate myself, to be in a due resolution' (i. 2).[8] The tempest at the heart of this tragedy may well symbolize the time described by Persons, 'when the fury of the Lord shall come forth as a whirlwind and shall rush and rest upon your heads as a tempest.' His repeated emphasis on human frailty and misery and on the vanity of this world is echoed no less here than in *Hamlet*, as when he observes how the world

> advanceth to authority poor men, that is, such as come naked into this life, and upon the sudden, when they look least for it, doth pull them down again and turn them off naked into their graves.

In a notable passage 'against the love of the world' he uses the very phrasing of Lear's comments on the mad beggar, and thus provides an alternative parallel to the more commonly cited passage from Montaigne's *Essays* : [9]

> We rob and spoil all sorts of creatures upon earth, to cover our backs and adorn our bodies. From one we take his wool; from another, his skin; from another, his hair and fur; and from some other, their very excrements, as the silk, which is nothing else but the excrements of worms. . . . When cats' dung doth smell in our garments, we would have men think that we send forth sweet odour from ourselves.

Finally, his pregnant remark on the pain of loss suffered by the damned soul : 'This word *never* breaketh his heart', may well have inspired Lear's heart-broken repetition of the simple word 'Never' in the concluding scene.

Another work commonly attributed to Persons, both then and now – though he probably had no more than a hand in it – the pseudonymous *Conference about the Next Succession* (1594), has an important connection with the political thought in Shakespeare's history plays.[10] The author attacks the Anglican doctrine of the 'divine right' of kings with many

formidable arguments, which were subsequently taken up by
Milton and the Whig philosophers and used in their resistance
to royal absolutism.[11] Shakespeare's own attitude to this doctrine has often been identified with the one-sided declarations
of John of Gaunt and the Bishop of Carlisle in *Richard II*;
but his characteristic myriad-mindedness emerges out of a
deeper study both of this and of other plays in which the theme
of kingship is dealt with.[12] The official propaganda of the age,
as expressed in the *Homilies*, was naturally in favour of the
doctrine; but the opposite – and, indeed, more traditional –
point of view could not be wholly repressed, least of all when
uttered, as in this book, in connection with the major political
problem of the nineties, that of the succession to the throne of
England. Here the dramatist could have found a lucid statement of the other side of the question, for the nourishment of
his favoured ambiguity; and there are signs here and there
that he not merely depended on hearsay, but actually read and
made use of the ideas of the pseudonymous author.

From the beginning of *The Conference* the author himself
professes to follow a middle line. On the one hand, with evident allusion to the sixteenth-century Puritans, he considers
himself 'far from the opinion of those people of our days, or
of old, who make so little accompt of their duty towards
princes, as be their title what it will, yet for every mislike of
their own they are ready to band against them wheresoever
they think they may make their party good.' On the other
hand, in his opposition to the Anglican doctrine of 'divine
right', he declares that he is equally 'far from the abject and
wicked flattery of such as affirm princes to be subject to no
law or limitation at all.' Such flatterers, he maintains – in
words to be echoed later by Laertes – free princes 'from all
obligation, duty, reverence or respect unto the whole body
whereof they are the heads'. In general, he agrees with Ulysses
in *Troilus and Cressida* that monarchy is the most perfect
form of government. 'It resembleth most of all the government
of God that is but one; it representeth the excellency of one
sun that lighteneth all the planets, of one soul in the body that
governeth all the powers and members thereof.' But, like
Henry V on the eve of Agincourt, he reminds his readers of
the plain truth that, 'A king or prince is a man as others be,

and thereby not only subject to errors in judgement, but also to passionate affections in his will.' He adds, moreover, in words that might well be taken as a text for *King Lear*: 'The greatest plague of all to a prince were to lose the way of righteousness, law and reason in his government, and to give himself over to passion and his own will.' Consequently, he defends the right of subjects, under certain circumstances, even to rise up against their ruler and depose him, adducing the examples of many English kings – John, Edward II, Richard II, Henry VI and Richard III – precisely those whose reigns are covered by the history plays of Shakespeare and Marlowe. Against the contention of the Homily 'Of Obedience', that subjects ought to submit patiently to evil princes 'for their sins' and 'cry to God for remedy', he points out a truth that is echoed in a different context by Helena in *All's Well That Ends Well*: 'God will not always bind himself to work miracles, or to use extraordinary means in bringing those things to pass which he hath left in the hands of men.'

Persons is also associated with Shakespeare in connection with a later work, entitled *Of Three Conversions of England* and published in three parts in 1603–4. In the third part he subjects Foxe's *Book of Martyrs* to a thorough criticism, in the course of which he speaks of Sir John Oldcastle, the champion of the early fifteenth-century Lollards, and his claim to be considered the 'morning-star of the Reformation'. In opposition to Foxe, he dismisses Oldcastle as 'a ruffian knight, as all England knoweth, and commonly brought in by comedians on their stages'.[13] Here the particular 'comedian', or writer of comedies, he has in mind is evidently Shakespeare, whose character of Sir John Falstaff in the two Parts of *Henry IV* grew out of the historical figure of Sir John Oldcastle. The original name, which Shakespeare would have found in the earlier play of *The Famous Victories of Henry the Fifth*, is still apparent in the beginning of Part I, where Prince Hal addresses Falstaff as 'my old lad of the castle' (i. 2), and in the 1600 quarto of Part II, where the abbreviation 'Old' is prefixed to one of Falstaff's speeches. It was probably altered to its present form at the instance of Lord Cobham, a descendant of Oldcastle, and one whose wishes had to be respected by the Chamberlain's Men – as he himself had just been

appointed Lord Chamberlain in August 1596.[14] The defence
of Oldcastle, and of the Protestant cause, was subsequently
taken up by a group of dramatists writing for the Admiral's
Men. In the prologue to this new play of *Sir John Oldcastle*,
they indignantly reject Shakespeare's picture of a 'pampered
glutton' and 'aged counsellor to youthful sin'. Subsequently,
the defence of Oldcastle was also undertaken by the Jacobean
historian, John Speed, in his *History of Great Britain* (1611),
where he directs his criticism equally against the Jesuit and
the dramatist: 'That N.D. [i.e. Nicholas Doleman, pseudo-
nym of Robert Persons], author of The Three Conversions,
hath made Oldcastle a ruffian, a robber and a rebel, and his
authority taken from the stage-players, is more befitting the
pen of his slanderous report than the credit of the judicious,
being only grounded from this papist and his poet, of like conscience for lies, the one ever feigning and the other ever
falsifying the truth.'[15]

A punning reference to Persons has, moreover, been
detected in a somewhat obscure jest in *Love's Labour's Lost*
between Holofernes, Sir Nathaniel, and Costard (iv. 2).
Jacquenetta enters and greets Sir Nathaniel, 'God give you a
good morrow, master parson,' to which Holofernes replies
with a punning conundrum: 'Master parson, quasi pers-on;
an if one should be pierced, which is the one?' Costard
answers: 'Marry, master schoolmaster, he that is likest to a
hogshead.' This exchange is interpreted as a jest against
Robert Persons, who was widely regarded as an arch-traitor,
the instigator of Jesuit plots against the Queen, and worthy of
having his head cut off, pierced and exposed on a pike to
public contempt.[16] The allusion would have particular relevance about the year 1595, when the notoriety of Persons was
increased by his association with Doleman's *Conference on the
Next Succession*. Further substantiation seems to be provided
by more punning later on in the scene. On the exit of Costard
and Jacquenetta, Sir Nathaniel compliments Holofernes on
his handling of the situation: 'Sir, you have done this in the
fear of God, very religiously; and, as a certain Father saith – ';
but he is abruptly checked by the other: 'Sir, tell me not of
the Father; I do fear colourable colours'. The pun is said to
consist in Holofernes's identification of the 'certain Father'

with Father Persons, whose name suggests 'colourable colours' – that is to say (in the words of Cecil's *Execution of Justice in England*, with precise reference to Seminaries and Jesuits), 'manifest and dangerous colourable practices and works of sedition'.

The ingenuity of this interpretation is, however, irrelevant to the total context of this play and its continual reference to the contemporary controversy between Gabriel Harvey and Thomas Nash.[17] A less ingenious, but more satisfying explanation of the above-mentioned passage is, in fact, to be found in Harvey's *Pierces Supererogation*, which he wrote in reply to Nash's *Pierce Penniless*. Here occurs the following sentence, which is used by Shakespeare in this scene : 'She knew what she said that intituled Pierce "the hogshead of wit", Penniless "the tosspot of eloquence", and Nash "the very inventor of asses"; she it is that must broach the barrel of thy frisking conceit and canonize the patriarch of new writers.' These words seem to contain a sufficient explanation of Holofernes's punning; but it is, of course, still open to conjecture as to whether a further reference to Persons is intended or not.

When Persons had to leave the country after Campion's arrest, his place as superior of the few Jesuits in England was occupied for a time by Jasper Heywood, son of John Heywood the dramatist, and uncle of John Donne the poet. In other respects, too, Heywood was indirectly connected with Shakespeare, through his translations of the Senecan tragedies, *Troas* (1559), *Thyestes* (1560) and *Hercules Furens*, which were incorporated in *Seneca his ten Tragedies* and published in 1581. His successor, William Weston, who arrived in England in the late summer of 1584 (after the arrest and imprisonment of Heywood), came to have a connection of a less literary kind with Shakespeare's plays. This was on account of certain exorcisms in which he engaged soon after his arrival at the house of a Catholic gentleman, with the assistance of some Seminary priests, including Shakespeare's former school companion, Robert Dibdale.[18] These exorcisms became notorious at the time and produced many conversions, but they also led to the arrest and execution of Robert Dibdale in 1586. It is possible that they are parodied in *The Comedy of Errors* in the efforts of Pinch the schoolmaster to exorcize devils out of Antipholus of Ephesus (iv. 4).[19] Subsequently, Pinch is described by the indignant Antipholus as

> *a hungry lean-faced villain,*
> *A mere anatomy, a mountebank,*
> *A threadbare juggler, a fortune-teller,*
> *A needy, hollow-eyed, sharp-looking wretch,*
> *A living-dead man.* (v. 1)

In this case, however, the reference to Weston and his associates is less than certain. About this time Puritans, as well as Jesuits and Seminary priests, were being called upon to practise exorcism of devils in other parts of the country. The feats of John Darrel, in particular, were hardly less notorious than those of Weston; and an allusion to them has been discerned in the baiting of Malvolio by Sir Topas in *Twelfth Night* (iv. 2).[20] Of greater significance, perhaps, is the name Shakespeare gives to the exorcist-schoolmaster, which is almost identical with that of a contemporary critic of 'popish jugglings', R. Phinch. In his book, *The Knowledge and Appearance of the Church*, which came out in 1590, he makes scornful reference to the 'false miracles, lying powers and wonders' of the Papists, adding : 'By the which feats they have increased and grown into the greater number. For when by the help of the devil, with their conjurations, charms and divers other false sleights, they wrought miracles and wonders in divers and sundry places, then the people (regarding not the simple word of God) forsook their faith and ran a-gadding from place to place, to gaze upon signs and wonders.' Thus it would seem that in his comedy Shakespeare is turning the tables on Phinch by making him the conjuror.

A more substantial outcome of Weston's exorcizing activities, in dramatic form, is to be found later on in *King Lear* – by way of Samuel Harsnett's account of them in his heavily biased *Declaration of Egregious Popish Impostures* (1604).[21] The same author had already exposed the Puritan exorcisms in his *Discovery of the Fraudulent Practises of John Darrell* (1599), which may have entered into *Twelfth Night*; and he went on to expose the Catholic priests in vivid language, whose influence on *King Lear* may be taken as certain – especially for the characterization of Edgar as Tom o' Bedlam. It is sometimes made a matter of wonder that Shakespeare should have derived material for this greatest of his plays from such an out-of-the-way source; and it is even assumed that he would hardly have read the book if he had not been to some extent in sympathy with its contents. But his interest is sufficiently explained by the fact that a principal character in the narrative was a former school companion, and by the probability that he was curious to know the subsequent fate of his friend as it had recently come to light through the investigations of Harsnett. It is even possible that the lot of such priests as Weston and Dibdale provided Shakespeare with a suggestion for his portrayal of Edgar in hiding – as will be considered in the following chapter.

In the same year that Weston was conducting his exorcisms, there came to England another Jesuit, Robert Southwell, who was to have a closer connection not only with the drama of Shakespeare, but in general with the literature of his time. His position for some time was that of chaplain to the Countess of Arundel, whose husband had been imprisoned in the Tower on account of his conversion to the Catholic faith. As such he came to exercise considerable influence on his contemporaries in London, not only by means of personal contact, but also by his poems and other writings, which were widely circulated in manuscript before being eventually published.[22] It has been suggested, on the basis of an interesting accumulation of evidence, that his popular prose work *Mary Magdalen's Funeral Tears* and his equally popular poem *Saint Peter's Complaint* gave rise to a 'literature of tears' which flooded the literature of the nineties.[23] Through the marriages both of his brother and of his sister he came to be related to the young Earl of Southampton, the Catholic nobleman who was soon to grant his patronage and other favours to Shakespeare; and so he may well have made the acquaintance of Shakespeare himself. A distant blood-relationship has even been traced between the poet and the dramatist through the family of Belknap, which might have entitled them to regard each other as cousins.[24]

Southwell's first book of poems, entitled *Saint Peter's Complaint* after its longest poem, was published posthumously in 1595 by James Roberts, who also published several of Shakespeare's plays. It is prefaced by an interesting dedication 'to my worthy good cousin, Master W.S.', in which the author laments the present state of English poetry. He complains, in particular, that 'poets, by abusing their talents and making the follies and feignings of love the customary subject of their base endeavours, have so discredited this faculty that a poet, a lover and a liar are by many reckoned but three words of one signification'. Here he seems to agree, at least in part, with those Puritan criticisms of poetry which were taken so seriously by Sir Philip Sidney in his *Apology for Poetry* (published, interestingly enough, in the same year), and also to anticipate the remarks of Theseus on 'the lunatic, the lover and the poet' in *A Midsummer Night's Dream* (v. i). He further continues, after presenting his ideal of religious poetry, with an appeal to 'some skilfuller wits to go forward in the same, or to begin some finer piece, wherein it may be seen how well verse and virtue suit together'. The effect of this appeal may be seen, more generally, in the above-mentioned 'literature of tears'; but it may also be studied in the particular case of Shakespeare.

The prose dedication is followed by a further 'dedicatory verse' to the reader, in which Southwell pursues his theme of complaint:

> *This makes my mourning muse dissolve in tears;*
> *This themes my heavy pen – too plain in prose;*
> *Christ's thorn is sharp, no head his garland wears;*
> *Still finest wits are stilling Venus' rose;*
> *In paynim toys the sweetest veins are spent;*
> *To Christian works few have their talents lent.*

The mention of 'Venus' rose' in this passage has been taken as pointing to Shakespeare's *Venus and Adonis*, which was published in 1593 and dedicated to the Earl of Southampton, but probably circulated beforehand, like the *Sonnets* (and Southwell's poem as well), 'among his private friends'. In 'the sweetest veins' there may also be a reference to Shakespeare, whose poetry was particularly praised by his contemporaries for its 'sweetness' and its 'honey-flowing vein'.[25] The very stanza chosen by Southwell (a b a b c c) echoes, perhaps of set purpose, that employed in Shakespeare's poem. For these

reasons it has been conjectured that 'Master W.S.' is no other
than William Shakespeare.[26] As for the reader to whom the
'dedicatory verse' is addressed, it may have been the Earl of
Southampton, who was in a position to grant the concluding
request:

> *Favour my wish, well-wishing works no ill;*
> *I move the suit, the grant rests in your will.*

Here the possible pun on Shakespeare's name is seen to accord
with Shakespeare's own practice in his 'Will' sonnets (135–6);
and the language seems to be echoed in the cryptic dedication
to the 1609 volume: '. . . wisheth the well-wishing adventurer
in setting forth'. The conclusion of all these conjectures is that
Southwell wished to protest against the 'paynim toys' of *Venus
and Adonis* (among other poems) and that Shakespeare
responded with his nobler *Rape of Lucrece*. The subject of the
latter poem is, of course, not openly Christian; but it may be
seen as corresponding to Southwell's own suggestion, stated in
his preface to *Mary Magdalen's Funeral Tears*: 'In fables are
often figured moral truths, and that covertly uttered to a
common good, which without mask would not find so free a
passage.'

A careful study of *The Rape of Lucrece* in conjunction with
Saint Peter's Complaint does indeed serve to bring out some
parallelism between the two poems – as if it was Shakespeare's
intention not only to respond to Southwell's challenge, but
also to outrival him in poetical skill.[27] From this time onwards,
moreover, we may find echoes of the poem not only in some of
the early comedies, but also and especially in the later tragedies
which are to some extent foreshadowed in *The Rape*. For
example, Berowne's lengthy speech on love and 'women's
eyes' in *Love's Labour's Lost* (iv. 3) may well owe something
to the series of stanzas in *The Complaint* apostrophizing the
sacred eyes of Christ:

> *Sweet volumes stored with learning fit for saints,*
> *Where blissful choirs imparadise their minds,*
> *Wherein eternal study never faints,*
> *Still finding all, yet seeking all it finds . . .*

O eyes, whose glances are a silent speech,
In ciphered works high mysteries disclosing,
Which, with a look, all sciences can teach,
Whose text to faithful hearts needs little glozing.

The similar conceits of Valentine in *Two Gentlemen of Verona*, such as his speech beginning, 'And why not death rather than living torment?' (iii. 1), seem to recall the artificial manner of Southwell in such lines as :

> *How can I live that thus my life denied?*

and

> *Whose presence day, whose absence causeth night.*

As for the great tragedies, *Hamlet* is foreshadowed in expressions such as 'the scorn of time' (*cf.* iii. 1 : 'the whips and scorns of time'), 'unkind in kindness' (*cf.* i. 2 : 'a little more than kin and less than kind'; iii. 4 : 'I must be cruel only to be kind'), 'the undermining ill' (*cf.* iii. 4 : 'rank corruption, mining all within'), 'wakeful bird, proclaimer of the day' (*cf.* i. 1 : 'the cock, that is the trumpet of the morn, doth . . . awake the god of day'), 'lancing impostum'd sore' (*cf.* iv. 4 : 'This is the impostume of much wealth and peace'), and 'these scornful words upbraid my inward thought' (*cf.* iv. 4 : 'How all occasions do inform against me'). Likewise in *Othello* are to be found echoes of the following lines :

> *Didst thou to spare his foes put up thy sword?*

(*cf.* i. 2 : 'Keep up your bright swords'),

> *O portress of the door of my disgrace!*

(*cf.* iv. 2 : 'You mistress, that have the office opposite to Saint Peter, and keep the gate of hell'),

> *O women, woe to men, traps for their falls,*
> *Earth's necessary ills, enchanting thralls!*

(*cf.* iii. 3 : 'O curse of marriage! that we can call these delicate creatures ours, and not their appetites.'); while the phrase, 'the scorn of time', already noted in relation to *Hamlet*, recurs in Othello's 'the time of scorn' (iv. 2). Other lines of Southwell's poem are echoed in *Macbeth*, such as :

> *Scarce will a sea cleanse my polluted soul,*
> *Huge horrors in huge tides must drowned be.*

(*cf*. ii. 2 : 'Will all great Neptune's ocean wash this blood clean from my hand?'),

> *Sleep, Death's ally, oblivion of tears,*
> *Silence of passions, balm of angry sore.*

(*cf*. ii. 2 : 'Sleep, that knits up the ravell'd sleave of care, the death of each day's life, sore labour's bath, balm of hurt minds.'),

> *Not such my sleep, but whisperer. of dreams,*
> *Creating strange chimeras, feigning frights.*

(*cf*. iii. 2 : '. . . sleep in the affliction of these terrible dreams that shake us nightly'),

> *Christ, as my God, was templed in my thought.*

(*cf*. ii. 3 : 'Most sacrilegious murder hath broke ope the Lord's anointed temple').

Besides this long poem of Southwell, there is another storehouse of Shakespearian phrases in his prose *Triumphs over Death* – as contrasted with his more popular *Mary Magdalen's Funeral Tears*, which contains relatively few such phrases. In the Preface there is yet another foreshadowing of the dedication to Shakespeare's *Sonnets*, when he speaks of 'as many good wishes as good-will can measure from a best meaning mind'. What is particularly interesting in this book is the large number of parallels with *Hamlet*, no doubt on account of its subject-matter. The author's words of comfort to his noble patroness, 'If this departure be grievous, it is also common', are taken up by Gertrude in her attempt to console her mourning son : 'Thou know'st 'tis common' (i. 2). His observation that 'some live till they be weary of life' seems to foreshadow the weariness of Hamlet, as expressed in his two great soliloquies (i. 2, iii. 1). His attitude to this life, where 'as prisoners we are kept in ward', is also that of Hamlet, when he complains that this world is a prison 'in which there are many confines, wards and dungeons' (ii. 2). He uses several expressions which are later echoed in Hamlet's 'To be or not to be' :

You still float in a troublesome sea . . .
As one rather falling asleep than dying, she most happily
took her leave of all mortal miseries . . .
The general tide wafteth all passengers to the same shore.

His explanation of the uncertainty of death,

that fear of a speedy passage might keep us in readiness,
and hope of longer continuance cut off unripe cares,

seems to enter into Hamlet's words of resignation, 'The readiness is all' (v. 2) – as also into the parallel words of Edgar in
King Lear, 'Ripeness is all' (v. 2). Lastly, his remark that
some men 'are cut off in the middle of their course' may be
echoed in the ghost's complaint : 'Cut off even in the blossoms
of my sin' (i. 5). Such resemblances may well, of course, be
mere coincidences of phrase; but taken together they seem to
point to a pervasive influence of Southwell on Shakespeare.

The execution of Robert Southwell in 1595, about the same
time as two other Jesuits, John Cornelius and Henry Walpole,
who suffered in other parts of the country, is not infrequently
mentioned in explanation of the cryptic couplet with which
Sonnet 124 concludes :

To this I witness call the fools of time,
Which die for goodness, who have lived for crime.[28]

According to this explanation, in the view of their fellow-
Catholics these Jesuit priests died 'for goodness' as martyrs of
Christ, but in the view of their Protestant fellow-countrymen
they had 'lived for crime' as traitors to their queen and country. It is, however, only one among many explanations. Other
commentators, for example, identify the 'fools of time' as the
Protestant martyrs described by John Foxe, or as the companions of the ill-fated Earl of Essex, or more generally as
those who, 'having lived a life of crime, give on their death-
beds a legacy or donation for some religious purpose'.[29]
Nevertheless, the former explanation, understood of all Catholic martyrs who were regularly sentenced on the charge of
treason, derives unexpected support from Southwell himself.
Describing the plight of his fellow-Catholics in his *Humble
Supplication to her Majesty* (not published till 1600, though

with the imprint of 1595), he says: 'We, like God almighty's fools (as some scornfully call us), lay our shoulders under every load.' Shakespeare's words, however, need not be understood in this scornful sense, if we consider the context of his Sonnet. He takes the 'fools of time' as witnesses to the permanence of his love which, like theirs, rises above the changes of time and policy. His following words, 'who have lived for crime', may therefore be interpreted not as an expression of the poet's own opinion, but as an allusion to the legal grounds of their execution.

Another of the above-mentioned martyrs, John Cornelius, is connected with an interesting ghost-story, which has been given as a contemporary parallel to Hamlet's vision of his father's ghost. The story concerns the death of Lord Stourton, a Catholic peer who had temporized with the established religion against his conscience; and it is related by an eye-witness, Dorothy Arundell, half-sister of the dead man.[30] The parallel with Hamlet may not seem particularly close; but it has, at least, some significance, especially in view of its proximity in time (Lord Stourton died on 13 October 1588) to the probable date of the Ur-Hamlet.

> One day my mother, Lady Arundell, begged Father Cornelius to offer up Mass for the soul of her son John, Lord Stourton, which he consented to do. When at the altar he remained for a considerable time in prayer between the consecration and the memento for the dead. After Mass he made an exhortation on the words, Beati mortui qui in Domino moriuntur, and then told us he had just seen a vision. Before him was presented a forest of immense size, in which all was fire and flame, and in the midst he perceived the soul of the deceased Lord. . . . Father Cornelius wept much in relating his vision to us, and all the household, who to the number of about eighty persons were listening to him, united their tears with his. The server of the Mass, afterwards a sufferer for the faith with Father Cornelius, saw and heard all that passed in the vision; but as for myself and the rest of those present, we only perceived, while it was manifested, a glimmering reflection like that of live coals on the wall against which the altar stood.

It was at the trial of Robert Southwell in 1595 that the issue of equivocation was raised, which subsequently became an important part of the official propaganda against the Jesuits.[31] It was there brought to light that he had instructed the daughter of the family with whom he had been staying at the time of his arrest, that she might freely deny having seen him (that is, with the intent to betray him) – even under oath. He tried to explain his reasons for giving such an instruction : namely, in the words of his contemporary, John Gerard : 'In equivocation the intention was not to deceive, which was the essence of a lie, but simply to withhold the truth in cases where the questioned party is not bound to reveal it. To deny a man what he has no claim to was not deception.' But he failed to impress his judges, who were already prejudiced against him; and his defence only served to establish the Jesuits' reputation for duplicity. It has, therefore, been suggested that this was in Shakespeare's mind, when he makes Hamlet protest against the disputatious grave-digger : 'How absolute the knave is! We must speak by the card, or equivocation will undo us' (v. 1).[32] But here, it seems, the word is used by Hamlet not in its technical, but in its general meaning, as defined about this time by Bacon in his *Advancement of Learning* (1605) as 'ambiguity of words and phrase' – with no special reference to the doctrine of Jesuit moralists.

The issue of equivocation was, however, revived in the aftermath of the Gunpowder Plot, when the Jesuit superior in England, Henry Garnet, was put on trial in 1606. After he had denied any previous knowledge of the Plot, it was proved against him that he had received full details of it in confession from Robert Catesby, the leader of the conspirators. He therefore explained that he had resorted to equivocation in order to safeguard a secret of the confessional, which may under no circumstances be revealed by a priest without the consent of the penitent.[33] But his explanation, like that of Robert Southwell, passed unheeded; and he was treated not only as an accomplice, but even as the ring-leader of the conspiracy. All these circumstances are implied in one of the ribald jests of the Porter in *Macbeth*, where mention is made not only of an equivocator, like Henry Garnet, but also of a farmer, with possible reference to one of Garnet's aliases.

> *Here's a farmer, who hanged himself on the expectation*
> *of plenty . . . Here's an equivocator that could swear in*
> *both the scales against either scale, who committed*
> *treason enough for God's sake, yet could not equivocate*
> *to heaven. O, come in, equivocator!* (ii. 3)

The mention of the farmer may also, it is true, have been suggested by Rabelais's description of the usurers of Landerousse, 'who not long since hanged themselves when they saw the price of corn and wine falling and good times returning'; but the general context seems to point clearly enough to Henry Garnet. Coleridge indeed considered the scene an artistic blemish and an interpolation by another hand; but modern critics generally agree with De Quincey, whose outstanding essay 'On the Knocking at the Gate in Macbeth' has proved its deep psychological relevance to the main theme of the play.

Not only the Porter scene in *Macbeth*, but the play as a whole, with its pervading emphasis on the sense of horror and 'the equivocation of the fiend' (v. 5), is related to the impression made on Shakespeare's mind by the trial of Henry Garnet.[34] A full report of the trial was published in the summer of 1606 in an anonymous pamphlet, entitled *A True and Perfect Relation of the Whole Proceedings against the late most Barbarous Traitors, Garnet a Jesuit and his Confederates*. Between this pamphlet and the play there are a striking number of parallels in thought and phraseology. Above all, the sense of horror in Macbeth's 'horrible imaginings' (i. 3), in his 'horrid deed' (i. 7), and in Macduff's horrified discovery of the crime:

> *O horror, horror, horror! Tongue nor heart*
> *Cannot conceive nor name thee!* (ii. 3)

corresponds with remarkable closeness to the wording of the pamphlet. There it is declared in the preliminary indictment: 'The matter now to be offered is matter of treason; but of such horror and monstrous nature, that before now the tongue of man never delivered, the ear of man never heard, the heart of man never conceived, nor the malice of hellish or earthly devil ever practised.' This idea is repeated by Sir Edward Coke in his speech for the prosecution: 'Considering the mon-

strousness and continual horror of this so desperate a cause . . .
neither hath the eye of man seen, nor the ear of man heard the
like things to these . . . This offence is Primae impressionis, and
therefore Sine nomine, without any name which might be
Adaequatum, sufficient to express it . . . This offence is such as
no man can express it, no pattern example it, no measure contain it.' The secrecy and 'unnatural' character of Macbeth's
crime similarly corresponds to the nature of the Gunpowder
Plot as described at the trial of Garnet. 'For treason is like a
tree whose root is full of poison, and lieth secret and hid within
the earth, resembling the imagination of the heart of man,
which is so secret as only God knoweth it . . . Now as this
powder treason is in itself prodigious and unnatural, so is it in
the conception and birth most monstrous, as arising out of the
dead ashes of former treasons.' Parallels with *Macbeth* cluster,
above all, in the words addressed by the attorney-general to
Garnet himself. He pretends to excuse Garnet's conduct by
suggesting that 'your mind was perplexed and disquieted upon
the meditation of strange events' (*cf.* ii. 3 : 'Strange screams
of death . . . confus'd events new hatch'd to the woeful time').
He warns him that 'washing can avail no man' (*cf.* ii. 2 :
'Will all great Neptune's ocean wash this blood clean from
my hand?'). He declares, almost in Macbeth's very words (in
iii. 4): 'Such acts as this is, Non laudantur nisi peracta, are
then only commended when they are performed . . . The more
you labour to get out of the wood, having once lost the right
way, the further you creep in.' He even alludes in open terms
to 'the equivocation of the fiend'. 'The devil now draws the
grounds of equivocation concerning princes' lives out of the
very scripture, and by scholastic authority.'

If Shakespeare used this pamphlet as source-material for his
play, then he must have composed *Macbeth* in a white heat of
inspiration. For Garnet was tried on 28 March, found guilty
soon after, and executed on 3 May. The pamphlet must have
been published in the summer. It is probable that Shakespeare's play was performed at Hampton Court on 7 August in
the presence of James I and Christian IV of Denmark. But we
also have to take into account the probability that it was also
acted earlier in 1606, in view of certain echoes of the play in
Marston's *Sophonisba*, which was entered in the Stationers'

Register on 17 March. In which case the influence may have been the other way round, if at all; and the Porter scene added as an inspired after-thought. Anyhow, *a priori* Shakespeare must have been deeply moved by the recent events of the Gunpowder Plot and the trial of Garnet. He was no mere outsider, startled by the sudden discovery of a crime whose causes and implications he could only conjecture, magnifying them in his horrified imagination. He was himself intimately connected in a variety of ways with these events. The conspirators were for the most part sons of Catholic families in Warwickshire and Worcestershire, the Catesbys, the Treshams, the Winters, the Throckmortons; and through his mother, Mary Arden, Shakespeare was, if distantly, related to each one of them.[35] Many of them, too, had been followers of the Earl of Essex, hoping through his influence to obtain a measure of toleration for their persecuted fellow-Catholics; and through his patron, the Earl of Southampton, Shakespeare was also connected with Essex's entourage – even to the extent of being implicated, if indirectly, in the rising of 1601. Thirdly, the conspirators had frequent meetings at the Mermaid Tavern in London, the very place where Shakespeare used to meet with Ben Jonson and other poets; and Jonson himself was very much in their confidence. Moreover, on the eve of the Plot they held a secret meeting with Robert Catesby, their leader, at Clopton House just outside Stratford. For all these reasons, it may be imagined how Shakespeare would have been horrified at the news of the Plot and the further revelations made at Garnet's trial.

It is, however, too easily assumed that the horror of Shakespeare was that shared by all English Protestants in face of the threat of destruction by Catholic forces. It is forgotten that the horror of English Catholics on hearing the news must have been immeasurably greater. The Protestants, though appalled by the Plot, would have felt only relief at its providential discovery. The Catholics, while appalled (as they were) by the Plot, would have felt still more fearful of its consequences, which were not slow to manifest themselves. They had become inured to persecution during the latter years of Elizabeth's long reign; but on James's accession in 1603 they had hoped for some toleration, at least for his Catholic mother's sake.

Instead, they had received even harsher treatment than before, particularly during the year preceding the Plot; and even Sir Edward Coke admitted at Garnet's trial: 'If any one green leaf for Catholics could have been visibly discerned by the eye of Catesby, Winter, Garnet, Vaux, etc., they would never have entered into practice with foreign princes.' Now, after the discovery of the Plot, they could expect little mercy, whether at the hands of the authorities or of their fellow-countrymen. In the past they had experienced a considerable amount of sympathy for their undeserved sufferings, but even this now disappeared; and they became, as never before, hated outcasts in their own country.

As for the anti-Jesuit feeling implicit in the Porter's scornful words on the 'equivocator', various conjectures may be made concerning the dramatist's own attitude. The words may have been (as Coleridge thought) a later addition to the text of the play, possibly without the consent of the dramatist himself. Or he may have added them as a topical reflection of the feelings of his audience, without necessarily sharing those feelings himself. Or he may have used them in agreement with those English Catholics who disagreed with the moral teaching and political activities of the Jesuits. For some time previous to the Gunpowder Plot there had arisen a fierce dispute between a group of priests known as 'appellants' and the Jesuits over the appointment of an Archpriest for the Catholics in England; and in the course of this dispute many of the methods and teachings of the Jesuits, particularly of Father Persons, had been called in question.[36] Now, therefore, at the trial of Garnet it seemed as if their criticisms of the Jesuits were amply justified; and Shakespeare may well, for the time at least, have felt in agreement with them, especially in their rejection of the Jesuit teaching on equivocation.

On the other hand, there are indications in several plays more or less contemporary with *Macbeth* that Shakespeare was much less ready to reject this teaching on equivocation than is commonly supposed. If anything, he seems in these plays to approve of an attitude that 'out-Jesuits the Jesuits'. In *Measure for Measure* the Duke explains his plan to outwit Angelo, saying:

> *So disguise shall by the disguis'd*
> *Pay with falsehood false exacting.* (iii. 2)

In similar circumstances in *All's Well That Ends Well*, Diana reflects after her interview with Bertram, whom she is likewise planning to outwit:

> *Only in this disguise I think 't no sin*
> *To cozen him that would unjustly win.* (iv. 2)

In a different context in *Coriolanus*, Volumnia declares to her too blunt and forthright son:

> *I would dissemble with my nature where*
> *My fortune and my friends at stake required*
> *I should do so in honour.* (iii. 2)

In each of these instances, it is to be noted, the defence of equivocation (or its rough equivalent) is put into the mouth not of a villain, but of a sympathetic character. In the two comedies it is, moreover, the means of bringing about a happy ending; whereas Coriolanus's neglect of his mother's advice leads directly to his tragedy. In all these cases, equivocation is used for a good end and as such seems to be justified by the dramatist himself.

But there is another kind of equivocation, or quibbling, which is clearly reprobated in *Macbeth*, namely, 'the equivocation of the fiend' – consisting, strangely enough, in the telling not of lies (or apparent lies), but of the truth (or rather, the apparent truth). As Banquo warns Macbeth at the beginning:

> *And oftentimes, to win us to our harm,*
> *The instruments of darkness tell us truths,*
> *Win us with honest trifles, to betray's*
> *In deepest consequence.* (i. 3)

And this is what Macbeth himself comes to realize at the end, when it is too late:

> *I pull in resolution and begin*
> *To doubt the equivocation of the fiend*
> *That lies like truth.* (v. 5)

This was never shown to be the method of the Jesuits, nor even of the dare-devil conspirators in the Gunpowder Plot. If anything, it was the method of their enemies, who had for a quarter of a century been waging a campaign of half-truths against them, supported by sham plots and provocations of various kinds.[37] From the time of the Armada onwards, such plots were particularly numerous and were invariably attributed to Jesuits lurking in the background; but in no case could any allegation be proved by real evidence. It was, in fact, a campaign that might well be described in the words of Bassanio as 'the seeming truth which cunning times put on to entrap the wisest' (*Merchant of Venice* iii. 2).

In view of these considerations, one may find in the plays of Shakespeare as a whole, and even in *Macbeth*, an attitude that is generally favourable to the Jesuits. Admittedly, in this matter one has to observe the method of Polonius and 'by indirections find directions out', by taking into account the various allusions and echoes that have been discovered or conjectured here and there in the plays and poems. What is certain is that Shakespeare was very much alive to everything that was going on around him, not omitting the intense activity of the Jesuits and the even more intense propaganda of their enemies against them. The evidence of the plays tends to show that he sympathized with the former rather than with the latter, and that when he seems to incline towards the latter it is perhaps more a case of seeming than of being.

IV

Catholic Clergy

BETWEEN SHAKESPEARE and the early English Jesuits
there are, as we have seen, not a few probable points of connection; but with the Seminary priests, who were far more
numerous than the Jesuits, the links are considerably fewer.
Mention has already been made of one such priest, Shakespeare's companion at school, Robert Dibdale, who was put to
death in 1586. Perhaps it was in memory of him that the
dramatist makes Lucentio in *The Taming of the Shrew*
masquerade as a 'young scholar that has been long studying at
Rheims' – with reference not so much to the university of
Rheims, as to Allen's Seminary which had moved thither from
Douai in 1578. It has been suggested that Shakespeare was
impressed by one of the few executions of a Catholic priest
that took place in Warwickshire, the hanging of William
Freeman in 1595; but there is no evidence that he was in his
home county at the time.[1] In any case, for one such execution
he might have witnessed or heard about in the neighbourhood
of Stratford, there were many he could see every year in
London at the gallows of Tyburn (near the present Marble
Arch). In *Love's Labour's Lost* there is, in fact, an allusion to
the triple beam of the gallows in Berowne's words: 'The shape
of love's Tyburn, that hangs up simplicity' (iv. 3) – where the
last word seems to refer to the innocence of so many of its
victims, the 'fools of time' (as in *Sonnet* 124).

At least one topical reference to the execution of a Seminary
priest has been discovered, with much circumstantial evidence,

in the final Act of *The Comedy of Errors*.[2] The place to which
the hapless merchant Aegeon is taken for execution, according
to the harsh penal laws of Ephesus, is described as

> *The melancholy vale,*
> *The place of death and sorry execution,*
> *Behind the ditches of the abbey here.* (v. 1)

It is noted that this exactly describes the site chosen for the
hanging of William Hartley, a Catholic priest, shortly after
the failure of the Spanish Armada in 1588 – not Tyburn, as
was usual, but Shoreditch, which was just outside the city and
'behind' the walls of the dismantled Holywell Priory. Here
were situated the Theatre and the Curtain, and here, according to John Aubrey, Shakespeare himself lived during his early
years in London.[3] The proposed identification of Aegeon with
Hartley is supported by the common practice of Seminary
priests and Jesuits to enter the country disguised as merchants
and to correspond with each other using the language of merchants (in case their letters were intercepted by government
agents) – following the suggestion of Christ's parable of the
pearl in *Matthew* xiii. 45–6.[4] The enmity between Ephesus
and Syracuse that forms the background of the play might
well be understood as implying a topical allusion to the political and religious opposition between Protestant England and
Catholic Spain or Rome. The point of the allusion may have
been a veiled plea for toleration at a time when anti-Catholic
penal proceedings were exceeding all bounds.[5]

Apart from this one instance, which is itself no more than
probable, there are no certain references in Shakespeare's
plays to the sufferings of English Catholics – though he must
have been well aware of them and even, as we have seen, to
some extent shared in them. It is this apparent silence of his
that prompted the Catholic novelist, Graham Greene, to
exclaim in his Introduction to *John Gerard, the Autobiography of an Elizabethan* : 'Isn't there one whole area of
the Elizabethan scene that we miss even in Shakespeare's huge
world of comedy and despair? The kings speak, the adven-
turers speak . . . the madmen and the lovers, the soldiers and
the poets; but the martyrs are quite silent.' To his implied
question it might, of course, be answered that none of the plays

have a contemporary English setting, and so there is no occasion for mentioning the martyrs. But this is not quite to the point. For in spite of their romantic settings in distant ages and nations, the plays all reflect – as Hamlet says they should – 'the very age and body of the time' (iii. 2), and may thus be called 'the abstracts and brief chronicles of the time' (ii. 2). It may be said that Shakespeare himself was nothing if not contemporary in his writings; and it was, as Shaw says, by writing about himself and his own time that he came to write 'about all people and about all time'.[6] The expectation of Graham Greene is, therefore, a just one; but it is not satisfied on the surface of the plays.

Some significance may be found in the frequent mention of various kinds of torment to which Catholic priests were regularly subjected after their arrest as 'traitors' – though they were not the only victims. In general, the unjust bloodshed of innocent men is a common theme in the history plays, which present a wide prospect of 'England's lawful earth unlawfully made drunk with innocent blood' (*Richard III* iv. 4). Its continuing reality in Shakespeare's own time may well have prompted the indignant irony in Timon's advice to Alcibiades :

> *Put armour on thine ears and on thine eyes,*
> *Whose proof nor yells of mothers, maids, nor babes,*
> *Nor sight of priests in holy vestments bleeding,*
> *Shall pierce a jot.* (iv. 3)

In particular, the torture of the rack as a means of extracting confessions from traitors is mentioned in *Richard II* (iii. 2), *Twelfth Night* (v. 1), *Othello* (iii. 3) and *King Lear* (v. 3).[7] Above all, in *The Merchant of Venice* it is extended into a lengthy metaphor in an exchange of wit between Bassanio and Portia :

> B.   *Let me choose;*
>   *For as I am, I live upon the rack.*
> P.   *Upon the rack, Bassanio! Then, confess*
>   *What treason there is mingled with your love.*
> B.   *None but that ugly treason of mistrust,*
>   *Which makes me fear th' enjoying of my love:*

> *There may as well be amity and life*
> *'Tween snow and fire, as treason and my love.*
> P. *Ay, but I fear you speak upon the rack,*
> *Where men enforced do speak anything.*
> B. *Promise me life, and I'll confess the truth.*
> P. *Well then, confess and live.*
> B. *'Confess' and 'love'*
> *Had been the very sum of my confession.* (iii. 2)

The cruel form of execution for traitors, by being hanged, drawn and quartered, is mentioned in a bantering context in both *Much Ado About Nothing* (iii. 2) and *King John* (ii. 1). The preliminary dragging of the victim on a hurdle to the place of execution is also alluded to in *Romeo and Juliet*, where Capulet warns his daughter that she must go to church for her wedding with Count Paris, 'or I will drag thee on a hurdle thither' (iii. 5).

The unjust accusation of treason commonly made against Catholics in Elizabethan England, and particularly against all priests since the harsh penal laws of 1585, is interestingly reflected in quite a number of the plays. There is, for instance, the indignant remark of the Duke of York in *Richard II*: 'The traitor lives, the true man's put to death' (v. 3). Of greater interest – in view of the Warwickshire associations of Arden – are the words of the usurping Duke in *As You Like It* where he retorts against Rosalind's protestations of innocence :

> *Thus do all traitors;*
> *If their purgation did consist in words,*
> *They are as innocent as grace itself.* (i. 3)

His words seem to echo those of Lord Burghley himself, in his self-justifying pamphlet on *The Execution of Justice in England* (1583): 'It hath been in all ages and in all countries a common usage of all offenders for the most part, both great and small, to make defence of their lewd and unlawful facts by untruths and by colouring and covering their deeds (were they never so vile) with pretences of some other causes of contrary operations or effects.' In contrast, there is this contemporary complaint of a Catholic against Elizabethan judges: 'It is ordinary with them to call Catholics traitors, and to proceed against them in their judgements as on cases of treason, not-withstanding that the case be directly conscience.'[8]

Clearest of all, however, is the reflection in *King Lear*. The rejection of Cordelia and the banishment of Kent, merely for their truth and honesty (i. 1); the machinations of Edmund against his brother and then against his father, reminiscent of the notorious case of Thomas Fitzherbert; the inversion by Cornwall of the names of 'traitor' and 'loyal servant', thereby turning 'the wrong side out' (iv. 2); the miserable plight of the faithful Edgar – all these elements in the play have precise correspondences in the contemporary sufferings of English Catholics.[9] Edgar, in particular, is much like the hunted priest, who was the object of frequent proclamations, was obliged to go about in disguise under an assumed name, and lived in continual fear of intelligence being given as to his whereabouts. With Edgar, the priest could truly say:

> *No port is free; no place*
> *That guard, and most unusual vigilance,*
> *Does not attend my taking.* (ii. 3)

With Edgar, he could describe himself as 'a most poor man, made tame to fortune's blows' (iv. 6), and even at times as 'the lowest and most dejected thing of fortune' (iv. 1). Edgar's realization of his need to 'lurk, lurk' (iii. 6) echoes the 'secret lurkings' of the priests condemned by Burghley in the above-mentioned pamphlet, where they are characterized as 'wandering up and down in corners, in disguised sort, changing their titles, names and manner of apparel'.[10] Their plight is set forth by Edmund Campion in a letter to the General of the Jesuits, in 1580: 'I cannot long escape the hands of the heretics; the enemy have so many eyes, so many tongues, so many scouts and crafts. I am in apparel to myself very ridiculous; I often change my name also . . . Threatening edicts come forth against us daily.' Robert Southwell several years later elaborates on the same theme in his *Humble Supplication*, published in 1600, which almost reads like a blueprint for Shakespeare's characterization of Edgar: 'We are made the common theme of every railing declaimer, abused without hope or means of remedy, by every wretch with most infamous names; no tongue so forsworn but it is of credit against us;

none so true, but it is thought false in our defence . . . So heavy is the hand of our superiors against us, that we generally are accounted men whom it is a credit to pursue, a disgrace to protect, a commodity to spoil, a gain to torture, and a glory to kill.'

More precise portrayals of Catholic priests – without allegorical disguise – are to be found in the three friars who appear in *Romeo and Juliet, Much Ado About Nothing* and *Measure for Measure.* In their portrayals it is interesting to notice the contrast between Shakespeare's apparent fondness for these friars 'of orders grey' (*The Taming of the Shrew* iv. 1) and the undisguised antipathy of many contemporary dramatists, such as Robert Greene and George Chapman. Even Chaucer in the Catholic Middle Ages seems none too fond of the friars, whom he could see at close quarters; whereas Shakespeare, living in Protestant England, evinces a certain nostalgia for them – as it were applying to himself and his own age the general truth enunciated by the friar in *Much Ado* :

> It so falls out
> That what we have we prize not to the worth
> Whiles we enjoy it; but being lack'd and lost,
> Why, then we rack the value, then we find
> The virtue that possession would not show us
> Whiles it was ours. (iv. 1)

There is also a further contrast between the comparatively favourable portrayal of these friars and the less than favourable portrayal of the few Protestant clergymen who appear in the plays – and who will be examined in a later chapter. Whereas the former speak with authority, within the sphere of their religious vocation, and command the respect of the other characters, the latter are invariably ridiculed in one way or another.

In *Romeo and Juliet* Friar Laurence is introduced as 'ghostly father' or 'ghostly confessor' – with the word 'ghostly' used in its medieval sense of 'spiritual' in a religious context – to both hero and heroine. To him they have recourse not merely for the ceremony of marriage, whereby holy church must 'incorporate two in one' (ii. 6), but also for comfort and advice in their human problems. His replies to their questions consist not merely of pious platitudes, but also of practical suggestions, and even at times of severe, though kindly, reprehensions. If his scheme to assist them meets with failure, it is through no fault of his own, but by a sad mischance. To the end, his reputation for holiness remains unshaken, even when the story of his scheme has been fully unfolded. In the eyes of Romeo, he is 'a divine, a ghostly confessor, a sin-absolver' (iii. 3); in the opinion of Juliet's father, he is a 'reverend holy friar' (iv. 2); in the conviction of Juliet herself, when a doubt assails her mind, 'he hath still been tried a holy man' (iv. 3); and in the final unfolding of the story, he is yet recognized by the Prince 'for a holy man' (v. 3). Not without reason he has been interpreted by several modern critics as a figure of Divine Providence, analogous to the Duke in *Measure for Measure* and Prospero in *The Tempest*.[11] Though his plans fail in their earthly purpose, they are connected, in his own words, with 'a greater power than we can contradict', the very power of which he is the earthly representative (v. 3). There is, it is true, something ambivalent about his character, which makes it possible for some producers to present him as a doddering old man who makes needless trouble for everyone, or as a male figure of farce (on Romeo's side) to balance the female figure of the Nurse (on Juliet's side). Such an interpretation adds, no doubt, to the amusement of the audience; but it is less justified by Shakespeare's text, and deprives the tragedy of much of its deep significance. The fact that it still remains possible may well be due not to Shakespeare himself, but to his Protestant source, Arthur Brooke's *Tragical History of Romeus and Juliet*, where the 'superstitious friar' is introduced as 'the naturally fit instrument of unchastity'.

In his characterization of Friar Francis in *Much Ado About Nothing*, Shakespeare is not limited by any bias in his source, Bandello's *Novelle*, and is therefore able to portray him without any ambiguity. In the source, in fact, the priest is merely brought in at the end to perform the wedding ceremony; and so in the play the character of Friar Francis is entirely the invention of the dramatist himself. There is, moreover, a clear connection between him and Friar Laurence.

From the moment of his first appearance at the wedding ceremony, where Claudio repudiates Hero (iv. 1), he takes charge of the situation, convinced of the lady's innocence. His insight into her character is matched by his resourcefulness in devising a scheme to vindicate her; and his scheme, unlike that of Friar Laurence (which, however, it closely resembles in kind), is crowned with success. Consequently, the play turns out to be, not a tragedy like *Romeo and Juliet*, but a comedy with a happy ending. It is almost as if what had befallen amiss in the former play is meant to be rectified in the latter, with a view to emphasizing the Christian principle of 'die to live' (iv. 1). The friar's advice is followed without question by the other characters; and in the final scene he is described by Claudio as 'this holy friar'. He then introduces Claudio to his new bride, who turns out to be the living Hero, as it were risen from the dead. In the subsequent dialogue, which is charged with Christian overtones, Claudio exclaims, 'Another Hero!', and she replies :

> *Nothing certainer;*
> *One Hero died de fil'd, but I do live,*
> *And surely as I live, I am a maid.* (v. 4)

The third friar, in *Measure for Measure*, is not indeed a real friar, but only an impersonation by the Duke – thereby providing a contrast with the impersonation of a parson by the Clown in *Twelfth Night*. Whereas in the latter play the impersonation of Sir Topas is mere fooling and serves to throw ridicule no less on parsons than on Malvolio, here the impersonation of a friar has a serious purpose, which proves to be a matter of life and death. In the other two plays where a friar appears among the major characters, he appears primarily in connection with marriage, and only secondarily in connection with death – pretended in *Much Ado*, but (ultimately) real in *Romeo and Juliet*. But in this play the Duke, in his character of Friar Lodowick, seems chiefly concerned with the task of preparing souls for death, and for a better life after death – though his ultimate aim is to *heal*. He advises Claudio (another Claudio, in love with another Juliet) :

> *Be absolute for death; either death or life*
> *Shall thereby be the sweeter.* (iii. 1)

In his reply, Claudio echoes the friar's words, to indicate their impact on his mind and to emphasize their deep meaning:

> *To sue to live, I find I seek to die,*
> *And seeking death, find life; let it come on.*

In spite of the apparent secularity of his advice, which has been criticized as unworthy of a friar,[12] it is, like many other such passages in Shakespeare, interwoven with Biblical echoes – from *Ecclesiasticus* xli. 3, *Job* xiv. 12, *Revelation* iii. 17, *Psalm* xlix. 17, I *Timothy* vi. 6; and it elicits from Claudio a similarly Biblical response – from *Matthew* xvi. 25. It also contains a noticeable echo of a constant theme of Robert Southwell in such poems as 'I die alive':

> *I live, but such a life as ever dies,*
> *I die, but such a death as never ends . . .*
> *Thus still I die, yet still I do revive,*
> *My living death by dying life is fed.*

His resourcefulness, moreover, is not inferior to that of Friar Francis; and his character is, even more than that of Friar Laurence, one of a father-figure and type of Divine Providence. So long as he remains a friar, he is presented as 'a brother of gracious order' (iii 2), acclaimed by others as 'a man of comfort' (iv. 1), and granted all his requests, to such an extent that the Provost on admitting him to the prison adds: 'I would do more than that if more were needful' (ii. 3). To some it has seemed strange, not only that the Duke should masquerade as a friar, but that he should be allowed to do so by other friars.[13] This criticism, however, is only justified in a naturalistic interpretation of the play; but a naturalistic interpretation is just what Shakespeare seems to be taking pains to prevent in *Measure for Measure* – as its very title seems to imply.

Between these three plays, in which a prominent part is assigned to a friar, there is, moreover, an unexpected connection in the names of the hero and heroine. The lovers in *Measure for Measure* – as has already been pointed out in part – derive their names, not from Giraldi's tale or Whetstone's play, but in one case from the hero of *Much Ado About Nothing* and in the other from the heroine of *Romeo and Juliet.*[14] The reason for Shakespeare's selection of these names is uncertain. But that of Claudio may be connected with his 'closure' in prison as a result of his 'too much liberty' (i. 2), and that of Juliet with the 'jewel' of her chastity which Claudio has found and stooped to take (ii. 1).[15] Their clandestine marriage points – as noted in a previous chapter – to the circumstances of Shakespeare's own marriage with Anne Hathwey, which may have been celebrated before Sir John Frith, the old Marian priest at Temple Grafton.[16] Sir John rather resembles the friar in *Romeo and Juliet*, with his skill in natural remedies; but the Duke as Friar Lodowick, who is described by Lucio as 'the old fantastical duke of dark corners', may be more aptly compared with those Jesuits and Seminary priests of whom Lord Burghley speaks in his *Execution of Justice in England* as wandering 'up and down in corners, in disguised sort, changing their titles, names and manner of apparel'. The theme of 'die to live', in particular, as taken up by Friar Lodowick from Friar Francis, recalls the constant exhortations of the priests to their fellow-Catholics – as in Southwell's *Epistle of Comfort* – to face with courage not only the hardships and vexations of life under the penal laws, but also the prospect of martyrdom.

In addition to the three friars who figure prominently in their respective plays, there are many other friars, monks, priests and religious men, as well as abbesses and sisters, who move about in the background. In *Two Gentlemen of Verona*, besides the unnamed monk who sends advice from his cloister about his nephew's education (i. 3), there is a Friar Patrick, whose cell is visited by Silvia, like another Juliet, for the purpose of 'holy confession' (iv. 3) – and to join her lover. In *Romeo and Juliet* there is also Friar John, who goes on the vital errand to Mantua for Friar Laurence, but fails to deliver his message to Romeo on account of his charitable visit to a plague-stricken house (v. 2). In *Measure for Measure* the Duke is assisted in his schemes by two real friars – Friar Thomas, who is called a 'holy father' and instructs the Duke in the way of life of a 'true friar' (i. 3); and Friar Peter, who helps the Duke to expose Angelo's misdeeds (v. 1). In *As You Like It* Rosalind refers to 'an old religious uncle of mine', who taught her to speak with a fine accent and to beware of love

(iii. 2); and there is the mysterious 'old religious man' at the end of the play, whose conversation succeeds in turning the usurping Duke 'both from his enterprise and from the world' (v. 4). In *Twelfth Night* there is the priest who performs the marriage ceremony between Sebastian and Olivia : he is called a 'holy man' and a 'good father' (iv. 3), and his holy thoughts are expressed in the simple statement that since he performed the ceremony 'toward my grave I have travell'd but two hours' (v. 1).

Behind all such references to Catholic priests and religious there appears a feeling of nostalgia for the Catholic past of England, now dissolved and fallen into ruin like the medieval monasteries. This is fully in keeping with the repeated suggestion in Shakespeare's plays of preference for 'old fashions' (*The Taming of the Shrew* iii. 1), 'old custom' (*As You Like It* ii. 1) and 'the constant service of the antique world' (*ibid.* ii. 3), for 'plain old form' (*King John* iv. 2) and 'our former state' which now seems but 'a happy dream' (*Richard II* v. 1). He speaks with affection of 'nooks merely monastic' (*As You Like It* iii. 2), of hermitages and 'holy edifices of stone' (*The Merchant of Venice* i. 1), of 'reclusive and religious life' (*Much Ado About Nothing* iv. 1), and of a life spent 'remote from all the pleasures of the world' (*Love's Labour's Lost* v. 2). In the suppression of the monasteries, he implies, charity has been offended (*King John* iii. 4), commodity has extended her sway (*ibid.* ii. 1), and country folk are increasingly oppressed by new owners, who 'little reck to find the way to heaven by doing deeds of hospitality' (*As You Like It* ii. 4). This is all aptly summed up in the melancholy *Sonnet* 73, where the poet (though barely thirty years of age, if we accept the common dating of 1594) seems to identify himself with that past and makes a significant allusion to the monastic ruins :

> *That time of year thou mayst in me behold*
> *When yellow leaves, or none, or few, do hang*
> *Upon those boughs which shake against the cold,*
> *Bare ruin'd choirs, where late the sweet birds sang.*[17]

On the other hand, it is necessary to take note of some anti-Papal passages in three of the history plays, connected with certain Cardinals who played an important part in English events. In *Henry VI* Part I, Cardinal Beaufort is characterized as a proud, ambitious prelate in antagonism with the 'good Duke Humphrey'. He is openly defied by the latter, with language that must have been warmly applauded by a Protestant audience:

> *Under my feet I stamp thy cardinal's hat,*
> *In spite of pope or dignities of church.* (i. 3)

He is also called a 'wolf in sheep's array', and described by the Mayor of London as being 'more haughty than the devil' (*ibid.*). Such descriptions come, of course, from the mouths of his enemies; and for a time the play seems to show a certain ambivalence on either side. But in the outcome, as presented in Part II, the good Duke is murdered partly by 'the Cardinal Beaufort's means' (iii. 2), and is thus confirmed in the sympathy of the audience; whereas the Cardinal is shown in the following scene dying in a state of agonized delirium, which is said to argue 'a monstrous life' (iii. 3).[18]

In *King John*, the Papal Legate, Cardinal Pandulph, has to listen to similar words of defiance from the mouth of the King – only this time their object is not the Cardinal himself, but the Pope:

> *What earthly name to interrogatories*
> *Can task the free breath of a sacred king?*
> *Thou canst not, cardinal, devise a name*
> *So slight, unworthy and ridiculous,*
> *To charge me to an answer, as the pope.* (iii. 1)

These are words, echoed from the earlier play of *The Troublesome Reign of John King of England*, in which John is represented as foreshadowing Henry VIII and the English Reformation.[19] In the same vein there follows a statement of the Anglican doctrine of the royal supremacy in ecclesiastical affairs, in what amounts to a paraphrase of Article 37 of the Thirty-Nine Articles:[20]

> *Tell him this tale, and from the mouth of England*
> *Add thus much more, that no Italian priest*
> *Shall tithe or toll in our dominions;*

But as we, under heaven, are supreme head,
So under him that great supremacy,
Where we do reign, we will alone uphold,
Without the assistance of a mortal hand;
So tell the pope, all reverence set apart
To him and his usurp'd authority. (ibid.)

The King goes on with a Protestant tirade, typical of the age, in which he sets at nought the leadership of 'this meddling priest', with his sale of 'corrupted pardon' (or indulgences) and his 'juggling witchcraft' (referring to Masses for the dead). It is interesting to note that this whole speech was deleted by a Jesuit, Father William Sankey, in his censorship of the 1632 folio edition of Shakespeare's plays for the Spanish Inquisition.[21] Pandulph himself is not, however, an evil man like Cardinal Beaufort; but he seems too ready to invoke 'the curse of Rome' and to involve himself in political quarrels, first against England, and then against France. He is somewhat surprised to find the Dauphin 'too wilful-opposite' to his entreaties on behalf of England, but even more surprised when the Bastard supports the Dauphin :

By all the blood that ever fury breath'd,
The youth says well. (v. 2)

– not for opposing England, but for opposing the Papal Legate. In other words, Shakespeare seems to level his criticism both at the ecclesiastical pretensions of the King and at the political pretensions of the Cardinal – considering the true interests both of the Church and of the State.

Thirdly, in the final history play of *Henry VIII*, there appear two Cardinals, Wolsey and Campeius, as the Papal Legates appointed to preside over the divorce proceedings between the King and the Queen. Their delaying tactics lead the King to complain indignantly of 'this dilatory sloth and tricks of Rome' (ii. 4). Of the two, Campeius is very lightly sketched, but he is courteous and kind of speech. Wolsey, however, is seen by the Queen, and by most others besides, as 'cramm'd with arrogancy, spleen and pride' (ii. 4). Yet in his downfall he redeems his former faults by a sincere repentance; and then, in the words of Griffith to the Queen, 'he felt himself, and found the blessedness of being little' (iv. 2). The final

Act of the play is to some extent taken up with the quarrel between two ecclesiastics, the Catholic Gardiner, Bishop of Winchester, and the Protestant Cranmer, Archbishop of Canterbury. The King judges between the two, and his preference falls on the latter, whom he calls 'true-hearted' and 'a soul none better in my kingdom' (v. 1). For this episode the dramatist is mainly indebted to the somewhat biased account in Foxe's *Book of Martyrs*; and there is also good reason to doubt if he is indeed Shakespeare, and not another.[22]

A further episode in a history play that involves two time-serving prelates, this time presented not in opposition, but in collusion with each other, occurs in the first Act of *Henry V*. From the outset of the play the Archbishop of Canterbury and the Bishop of Ely are shown in conversation about a Bill soon to be proposed in the Commons about taking away 'all the temporal lands which men devout by testament have given to the church' (i. 1). In order to win over the King to their side, and so keep their possessions, they plan to lay open 'the several and hidden passages' of his pretended title to the French crown. This is what Canterbury proceeds to do in the following scene, in a long-winded explanation which would be pure comedy but that it subserves the harsh tragedy of war. On the surface, therefore, the play seems to be a celebration of patriotism triumphant; but beneath the surface there is an undercurrent of doubt about the motives of war, and in the concluding Chorus there is significant mention of the outcome – the loss of France and civil strife in England.

Other prelates in the history plays appear to better advantage. In *Richard III* both the Archbishop of York and Cardinal Bourchier are concerned for the safety of the young Duke of York and his right of sanctuary, though the latter is prepared to use means of persuasion – provided he does not 'infringe the holy privilege of blessed sanctuary' (iii. 1). There is also the Bishop of Ely, who attends a meeting of the council; but he is hardly characterized at all – save that he is perhaps overly anxious to please Richard. In *Richard II* the Bishop of Carlisle stands out for his loyalty to the King and his assertion of 'divine right'. He even appears, like John of Gaunt before him, in the function of a prophet, warning 'proud Hereford' that

> *The blood of English shall manure the ground*
> *And future ages groan for this foul act.* (iv. 1)

Subsequently, he joins with Aumerle and the Abbot of West-minster in a plot to restore Richard to the throne; but even when the plot is exposed and he is brought before the new king, Henry IV, the latter grants him his life in view of 'high sparks of honour' seen in him (v. 6). The place of Carlisle is to some extent taken in the two Parts of *Henry IV* by Richard Scroop, Archbishop of York – whose rebellion is presented in terms reminiscent of the rising of the Northern Earls in 1569.[23] In his case there appears a certain ambivalence, which is very characteristic of Shakespeare in his presentation of history. On the one hand, he is described as 'the gentle Arch-bishop of York' and is 'suppos'd sincere and holy in his thoughts', so that he 'turns insurrection to religion' (Part II i. 1). By virtue of his holy office he should be, as Westmoreland points out, a man of peace

> *Whose white investments figure innocence,*
> *The dove and very blessed spirit of peace.* (iv. 1)

And in the eyes of Prince John, who is sent out to check his rebellion, he appears as

> *the imagin'd voice of God himself,*
> *The very opener and intelligencer*
> *Between the grace, the sanctities of heaven*
> *And our dull workings.* (iv. 2)

On the other hand, he has committed the crime of treason, caught up in a political dilemma that makes him one of the 'fools of time', as mentioned in *Sonnet* 124.

In general, it may be said that the presentation of ecclesi-astical prelates, whether favourable or unfavourable, depends in large measure on the historical or dramatic source of each play. For the most part, Shakespeare presents them as he finds them, being concerned chiefly with their human and dramatic interest. Apart from their human qualities, whether worthy or unworthy, he always shows respect for their holy office – with no sign of the Protestant distaste for 'Popish prelates' or the Puritan hostility to 'Lord bishops'. As for his attitude to the

Pope, the long speech in *King John* which contains the only real evidence in the plays of anti-Papal feeling is conditioned partly by the dramatic context, partly by the stronger Protestant sentiment of its source, *The Troublesome Reign*. What Shakespeare has done is to tone down the religious bias of the earlier play, and to develop its plot along more political lines.[24] Other references to the See of Rome are either neutral or favourable, in keeping with the character of the speaker. In *King John* Pandulph speaks of 'the great metropolis and see of Rome' (v. 2). In *Measure for Measure* the Duke, as Friar Lodowick, professes to come 'from the See, in special business from his Holiness' (iii. 2). Finally, in *Henry VIII* Wolsey speaks of Rome as 'the nurse of judgment' (ii. 2), and the Queen, finding no justice in England, makes her 'appeal unto the pope' and brings her 'cause 'fore his holiness' (ii. 4).

In addition to these obvious references on the surface of the text, there are two interesting passages in the last plays which hint at an allegorical connection with the Papacy. In *Cymbeline*, where the situation of the aged King in many ways recalls that of Henry VIII, Posthumus is described by Iachimo in terms reminiscent of Papal dignity and prerogative, especially that of infallibility :

> *He sits among men like a descended god;*
> *He hath a kind of honour sets him off,*
> *More than a mortal seeming . . . A sir so rare,*
> *Which you know cannot err.* (i. 6)

Similarly, in *The Winter's Tale*, Leontes, whose character and deeds again correspond roughly to those of Henry VIII, confesses his former injustice to Polixenes in welcoming the latter's son, Florizel, to Sicily :

> *You have a holy father,*
> *A graceful gentleman, against whose person,*
> *So sacred as it is, I have done sin.* (v. 1)

A fuller examination of these and other plays in relation to the person of Henry VIII must be left to a later chapter. Here it is enough to point out that both these plays seem to look forward to a reconciliation between England and Rome, as expressed in the reunion of Leontes with Polixenes and in Cymbeline's unconstrained submission to the authority of Rome:

> *Publish we this peace*
> *To all our subjects. Set we forward: let*
> *A Roman and a British ensign wave*
> *Friendly together.* (v. 5)

V

The Bible

THE RELIGIOUS movements of the Reformation period in England may be said to have centred on the Bible, and on its successive English translations. In contrast to the Catholic emphasis on the tradition of the Church, Article 6 of the Thirty-Nine Articles declared: 'Holy Scripture containeth all things necessary to salvation; so that whatsoever is not read therein, nor may be proved thereby, is not to be required of any man, that it should be believed as an article of the faith, or be thought requisite or necessary to salvation.' Thereby a new emphasis was laid on the importance of reading the text of Holy Scripture; and a new incentive was given both to education in the elements of reading and writing and to translation of the Bible into the vernacular language. The pioneering work of translation into English was undertaken in the reign of Henry VIII by William Tyndale and Miles Coverdale, culminating in the Great Bible of 1539, often known as Cranmer's Bible. In the subsequent reign of Elizabeth the official version of the Church of England was the Bishops' Bible, which was published in 1568 under the supervision of Archbishop Parker. A more popular version for family use was the Geneva Bible, which had already appeared in 1560 and which maintained its popularity throughout the reign. The Catholics, for their part, were not uninfluenced by these translations, though they objected to a Protestant bias in them. Eventually, in 1582, they produced a scholarly version of the New Testament, mainly the work of Gregory Martin, a professor at the Seminary of Rheims. His version of the Old Testament was not added until 1609, when the Seminary had moved back to its original home at Douai. Finally, a crown was set on all these translations with the publication in 1611 of King James's Authorized Version, which superseded all others except the Douai Version for the Catholics.[1]

To this great movement of Biblical translation the plays of Shakespeare are by no means unresponsive. The two major versions of the Elizabethan Age, the Bishops' and the Geneva, are both clearly represented in them, though the later plays seem to contain a larger proportion of echoes from the Geneva.[2] Only, when he uses the phraseology of the *Psalms,* it has been noted that Shakespeare follows the Great Bible, as used for the *Psalms* in the *Book of Common Prayer.* This seems to indicate that, in spite of his probable Catholic upbringing, he attended the Anglican services at least for a time during the impressionable years of his youth; though it is true he might also have picked up many phrases of the *Psalms* that had passed into common parlance. The Catholic Rheims version of the New Testament was accessible, in spite of the general ban on Catholic books, through William Fulke's 1589 edition of its text with a detailed confutation of its notes. There are only a few indications of its influence on the plays, which may be briefly mentioned.[3] The Rheims use of the word 'cockle' in *Matthew* xiii. 25, where the Protestant versions have 'tares', may be echoed in *Love's Labour's Lost,* 'Sowed cockle reaps no corn' (iv. 3), and in *Coriolanus,* 'The cockle of rebellion' (iii. 1) – but these passages could also be explained with reference to a country proverb. Other echoes are clearer. In *All's Well That Ends Well* the Clown's distinction between the 'narrow gate' and the 'broad gate' (iv. 5) follows the wording of the Rheims version for *Matthew* vii. 13, where the Protestant versions have 'strait' and 'wide'. In *The Tempest* Ariel's assurance, 'Not a hair perish'd' (i. 2), is closer to the Rheims version for *Luke* xxi. 18 or *Acts* xxvii. 34 than to the Protestant versions, which have 'fall' instead of 'perish'. Shakespeare's use of these phrases from the Catholic version is perhaps to be explained rather by conversation with Catholic friends than by personal reading of the Rheims Testament.

His familiarity with the Bible is surprisingly extensive.

There is hardly a book of the Old or the New Testament which is not represented at least by some chance word or phrase in one or other of his plays. The books he seems to have known most thoroughly, and even in places by heart, are *Genesis, Job,* the *Psalms* and *Ecclesiasticus,* from the Old Testament, and the Gospels of St Matthew and St Luke, with the Epistle to the Romans, from the New Testament. In his use of them, he does not merely borrow an occasional phrase or allusion for the enrichment of his dramatic language, but he derives the central ideas and images that run through all his plays. One might, in fact, characterize each stage of his dramatic development in terms of some major aspect of Biblical influence. The comedies, for instance, would turn on the great texts from *Genesis, Matthew* and *Ephesians* on marriage; the history plays, on the treatment of kingship as a sacred institution in the books of *Samuel;* the problem plays, on the Pauline theology of sin and redemption; the great tragedies, on the accounts of Adam's sin and the passion of Christ; the final plays, on Christ's teaching of forgiveness and St Paul's proclamation of new life in Christ. Each play, it is true, treats of a secular subject in a secular manner; but its thought is invariably charged with religious overtones, largely in virtue of the frequent, though unobtrusive, Biblical references.[4]

To begin with the comedies, a prominent theme in the two early plays, *The Comedy of Errors* and *The Taming of the Shrew,* is the ideal relationship between husband and wife, which is expressed mainly in Biblical terms. In *The Comedy of Errors* the ideal is stated by Adriana, wife to Antipholus of Ephesus. She makes her appeal to two passages of which Shakespeare seems particularly fond – to *Psalm 8* in:

> *There's nothing situate under heaven's eye*
> *But hath his bound, in earth, in sea, in sky;*
> *The beasts, the fishes, and the winged fowls,*
> *Are their males' subjects and at their controls.*
> *Men, more divine, the masters of all these,*
> *Lords of the wide world, and wild wat'ry seas,*
> *Indued with intellectual sense and souls,*
> *Of more pre-eminence than fish and fowls,*
> *Are masters to their females and their lords.* (ii. 1)

and to *Ephesians* v in:

> *How comes it now, my husband, O! how comes it,*
> *That thou art thus estranged from thyself?*
> *Thyself I call it, being strange to me,*
> *That undividable, incorporate,*
> *Am better that thy dear self's better part . . .*
> *For if we two be one and thou play false,*
> *I do digest the poison of thy flesh.* (ii. 2)

This passage from *Ephesians* is also used by Katharina, at the climax of *The Taming of the Shrew*, in her impressive speech on the duty of wives to their husbands:

> *Thy husband is thy lord, thy life, thy keeper,*
> *Thy head, thy sovereign . . .*
> *Such duty as the subject owes the prince,*
> *Even such a woman oweth to her husband.* (v. 2)

Two other early comedies culminate in the Christian ideal of charity, as being the reality underlying the sacrament (sacred sign) of marriage. In *Two Gentlemen of Verona* emphasis is laid on the particular aspect of forgiveness, and the happy outcome hinges on Valentine's much criticized advertence to this deeply Christian concept:[5]

> *Who by repentance is not satisfied*
> *Is nor of heaven nor earth; for these are pleas'd.*
> *By penitence the Eternal's wrath's appeas'd.* (v. 4)

In *Love's Labour's Lost* Berowne's rhetorical speech in praise of 'lady's eyes' – which, as we have seen, may have been suggested by Southwell's lines on the eyes of Christ[6] – leads up to the Pauline declaration:

> *For charity itself fulfils the law;*
> *And who can sever love from charity.* (iv. 3)

His meaning is, it is true, somewhat frivolous on this occasion; but he is soon obliged to accept its practical implication, when his lady Rosaline enjoins him for his penance to

> *Visit the speechless sick, and still converse*
> *With groaning wretches.* (v. 2)

This done, he will be properly disposed for Christian marriage.

It is interesting to notice how the fools in these comedies derive much of their foolery from Biblical parodies. Dromio of Syracuse in *The Comedy of Errors* has 'odd old ends stol'n forth of holy writ' (*Richard III* i. 3) at the tip of his tongue, as in this passage which brings together some of Shakespeare's favourite texts:

> *Not that Adam that kept the Paradise, but that Adam that keeps the prison; he that goes in the calf's skin that was killed for the Prodigal; he that came behind you, sir, like an evil angel, and bid you forsake your liberty.* (iv. 3)[7]

A similar vein of Biblical humour appears in Lance in *Two Gentlemen of Verona*, who looks forward to Lancelot Gobbo in *The Merchant of Venice*. Like Dromio, Lance makes jesting allusion to the parable of the Prodigal Son, which evidently meant much to Shakespeare:

> *I have received my proportion, like the prodigious son, and am going with Sir Proteus to the imperial's court.*
> (ii. 3)

The same jesting vein is still apparent in *Henry IV* Part I, in the comment of Falstaff on his company of soldiers:

> *You would think that I had a hundred and fifty tattered prodigals, lately come from swine-keeping, from eating draff and husks.* (iv. 2)

A more serious vein emerges in Orlando's complaint to his brother at the beginning of *As You Like It*:

> *Shall I keep your hogs and eat husks with them? What prodigal portion have I spent, that I should come to such penury?* (i. 1)[8]

Such use, or abuse, of the Bible has been regarded by some critics as proof of the dramatist's fundamental agnosticism and irreverence towards sacred things.[9] But their criticism, besides being narrowly Puritanical, fails to do justice to the inner significance of Shakespeare's fools.[10] Their words may sound foolish; yet out of their mouths proceeds a higher wisdom than is found in most of the wiser characters. As the Clown says, apostrophizing wit, in *Twelfth Night* :

> *Those wits that think they have thee, do very oft prove fools; and I that am sure I lack thee, may pass for a wise man.* (i. 5)

Their function is best shown in *Much Ado About Nothing*, where it is the folly of Dogberry and his companions which uncovers the deep-laid plot of Don John and Borachio – as the latter admits :

> *What your wisdoms could not discover, these shallow fools have brought to light.* (v. 1)

All this has a deep Scriptural basis in I *Corinthians*, where St Paul declares : 'The foolish things of the world hath God chosen, that he may confound the wise' (i. 27).

The use of Biblical language in the mouths of fools is further manifested in the character of Falstaff; but in his case it is manifested with a difference. The lesser fools may be said to illustrate the truth of *Psalm* 8 : 'Out of the mouths of babes and sucklings thou hast perfected praise'; but Falstaff merely abuses the Bible to justify his own pursuit of the seven deadly sins. In this respect, he is more a villain than a fool. As he confesses to Prince Hal in *Henry IV* Part I :

> *Dost thou hear, Hal? Thou knowest in the state of inno-cency Adam fell; and what should poor Jack Falstaff do in the days of villainy? Thou seest I have more flesh than another man, and therefore more frailty.* (iii. 3)

Implicit in his frequent abuse of Scripture and religious ter-minology is the well-known fact – mentioned in an earlier chapter – of his derivation from the Lollard, Sir John Old-castle, who was hailed by John Foxe as morning-star of the Reformation.[11] He is thus connected in Shakespeare's mind with the popular acceptance of Luther's doctrine of 'justifica-tion by faith alone', to which he alludes in speaking of Poins :

> *O, if men were to be saved by merit, what hole in hell were hot enough for him?* (i. 2)

This is also the doctrine echoed by his 'cousin', Sir Toby

Belch, when he drunkenly declares of Viola waiting at the gate :

Let him be the devil, an he will, I care not: give me faith,
say I! (Twelfth Night i. 5)

On the other hand, the noticeable difference between the Falstaff of the *Henry IV* plays and his name-sake in *The Merry Wives of Windsor* is due in no small measure to the decline of Biblical language in the latter.

As we see in the case of Falstaff, the abuse of Scripture is a characteristic not only of Shakespeare's fools, but also of his villains. In them the dramatist finds illustrated two of his favourite texts : Christ's warning against wolves in sheep's clothing (*Matt.* vii. 15), and that of St Paul against Satan who transforms himself into an angel of light (II *Cor.* xi. 14). It is interesting that these were also texts most frequently cited in the religious controversies of the period, on either side. In them, moreover, he emphasizes the contrast between fair appearances and ugly reality, which is one of his most recurrent themes. The prototype of such villains is Richard III, who, of set policy, clothes his naked villainy

With odd old ends stol'n forth of holy writ,
And seem a saint when most I play the devil. (i. 3)

Of the same type is Shylock, as seen through the eyes of Antonio, and described in words which are later adapted to Claudius in *Hamlet* :

The devil can cite Scripture for his purpose.
An evil soul, producing holy witness,
Is like a villain with a smiling cheek,
A goodly apple rotten at the heart.
O, what a goodly outside falsehood hath! (i. 3)

Antonio here makes a specific allusion to yet another passage in the Bible, where Satan tempts Christ by appealing to a variety of texts (*Matt.* iv. 1–10); and the same idea is repeated by Bassanio in the casket-scene, with reference to heretics in religion (iii. 2). There is, however, a fundamental difference between Richard and Shylock in their use of Scripture. Whereas the former's intention is merely to deceive, the latter naturally refers to the Bible in virtue of his Jewish character, even though he also uses it to justify his practice of usury and his pursuit of revenge.

In *The Merchant of Venice* it is not only the character of Shylock, but the general theme of the play, which has a Scriptural basis. Allusions to various texts are skilfully used to present the fundamental contrast between the Old Law of strict legal justice, as represented by Shylock, and the New Law of mercy and love, as represented by Antonio and Portia.[12] This contrast is emphasized, above all, in the culminating trial-scene. Whereas Shylock proclaims, 'I stand for judgment', and demands, 'What judgment shall I dread, doing no wrong?', Portia pleads for mercy in a speech which is a tissue of texts from the Old and the New Testaments:

> *The quality of mercy is not strain'd,*
> *It droppeth as the gentle rain from heaven*
> *Upon the place beneath . . .*
> *Though justice be thy plea, consider this,*
> *That in the course of justice none of us*
> *Should see salvation: we do pray for mercy,*
> *And that same prayer doth teach us all to render*
> *The deeds of mercy.* (iv. 1)

Here the comparison of divine mercy to rain is derived from *Ecclesiasticus* xxxv and *Deuteronomy* xxxii. 2; the warning that no man is just in God's sight, from *Psalm* 143; the phrase 'to see salvation', from *Isaiah* lii. 10 and the Canticle of Simeon in *Luke* ii. 30; and the prayer for mercy, from the latter half of the Lord's Prayer (*Matt.* vi. 12) and *Ecclesiasticus* xxviii. 2.

The same dramatic conflict between justice and mercy is at the thematic basis of *Measure for Measure*, whose very title echoes Christ's words in the Sermon on the Mount: 'With what measure you mete, it shall be measured to you again' (*Matt.* vii. 2). Here it is the judge, Lord Angelo, who stands for strict justice, though he makes no attempt to justify his position from the Bible; while the novice, Isabella, presents her plea for mercy on her brother in language that is both Scriptural and theological:

> *Why, all the souls that were were forfeit once;*
> *And he that might the vantage best have took,*
> *Found out the remedy. How would you be*
> *If he which is the top of judgment should*
> *But judge you as you are? O, think on that,*
> *And mercy then will breathe within your lips*
> *Like man new made.* (ii. 2)

Her opening words, which combine the doctrines of original sin and redemption, are followed by another echo of *Psalm* 143, as well as of *Ezekiel* vii. 27; while her closing reference to 'man new made' recalls numerous passages in St Paul's epistles about the making of a 'new man' in Christ (e.g. II *Cor.* iv. 17; *Eph.* iv. 24; *Col.* iii. 10).

Yet another heroine, Helena in *All's Well That Ends Well*, stands out for her Scriptural language. The speech in which she persuades the King to make trial of her remedy is no less replete with allusions to the Bible than those of Portia and Isabella:

> *He that of greatest works is finisher*
> *Oft does them by the weakest minister;*
> *So holy writ in babes hath judgment shown,*
> *When judges have been babes; great floods have flown*
> *From simple sources; and great seas have dried*
> *When miracles have by the greatest been denied.* (ii. 1)

Here the general principle of St Paul in I *Cor.* i. 27, already mentioned in connection with fools, is illustrated by three events from the Old Testament: the judgement of Daniel in defence of Susanna (*Dan.* xiii. 45); the miraculous drawing of water from the rock by Moses (*Exod.* xvii. 6; also *Num.* xx. 11); and the crossing of the Red Sea by the Israelites (*Exod.* xiv). There is also an echo of Mary's Canticle, the Magnificat, from *Luke* i. 46–55; and this echo is supported by other passages which serve – as mentioned in an earlier chapter – to relate Helena to the Virgin Mary.[13]

Not only Helena, but almost all the ideal heroines in Shakespeare's plays, have their setting not only in the Bible, but more precisely in relation to Mary, the Mother of God. It is significant that they are described, almost unfailingly, as 'full of grace', recalling the Angel's words of salutation to Mary in *Luke* i. 28. In *The Comedy of Errors* Antipholus of Syracuse thus addresses Luciana :

> *Less in your knowledge and your grace you show not*
> *Than our earth's wonder; more than earth, divine.*

> (iii. 2)

In *Love's Labour's Lost* the Princess of France is said to be 'a maid of grace and complete majesty' (i. 1); and she is implored by Boyet :

> *Be now as prodigal of all dear grace*
> *As Nature was in making graces dear.* (ii. 1)

In *Two Gentlemen of Verona* the song to Silvia includes these words :

> *Holy, fair, and wise is she;*
> *The heaven such grace did lend her,*
> *That she might admired be.* (iv. 2)

In *Much Ado About Nothing* Benedick swears that 'till all graces be in one woman, one woman shall not come in my grace' (ii. 3). In *As You Like It* this ideal is seen by Orlando as fulfilled in Rosalind, who is 'filled with all graces wide enlarged' at the command of heaven (iii. 2). In *Othello* Desdemona is greeted by Cassio on her safe arrival in Cyprus :

> *Hail to thee, lady! and the grace of heaven,*
> *Before, behind thee, and on every hand,*
> *Enwheel thee round.* (ii. 1)

In *The Winter's Tale* Perdita is declared by Time, as Chorus at the beginning of Act IV, to be 'now grown in grace equal with wondering'. Lastly, in *The Tempest* Miranda's 'noblest grace' is admired by Ferdinand as 'so perfect and peerless' that she must surely have been 'created of every creature's best' (iii. 1). Such declarations have been explained by the influence of Neo-Platonism, which became fashionable in England through the interest of Sidney and Spenser.[14] But they are closer to the language of the New Testament and of medieval devotion to the Blessed Virgin.

In the history plays, it is not only villains like Richard III, or buffoons like Falstaff, who monopolize the Scriptural phrases. Rather, it is here the kings who, appropriately, fulfil a Biblical function which is somewhat analogous to that of the heroines in the comedies. In the three Parts of *Henry VI* there are numerous echoes of the Bible; and most of them come from the mouth, not of Richard of Gloucester (who does not really come into his own, whether Biblically or politically, till *Richard III*), but of the pious King Henry. It is indeed precisely by means of these echoes that the dramatist portrays his royal character. One after another they occur to his mind, as one event succeeds another; and in one scene of Part II (ii. 1) we have the following series of pious reflections:

To see how God in all his creatures works!

(from I *Cor.* xii. 6: 'God is the same which worketh all in all');

The treasury of everlasting joy.

(from *Luke* xii. 33, *Matt.* vi. 20: 'Treasures in heaven');

Blessed are the peacemakers on earth.

(from *Matt.* v. 9: 'Blessed are the peacemakers');

Now God be prais'd, that to believing souls
Gives light in darkness, comfort in despair.

(from *Luke* i. 79 [Canticle of Zachary]: 'To give light to them that sit in darkness'; *cf.* II *Sam.* xxii. *Ps.* xviii. 28);

Although by his sight his sin be multiplied.

(from *John* ix. 41: 'If ye were blind, ye should not have sin; but now ye say, We see; therefore your sin remaineth');

Good fellow, tell us here the circumstance,
That we for thee may glorify the Lord.

(from *Matt.* v. 16: 'Let your light so shine before men, that they may see your good works, and glorify your Father which is in heaven');

O God, seest thou this, and bear'st so long?

(from *Ps.* lxxix. 5 : 'How long, Lord? wilt thou be angry for ever?');

> *O God! what mischiefs work the wicked ones,*
> *Heaping confusion on their own heads thereby.*

(from *Ps.* vii. 16 : 'His mischief shall return upon his own head'; *cf. Ps.* xiv. 8, cxl. 9).

The pious character of Henry VI is to some extent continued in Richard II, at least after his deposition. In his experience of temporal failure the words of Christ come spontaneously to the lips of Richard. Reflecting on himself in his imprisonment, he finds 'thoughts of things divine' mixed with baser scruples which 'set the word itself against the word' :

> *As thus, 'Come, little ones'; and then again,*
> *'It is as hard to come as for a camel*
> *To thread the postern of a needle's eye!'* (v. 5)[15]

Yet even before his deposition, in all his pride of royalty, Richard thinks and speaks in terms of Scripture. His fundamental assertion of 'divine right' is derived from the Old Testament ideal of the 'Lord's Anointed', as represented by Saul and David, and fulfilled in Christ himself. In virtue of his sacred kingship, he sees himself as another Christ and his enemies as the enemies of Christ, in the likeness of Pilate or Judas. It is indeed this self-identification with Christ in *Richard II* which may have suggested the story of the Passion as a 'paradigm' underlying Shakespeare's tragedies.[16] At the same time, the history of David enters no less into the characterization of Bolingbroke, who is on three occasions described in terms reminiscent of Absalom's quest for popularity (*cf. Richard II* v. 2; *Henry IV* Part I iii. 2, iv. 3).

The principal hero of the English histories, Henry V, likewise has his setting in Scripture, no less than in Morality, from the moment when

> *Consideration, like an angel came,*
> *And whipp'd the offending Adam out of him,*
> *Leaving his body as a Paradise,*
> *To envelop and contain celestial spirits.* (i. 1)

Like the heroines, he, too, is significantly described as 'full of grace and fair regard' (i. 1); and his words are, in fact, filled with the grace of Holy Scripture. This is evident above all in his reaction to the news of his great victory at Agincourt, the climax of the play, when he exclaims (with echoes of *Psalms* 44 and 115):

> *O God! thy arm was here;*
> *And not to us, but to thy arm alone*
> *Ascribe we all.* (iv. 8)

In such words of his we recognize a true family likeness to his son, the pious Henry VI.

From the history plays, which themselves incorporate a considerable amount of tragic matter, there is a direct line of development leading to the great tragedies, and culminating in *Macbeth* and *King Lear*. This line is, moreover, noticeably Biblical in its overtones. There is, in the first place, a significant series of references to the murder of Abel by his brother Cain, from *Genesis* iv, where his blood is said to cry out from the earth. As in *Richard II* the blood of Gloucester 'like sacrificing Abel's cries even from the tongueless caverns of the earth' (i. 1), so the 'spirit of the first-born Cain' (*Henry IV* Part II i. 1), with its implication of fratricidal strife, seems to hang like a dark shadow of evil over both tetralogies of history plays (*cf.* also *Henry VI* Part I i. 3; *Richard III* i. 2; *Richard II* v. 6). Even in the comedies it appears wherever, as so often happens, brothers are at variance with each other – Oliver and Orlando, and the two Dukes in *As You Like It*, Don John and Don Pedro in *Much Ado About Nothing*, Antonio and Prospero in *The Tempest*. In the tragedies, it looms behind the main action in *Hamlet*, where the old king has been assassinated and his royal power usurped by his wicked brother, Claudius. The outcome of the play-within-the-play is to expose the guilty conscience of Claudius, who is led to confess in his agonized soliloquy:

> *O, my offence is rank, it smells to heaven;*
> *It hath the primal eldest curse upon it,*
> *A brother's murder.* (iii. 3)

The same theme of division of brothers recurs in *King Lear,* with Edmund playing the part of Cain against Edgar, though there is no overt Biblical allusion.

Secondly, there is a parallel series of references to the Passion of Christ, particularly to the two episodes of his betrayal by Judas and his judgement by Pilate. Both episodes likewise make their first appearance in the history plays. That of Pilate washing his hands while declaring himself innocent of Christ's blood is mentioned by one of Clarence's murderers in *Richard III*:

> *How fain, like Pilate, would I wash my hands*
> *Of this most grievous murder.* (i. 4)

It recurs in *Richard II*, where the deposed King complains of his treatment, comparing his situation with that of Christ:

> *Though some of you with Pilate wash your hands,*
> *Showing an outward pity, yet you Pilates*
> *Have here delivered me to my sour cross,*
> *And water cannot wash away your sin.* (iv. 1)

It is mingled with the reference to Cain in the troubled soliloquy of Claudius in *Hamlet*:

> *What if this cursed hand*
> *Were thicker than itself with brother's blood,*
> *Is there not rain enough in the sweet heavens*
> *To wash it white as snow?* (iii. 3)

Above all, it has its culminating expression in Macbeth's reaction of guilt after murdering Duncan, which is also re-echoed in Lady Macbeth's sleep-walking:

> *Will all great Neptune's ocean wash this blood*
> *Clean from my hand? No, this my hand will rather*
> *The multitudinous seas incarnadine,*
> *Making the green one red.* (ii. 2)

This passage is often explained with reference to two parallels in Seneca's *Phaedra* and *Hercules Furens*, both well known in their Elizabethan translations; but, whether he used them or not, Shakespeare evidently retained the Biblical association of 'wash – hands – blood' at the back of his mind. Two other texts from the Old Testament may also have influenced him:

Ps. li. 7 : 'Wash me, and I shall be whiter than snow'; and *Isa.* i. 16, 18 : 'Wash you, make you clean . . . though your sins be as scarlet, they shall be as white as snow.'

The other episode of Judas betraying his Master seems to have made an even deeper impression on the dramatist's imagination. In it he sees not just the treachery of a disciple or a servant, but also the ingratitude of a friend – the sin which most moves his deep indignation in such plays as *As You Like It*, *King Lear* and *Timon of Athens*. It is mentioned once in *Henry VI Part III* (v. 7) and twice in *Richard II* (iii. 2 and iv. 1). In the latter play, as we have noticed, Richard compares himself to Christ in contrast to his opponents, whom he sees now as Pilate, now as Judas :

> *Did they not sometime cry 'All hail!' to me?*
> *So Judas did to Christ; but he, in twelve,*
> *Found truth in all but one; I, in twelve thousand, none.*
>
> (iv. 1)

In the tragedies, there is a significant reference to Judas – if we accept the Folio reading – in Othello's remorseful comparison of himself to the 'base Judean' who 'threw a pearl away, richer than all his tribe' (v. 2).[17] Just as Judas betrayed his Master with a kiss, and threw away the 'pearl of great price' (*Matt.* xiii. 46), so Othello realizes that he has betrayed Desdemona with a kiss – 'I kiss'd thee ere I kill'd thee' – and then continues his imitation of Judas by killing himself. Macbeth, too, implicitly compares himself to Judas, when he addresses to himself the words Christ addressed to Judas on the night of the betrayal (*John* xiii. 27 : 'That thou doest, do quickly') :

> *If it were done when 'tis done, then 'twere well*
> *It were done quickly.* (i. 7)

In two of the last plays, despite their pagan setting, there are clear allusions to Judas, on account of their connection with the dominant theme of ingratitude. In *Timon of Athens* Apemantus significantly comments on the behaviour of Timon's friends at the banquet in words that recall the Last Supper :

> *It grieves me to see so many dip their meat*
> *In one man's blood ...*
> *There's much example for't; the fellow that*
> *Sits next him now, parts bread with him, and pledges*
> *The breath of him in a divided draught,*
> *Is the readiest man to kill him: 't has been prov'd.* (i. 2)

In *The Winter's Tale* Polixenes indignantly rejects the imputa-
tion of treachery, cast on him by Leontes, whereby his name is
yoked 'with his that did betray the Best' (i. 2).

The use of a pagan setting in the last plays is probably to be
explained by the Act of 1606 in restraint of 'abuses of players',
by which any player jestingly or profanely using the name of
God, Jesus Christ, the Holy Ghost, or the Trinity, was liable
to a fine of £10.[18] This did not, however, prevent Shakespeare from making continued use of the Bible in his plays,
and with even deeper significance. Rather, in these very plays
he conveys his deepest religious and Christian meaning. In
many ways, the series may be said to begin with *King Lear*. In
the climax of the play there occurs an interesting, if veiled,
allusion to the parable of the Prodigal Son (developed perhaps from the comedies, particularly from the opening scene
of *As You Like It*) in Cordelia's words of pity for her 'child-
changed father':

> *And wast thou fain, poor father,*
> *To hovel thee with swine and rogues forlorn,*
> *In short and musty straw?* (iv. 7)

The Prodigal, too, 'would fain have filled his belly with the
husks the swine did eat' (*Luke* xv. 16). This points to an
extended interpretation of the play in the light of this parable,
with the erring father as the Prodigal Son, and the dutiful
daughter (conversely) as the merciful Father.[19] This interpretation is borne out by the earlier description of Lear's
knights as 'riotous' – so, too, the Prodigal Son 'wasted his
goods with riotous living' – and by Cordelia's later pity for her
father as 'poor perdu' – recalling the Father's joy that 'he was
lost, but he is found'. Other Biblical allusions connect Cordelia with Christ. France's words to her in the opening scene,
'Fairest Cordelia, that art most rich, being poor' (i. 1), echo

St Paul's commendation of Christ, 'who being rich, became poor for your sake' (II *Cor.* viii. 9). She herself, on her return to England, makes her own the words of the child Christ in the Temple, when she declares: 'O dear father! It is thy business that I go about' (iv. 4). She is later praised by the Gentleman as the one daughter of Lear

> *Who redeems nature from the general curse*
> *Which twain have brought her to.* (iv. 6)

While these words may be given a precise literal meaning in the context of the play, they also contain deeper Biblical and theological implications – with 'redeems', 'nature', 'general curse' and 'twain' all pointing in the same direction.[20] In the outcome of the play, moreover, Lear's lament over the dead body of Cordelia strongly suggests the feeling of Mary and the disciples at the death of Christ: his very posture has been compared to that of Michelangelo's *Pieta*.[21] This suggestion is reinforced by Kent's horrified question, 'Is this the promised end?' and Edgar's echo, 'Or image of that horror?' (v. 3) – with overtones of the Biblical end of the world.

To many critics this ending of *King Lear* seems intensely pessimistic, and of a piece with the famous soliloquies of Hamlet and Macbeth. In their opinion it makes 'a tragic mockery of all eschatologies', whether Christian or secular.[22] Yet, on the one hand, the pessimism, such as it is, has a precisely Biblical origin in the *Book of Job*, whose echoes abound in the play;[23] and, on the other, the pessimism is itself no more than a passing mood – not a final comment on life – and gives place, both in this and in the subsequent plays, to an optimistic view which looks, in a Christian spirit, beyond death to life and beyond passion to resurrection.[24] Here is the single inspiration which breathes through the last plays, and which derives from the touching scene of reunion between father and daughter in Act IV of *King Lear*. It is developed in the recurring theme of regeneration and new life, as sorrow is changed into joy in the climax of each play. This is nothing but the Pauline ideal of the 'new man', the 'new creation', the 'new life' in Christ which the Christian first receives in baptism.[25] It appears in such phrases as 'man new made' (*Measure for Measure* ii. 2), 'new heaven and new earth' (*Antony and*

Cleopatra i. 1), and 'brave new world' (*The Tempest* v. 1).
It is even embodied in the character of Paulina in *The
Winter's Tale*, whose name suggests St Paul,[26] and whose
words to the statue,

> *Bequeath to death your numbness, for from him
> Dear life redeems you.* (v. 3)

transform the appearance of death into the reality of life, not
only for Hermione, but also for Leontes, who is as it were a
lesser version of Lear. Finally, the theme of good drawn out of
evil, joy out of sorrow, and life out of death, has its climax in
Gonzalo's delighted epilogue on the events of *The Tempest*,
with its above-mentioned allusion to the *Exultet* of Holy
Saturday and the theme of '*felix culpa*'.[27]

The foregoing review of Shakespeare's dramatic use of
Biblical themes and phrases should be sufficient to disprove the
common assertion that his plays are 'pervasively secular'.[28] For
all their secular appearance, they conceal an undercurrent of
religious meaning which belongs to their deepest essence. In
this connection, the words of Bassanio in the casket-scene touch
on a fundamental idea of the dramatist :

> *So may the outward shows be least themselves;
> The world is still deceiv'd with ornament.* (iii. 2)

Even those speeches which most linger in the memory with a
pessimistic impression, such as the soliloquies of Hamlet and
Macbeth, and certain speeches of Lear and Prospero, are not
only countered by more optimistic sentiments within the play,
but reflect in themselves the close familiarity of the dramatist
with the Books of the Old Testament. A careful collation of
these speeches with parallel passages in the *Psalms* and the
Book of Job is enough to show how closely the thought of
Shakespeare follows the 'wisdom' of the Bible.[29] From the
Psalms, for example, come Macbeth's references to 'dusty
death' (*cf. Ps.* xxii. 15), to 'a walking shadow' (*cf. Ps.* xxxix.
7), and to 'a tale told by an idiot' (*cf. Ps.* xc. 9). From the
Book of Job come Hamlet's 'slings and arrows of outrageous
fortune' (*cf. Job* vi. 4, xli. 28), 'a consummation devoutly to
be wish'd' (*cf. Job* vi. 9–10), 'to die, to sleep' (*cf. Job* xiv. 10,
12), 'the oppressor's wrong' (*cf. Job* iii. 18), and 'the undis-

cover'd country from whose bourn no traveller returns' (*cf.* *Job* vii. 9–10, x. 21, xvi. 22). The comparison of death to sleep, in particular, which also recurs in Macbeth's 'Out, out, brief candle!' (v. 5) and Prospero's 'This our little life is rounded with a sleep' (*The Tempest*, iv. 1), so far from being evidence of agnosticism, is a commonplace of the Old Testament – as the Homily 'Against the Fear of Death' points out: 'Holy Scripture calleth this bodily death a sleep'. In brief, it may be said that Shakespeare's view of human life is neither more nor less than the Biblical view, with the imperfections of the Old Testament supplemented by the teaching and life of Christ in the New Testament.

VI

Anglican Liturgy

THERE IS no objective evidence, as there is for many of his fellow-actors, that Shakespeare attended the services of the Church of England – apart from the *argumentum ex silentio* that, unlike his father, he was never indicted for non-attendance, or recusancy.[1] At Stratford there are, indeed, various points of connection with the church of the Holy Trinity. Here he was baptized and buried, but not married. Here his children were all baptized, Susanna in 1583, Hamnet and Judith in 1585. Here his two daughters were married, Susanna in 1607, and Judith in 1616. Here he stood as god-father, at least by proxy, to William Walker in 1608. Here his son-in-law, Dr John Hall, was a leading parishioner and became churchwarden in 1628–9. At London, however, Shakespeare has no link with any of the city churches, except in connection with a list of tax assessments for the parish of St Helen's, Bishopsgate, between 1596 and 1599. Only in the plays do we find evidence of a familiarity with the Anglican services, such as he could hardly have gained merely by hear-say. His frequent references to the *Psalms*, as has been noted, usually follow the version of the Great Bible which was still used in the *Book of Common Prayer*.[2] He also refers, explicitly or implicitly, to almost all the ceremonies prescribed in the Prayer Book, and echoes many passages of the Elizabethan *Homilies* which were read aloud in church Sunday after Sunday to an often weary congregation.

The *Book of Common Prayer* opens with an order for

morning and for evening prayer, commonly known as Matins and Evensong. The two are mentioned together in *The Merry Wives of Windsor*, where Mistress Quickly commends Mistress Page as one 'that will not miss you morning nor evening prayer as any is in Windsor' (ii. 2). The words of the General Confession in Morning Prayer, 'We have left undone those things which we ought to have done', seem to be distinctly echoed in *Othello*, where Iago says of the Venetian women:

> *Their best conscience*
> *Is not to leave 't undone, but keep 't unknown.*
>
> (iii. 3)

The *Te Deum*, which follows the first Lesson, includes the verse, 'To thee Cherubin, and Seraphin continually do cry'. This seems to have given rise to no less than two strange mistakes in one line of *The Merchant of Venice*, Lorenzo's 'Still quiring to the young-eyed cherubins' (v. 1) – where 'to thee' is mistaken for 'to the', and the plural 'cherubin' is treated as a singular form (*cf. Othello* iv. 2: 'Thou young and rose-lipp'd cherubin').[3] There is also a possible echo of the Creed, where Christ is said to judge 'the quick and the dead', in Hamlet's words to the grave-digger: ' 'Tis for the dead, not for the quick' (v. 1).

The Litany, which is provided for Sundays, Wednesdays and Fridays, is echoed rather frequently in the plays. The opening invocations with the refrain, 'Have mercy upon us miserable sinners', form the dying words of Salisbury and Gargrave in *Henry VI* Part I:

> S. *O Lord! have mercy on us, wretched sinners.*
> G. *Lord! have mercy on me, woeful man.* (i. 4)

The subsequent reference to 'thy people, whom thou hast redeemed with thy most precious blood', which is itself derived from I *Pet.* i. 18–19, may be implied in the words with which Clarence adjures his murderers in *Richard III*:

> *I charge you, as you hope to have redemption*
> *By Christ's dear blood shed for our grievous sins.* (i. 4)

The petition, 'From all evil and mischief, from sin, from the crafts and assaults of the devil . . . good Lord, deliver us', is re-echoed twice: more directly, in *The Taming of the Shrew*: 'From all such devils, good Lord, deliver us' (i. 1); and indirectly, in *The Merchant of Venice*: 'Here to this devil, to deliver you' (iv. 1). The prayer, 'That it may please thee to give all thy people increase of grace, to hear meekly thy word', is echoed by Longaville in *Love's Labour's Lost*: 'To hear meekly' (i. 1). Likewise, the prayer, 'That it may please thee to give us true repentance . . . to amend our lives according to thy holy word', is reflected in the first appearance of Falstaff in *Henry IV* Part I, when he desires to 'give over this life', and Prince Hal ironically comments: 'I see a good amendment of life in thee' (i. 2). The petition, 'O lamb of God . . . grant us thy peace', is turned to a satirical purpose by the Gentleman in *Measure for Measure*: 'Heaven grant us its peace, but not the King of Hungary's' (i. 2). Finally, the Collect beginning with the words, 'Oh God, we have heard with our ears', and derived from the first verse of *Psalm* 44, is quoted by Pistol in *The Merry Wives of Windsor*: 'He hears with ears' – whereat the parson, Sir Hugh Evans, shows himself an unlearned minister by his derisive comment: 'What phrase is this? "He hears with ear". Why, it is affectations.' (i. 1).

On the other hand, there are surprisingly few echoes from the Communion Service in the plays – as if this was the section of the Prayer Book with which Shakespeare was either least familiar, or else least willing to show his familiarity. The opening words of the prayer, 'Almighty God, unto whom all hearts be open, all desires known, and from whom no secrets are hid', seem to enter into the thoughts of Claudius when caught in his conscience:

> *In the corrupted currents of this world*
> *Offence's gilded hand may shove by justice,*
> *. . . but 'tis not so above;*
> *There is no shuffling, there the action lies*
> *In his true nature.* (iii. 3)

The rehearsing of the Ten Commandments, which comes at this place and in the Catechism, differs in its wording from the printed versions for *Exodus* xx in two points: in the Second

Commandment, where it says, 'And visit the sins of the fathers . . .', and in the Sixth, 'Thou shalt do no murder.'[4] In each point Shakespeare follows the wording of the Prayer Book: for the first, in *The Merchant of Venice*: 'The sins of the father are to be laid upon the children' (iii. 5); and for the second, in *Richard III*, where Clarence warns his murderers:

> *The great King of kings*
> *Hath in the table of his law commanded*
> *That thou shalt do no murder.* (i. 4)

The exhortation before communion, 'to examine your lives and conversation . . . whereinsoever you shall perceive yourselves to have offended, either by will, word or deed, there bewail your own sinful lives, confess yourselves to Almighty God with full purpose of amendment of life,' has two apparent echoes in *Othello*: in Desdemona's protest:

> *If e'er my will did trespass 'gainst his love,*
> *Either in discourse of thought or actual deed.*
>
> (iv. 3)

and in Othello's warning to her:

> *If you bethink yourself of any crime*
> *Unreconcil'd as yet to heaven or grace . . .*
> *Confess thee freely of thy sin.* (v. 2)

It also appears in Hamlet's exhortation to his mother, 'Confess yourself to heaven' (iii. 4), and in Prince Hal's words to Falstaff, 'I see a good amendment of life in thee' (*Henry IV* Part I i. 2). The General Confession of sins which follows, where it is said that 'the remembrance of them is grievous unto us, the burden of them is intolerable', is echoed in *Romeo and Juliet*:

> *But O! it presses to my memory,*
> *Like damned guilty deeds to sinners' minds.* (iii. 2)

Finally, the concluding mention of the 'comfortable words' spoken by Our Saviour Christ seems to be recalled in *Richard II*, where the Queen implores York: 'Uncle, for God's sake, speak comfortable words' (ii. 2). A prayer in the form of a

Collect is also put into the mouth of Falstaff in *Henry IV* Part I:

> *Well, God give thee the spirit of persuasion and him the ears of profiting, that what thou speakest may move, and what he hears may be believed.* (i. 2)

From the ceremony for the Ministration of Baptism come several interesting echoes in the plays. The opening declaration, 'Forasmuch as all men be conceived and born in sin', is verbally reflected in *King John*, where Constance speaks of 'thy sin-conceiving womb', and indirectly in *All's Well That Ends Well*, where the Clown confesses to the Countess: 'I have been, madam, a wicked creature, as you and all flesh and blood are' (i. 3). The general truth it expresses is, of course, deeply present in such plays as *Hamlet*, *King Lear* and *The Winter's Tale*. The subsequent reference to baptism as 'the mystical washing away of sin' is echoed in the assurance of Henry V that what the Archbishop is to speak is in his conscience 'wash'd pure as sin with baptism' (i. 2). The question put by the priest, 'Dost thou forsake the devil and all his works, the vain pomp and glory of the world, with all covetous desires of the same, the carnal desires of the flesh', is developed in the opening scene of *Love's Labour's Lost*, where the King appeals to his lords as 'great conquerors'

> *That war against your own affections*
> *And the huge army of the world's desires;*

and Dumain responds in the required vein:

> *The grosser manner of these world's delights*
> *He throws upon the gross world's baser slaves:*
> *To love, to wealth, to pomp, I pine and die.* (i. 1)

Wolsey likewise, in *Henry VIII*, declares his hatred of the 'vain pomp and glory of the world' in his moment of conversion (iii. 2). The subsequent contrast between 'the old Adam' and 'the new man' combines with the teaching of St Paul in the various references to 'the old man' in *Timon of Athens* (iii. 6), 'the offending Adam' in *Henry V* (i. 1), and 'man new made' in *Measure for Measure* (ii. 2). The exhortation accompanying the sign of the cross, 'to continue Christ's faithful soldier and servant', is recalled in Richmond's prayer at the end of *Richard III* : 'O thou, whose captain I account myself' (v. 3), and in the description of Mowbray's death in *Richard II*, as giving

> *his pure soul unto his captain Christ,*
> *Under whose colours he had fought so long.* (ii. 4)

Finally, there is a general mention of baptism and 'all seals and symbols of redeemed sin' in *Othello* (ii. 3), though without any verbal echo of the ceremony.[5]

Under the next heading of Confirmation, there is a prefatory instruction about the time of ministering the sacrament, 'when children come to that age, that partly by the frailty of their own flesh, partly by the assaults of the world and the devil, they begin to be in danger to fall into sundry kinds of sin'. It is possibly this sentence which is parodied by Falstaff in his attempt to excuse himself : 'Thou seest I have more flesh than another man and therefore more frailty' (*Henry IV Part I* iii. 3). The actual ceremony seems to have no echoes in the plays; but there are several interesting ones from the Catechism that precedes it, particularly in the list of duties towards one's neighbour. In the first place, the words, 'My duty towards my neighbour is to love him as myself', are echoed by Phebe in *As You Like It* : 'Thou hast my love; is not that neighbourly' (iii. 5). Then, the successive duties, 'To love, honour and succour my father and mother; to honour and obey the king and his ministers', are combined in Cordelia's reply to Lear :

> *You have begot me, bred me, lov'd me: I*
> *Return those duties back as are right fit,*
> *Obey you, love you, and most honour you.* (i. 1)

The duty, 'To keep my hands from picking and stealing', enters into Hamlet's mocking reply to Rosencrantz : 'So do I still, by these pickers and stealers' (iii. 3). The concluding exhortation,

> My good child, know this, that thou art not able to do these things of thyself, nor to walk in the commandments of God, and to serve him, without his special grace,

is echoed by Berowne in *Love's Labour's Lost* :

For every man with his affects is born,
Not by might mastered, but by special grace. (i. 1)

The following section, the Solemnization of Matrimony, is naturally enough that which finds most frequent representation in the plays. The actual ceremony, or 'the plain form of marriage', is presented in the climax of *Much Ado About Nothing*, though it is broken off when Claudio cruelly rejects Hero's hand in marriage (iv. 1). It is carried through in pretence between Orlando and Rosalind in *As You Like It* (iv. 1), though their subsequent union in reality with the blessing of Hymen contains little of the Prayer Book ceremony. It is performed off-stage in *Romeo and Juliet*, when Friar Laurence brings the lovers to the chapel, to 'incorporate two in one'; in *The Taming of the Shrew*, when Gremio describes the 'mad marriage' of Petruchio and Katharina with little reference to 'the ceremonial rites' (iii. 2); in *All's Well That Ends Well*, when Bertram leaves the stage with Helena for the ceremony, and returns saying he has sworn 'before the solemn priest' (ii. 3); and in *Twelfth Night*, when Olivia brings Sebastian to a nearby chantry, to plight the full assurance of his faith (iv. 3). A detailed description of the ceremony is added by the priest in the same play :

> *A contract of eternal bond of love,*
> *Confirm'd by mutual joinder of your hands,*
> *Attested by the holy close of lips,*
> *Strengthen'd by interchangement of your rings;*
> *And all the ceremony of this compact*
> *Seal'd in my function, by my testimony.* (v. 1)

Similarly, the Prayer Book service prescribes that 'the minister shall cause the man to take the woman by the right hand, and so either to give their troth to other', which troth is signified by 'the ring given and received'. Then the minister pronounces them to be 'man and wife together', and joins their right hands saying, 'Those whom God hath joined together, let no man put asunder.' This last point is further echoed in *Romeo and Juliet*, in Juliet's declaration to the friar : 'God joined my heart and Romeo's, thou our hands' (iv. 1).

As regards various details of the ceremony, the opening

words of the minister describing 'holy matrimony' as 'an honourable estate, instituted of God in Paradise, in the time of man's innocency' are echoed in *Much Ado About Nothing*, when Margaret asks, 'Is not marriage honourable in a beggar?' (iii. 4), and also perhaps in Falstaff's reference to 'the state of innocency' in *Henry IV* Part I (iii. 3). The warning against entering into marriage 'unadvisedly, lightly or wantonly, to satisfy man's carnal lusts and appetites' is distinctly echoed by Touchstone in *As You Like It*:

> As the ox hath his bow, sir, the horse his curb, and the falcon her bells, so man hath his desires; and as pigeons bill, so wedlock would be nibbling. (iii. 3)

and by the Clown in *All's Well That Ends Well*:

> My poor body, madam, requires it: I am driven on by the flesh; and he must needs go that the devil drives. (i. 3)

and perhaps also in Iago's contemptuous allusion to 'our raging motions, our carnal stings, our unbitted lusts' (*Othello* i. 3). The further reference to the 'mutual society' which is one of the reasons of marriage is echoed by Sir Nathaniel in *Love's Labour's Lost*: 'For society (saith the text) is the happiness of life' (iv. 2), and by Paris in *Romeo and Juliet*, speaking of Juliet's tears,

> Which, too much minded by herself alone,
> May be put from her by society. (iv. 1)

The requirement to disclose if there be any impediment why the two persons 'may not be lawfully joined together in matrimony' is thrice re-echoed in *Much Ado About Nothing* (twice in iii. 2, and once in the marriage-scene of iv. 1). The phrase, 'thy wedded wife', recurs in two plays with a pagan context: in *Coriolanus*, as 'my wedded mistress' (iv. 5), and in *Cymbeline*, as 'your wedded lady' (v. 5). The phrase, 'for better, for worse', is parodied by Hamlet when, in response to Ophelia's 'Still better, and worse', he responds, 'So you must take your husbands' (iii. 2).

The concluding exhortation, with its numerous references to *Ephesians* v, contains many significant echoes. Thus it is declared that 'men are bound to love their own wives as their own bodies. He that loveth his own wife, loveth himself. For never did any man hate his own flesh, but nourisheth and cherisheth it.' These words are distorted by the Clown in the above-quoted passage from *All's Well That Ends Well*, where he continues:

> *He that comforts my wife is the cherisher of my flesh and blood; he that cherishes my flesh and blood loves my flesh and blood; he that loves my flesh and blood is my friend; ergo, he that kisses my wife is my friend.* (i. 3)

They are likewise parodied by Hamlet, in speaking to the King as 'dear mother'; for, he explains,

> *Father and mother is man and wife, man and wife is one flesh, and so, my mother.* (iv. 3)

The reference to the wife as 'the weaker vessel' is repeated on several occasions: by Sampson in *Romeo and Juliet*: 'Women, being the weaker vessels, are ever thrust to the wall' (i. 1), by Don Armado in *Love's Labour's Lost*, describing Jaquenetta as 'the weaker vessel' (i. 1), and by Rosalind in *As You Like It*, when in her man's apparel she comforts Celia saying, 'But I must comfort the weaker vessel' (ii. 4). Finally, the exhortation to wives, 'that the spirit be mild and quiet, which is a precious thing in the sight of God', is fulfilled in the cases of Desdemona, who is described by her father as

> *A maiden never bold;*
> *Of spirit so still and quiet, that her motion*
> *Blush'd at herself. (Othello* i. 3)

and of Cordelia, who is likewise described by her father:

> *Her voice was ever soft,*
> *Gentle and low, an excellent thing in woman.*
> (*King Lear* v. 3)

The following order for the Visitation of the Sick is generally reflected, or rather parodied, in the pretended visitation of the lunatic Malvolio by the parson Sir Topas, in *Twelfth Night*. There is a particular echo of the opening invocation, 'Peace be in this house, and to all that dwell in it', in the Clown's words: 'What ho, I say. Peace be in this prison!' (iv.

1). There is also a Collect, beginning with the words : 'O most merciful God, which according to the multitude of thy mercies dost so put away the sins of those which truly repent, that thou remembrest them no more', which is recalled in one of the early comedies, *Two Gentlemen of Verona*, where Valentine declares :

> *Who by repentance is not satisfied*
> *Is nor of heaven, nor earth; for these are pleas'd.*
> *By penitence the Eternal's wrath's appeas'd.* (v. 4)

and in one of the last plays, *The Winter's Tale*, where Cleomenes urges Leontes :

> *Do as the heavens have done, forget your evil;*
> *With them forgive yourself.* (v. 1)

The order for the Burial of the Dead which follows in the Prayer Book provides suitable material for the tragedies, though not in such abundance as the Marriage service for the romantic comedies. One of its opening themes, from the words of St Paul in I *Tim.* vi : 'We brought nothing into this world, neither may we carry anything out of this world,' may be said to enter into the brooding reflections of Hamlet (v. 2), Macbeth (v. 5) and Lear (iv. 6) on human mortality. In particular, Macbeth's comparison of human life to 'a walking shadow', besides echoing the *Book of Job* and the *Psalms*, may come even more directly from the prayer in which the words of Job are quoted : 'Man that is born of a woman, hath but a short time to live, and is full of misery . . . he flieth as it were a shadow, and never continueth in one stay.' The direction that 'earth shall be cast upon the body, by some standing by', is explicitly referred to in *Hamlet*, where Laertes leaps into Ophelia's grave, exclaiming :

> *Hold off the earth awhile,*
> *Till I have caught her once more in mine arms.*
> *Now pile your dust upon the quick and dead.* (v. 1)

Meanwhile, the priest says the words : 'We therefore commit his body to the ground, earth to earth, ashes to ashes, dust to dust', which are recalled in Hamlet's 'quintessence of dust' (ii. 2), Macbeth's 'way to dusty death' (v. 5), and the refrain of

the Dirge in *Cymbeline*, 'come to dust' (iv. 2). The pattern of
the phrase is further parodied in Gertrude's 'sweets to the
sweet', as she throws not earth, but flowers on Ophelia's grave
(v. 1). One of the final prayers, which draws a contrast
between the 'joy and felicity' of heaven and 'the miseries of
this sinful world', may also be recalled in Hamlet's dying words
to Horatio :

> *Absent thee from felicity awhile,*
> *And in this harsh world draw thy breath in pain.*
>
> (v. 1)

and in Kent's last words over the corpse of Lear :

> *Vex not his ghost: O, let him pass; he hates him*
> *That would upon the rack of this tough world*
> *Stretch him out longer.* (v. 3)

In the Prayer Book there follow two services of minor
importance, which are both echoed in the plays : the Church-
ing of Women, and a Commination against Sinners. In the
former occur the words of *Psalm* 121 : 'The sun shall not burn
thee by day', which are parodied by Beatrice in *Much Ado
About Nothing* with reference to marriage : 'Thus goes everyone to the world but I, and I am sunburnt' – that is, because
unmarried (ii. 1).[6] The influence of the Commination may be
seen in the early histories, where the theme of cursing occupies
an important function. The general form, 'Cursed is he
that . . .' followed by the response 'Amen', is echoed by Constance in *King John* :

> *O, lawful let it be*
> *That I have room with Rome to curse awhile.*
> *Good father Cardinal, cry thou 'Amen'*
> *To my keen curses.* (iii. 1)

The particular curse, 'Cursed is he that lieth with his neighbour's wife', is recalled by the Second Murderer in *Richard
III* in his droll reflections on conscience : 'A man cannot lie
with his neighbour's wife, but it detects him' (i. 4). In the final
Collect, the words, 'Thy property is to have mercy', come closer
to Portia's speech on 'The quality of mercy', which is said to

be 'an attribute to God himself', than any of the Scriptural texts usually cited – though the use of the word 'attribute' may well come from the Homily 'Of Repentance', which says of God : 'He doth attribute unto him mercy'.

To turn now to the *Homilies*, it may be said that their influence on the dramatist was hardly less considerable than that of the Prayer Book, as well in their general themes as in their particular phrases and sentences. They may at times have induced a feeling of weariness through their continual repetition, as Rosalind implies in *As You Like It* (iii. 2), but their deep effect on the dramatist's mind is sufficiently witnessed by their frequent echoes in his plays. There are indeed few plays which are not governed to some extent by the ideas of one or other Homily. Yet it is only in recent times that the importance of their influence has come to be recognized by some Shakespearian scholars, together with an increasing recognition of his indebtedness to the homiletic tradition of the Middle Ages – which lingers on in these homilies.[7] Even so, their attention has mainly been devoted to the two political Homilies, those 'On Order and Obedience' and 'Against Disobedience and Rebellion', which were mainly insisted on during the Elizabethan Age.[8] But the others, which have largely been neglected, are no less amply stored with Shakespearian themes.[9]

As with the corresponding service in the Prayer Book, the Homily which is most richly represented in the plays, especially the comedies, is naturally that 'Of the State of Matrimony'. Here, for example, is portrayed the ideal wife in terms that anticipate the speech of Katharina at the climax of *The Taming of the Shrew* :

> When the wife is ready to hand at her husband's commandment, when she will apply herself to his will, when she endeavoureth herself to seek his contention and to do him pleasure.

Like Katharina, the homilist says of the husband that he is 'made the ruler and head over' his wife; and like Adriana in *The Comedy of Errors* (ii. 2), he says of the wife that she is her husband's 'body and made one flesh' with him. He lays noticeable emphasis on the weakness of women, in words that are echoed though rejected by the Duke in *Twelfth Night* (ii. 4):

> The woman is a weak creature, not endued with like strength and constancy of mind; therefore they be the sooner disquieted. They be the more prone to all weak affections and dispositions of mind, more than men be; and lighter they be, and more vain in their fantasies and opinions.

Hamlet, on the other hand, deeply agrees with these sentiments; and his general comment, 'Frailty, thy name is woman' (i. 2), however much it may resemble the *puerilis sententia*, '*Varia et mutabilis, femina*', comes closer to the repeated teaching of the Homily that woman is 'the weaker vessel, of a frail heart, inconstant', 'the more frail part', 'a frail vessel'. Viola herself admits as much when she exclaims:

> *How easy is it for the proper-false*
> *In women's waxen hearts to set their forms!*
> *Alas, our frailty is the cause, not we!*
> *For such as we are made of, such we be.*
> *(Twelfth Night* ii. 2)

The homilist, therefore, advises the husband, in words which are interestingly recalled by Hamlet and adapted to his parents:

> Apply thyself to weed out little by little the noisome weeds of uncomely manners out of her mind with wholesome precepts.

The important contrast between appearance and reality, between shadow and substance, between outward show and inward truth, which is developed by Shakespeare both in his *Sonnets* and throughout his plays, had previously been instilled into his mind by such homilies as that 'Of Good Works'. The idea of a painted picture as but a poor substitute for the real thing, which recurs in *Sonnet* 24 and in *Two Gentlemen of Verona* (iv. 2), is already expressed in this Homily: 'Even as the picture graven or painted is but a dead representation of the thing itself, and is without life or any manner of moving, so be the works of all unfaithful persons before God. . . . They be but shadows and shows of lively and good things, and not good and lively things indeed.' The notable contrast drawn by Bassanio in the casket-scene of *The Merchant of Venice* between 'the outward shows' and 'themselves', between that 'ornament' which deceives the world and the 'truth', especially with its significant reference to hypocrisy in religion, recalls the words in the second part of this Homily : 'Notwithstanding all the goodly traditions and outward show of good works devised of their own imagination, whereby they appeared to the world most religious and holy of all men, yet Christ, who saw their hearts, knew that they were inwardly in the sight of God most unholy, most abominable, and furthest from God of all men.' It is interesting, however, to note that, whereas the Homily expresses a Protestant rejection of 'goodly traditions and outward show of good works', Bassanio rather associates religious hypocrisy with the abuse of Biblical texts. This theme of 'good works' is further continued in the Homily 'Of Fasting', which warns us 'not to put any confidence in our works, as by the merit and deserving of them to purchase to ourselves and others remission of sin . . . for that were mere blasphemy. It is of the free grace and mercy of God, without merit or deserving on our part, that our sins are forgiven us.' This is also one of the themes in *Love's Labour's Lost*, which vindicates Berowne's contention against the other lords, as echoed from the Catechism :

> For every man with his affects is born,
> Not by might master'd, but by special grace. (i. 1)

The Princess of France, too, in a lighter mood, refers to the 'heresy' of merit, after having given the Forester 'fair payment for foul words' (iv. 1).

Another theme, common to both *Love's Labour's Lost* and *King John*, is that of swearing and forswearing, which is developed in the Homily 'Against Swearing and Perjury'. Here it is emphasized 'what peril and danger it is vainly to swear or to be forsworn', and also 'how damnable a thing it is either to forswear ourselves or to keep an unlawful and unadvised oath'. It is along these lines that Berowne in the former play uses sophistical arguments to persuade the lords to break their former oath (iv. 3); and Cardinal Pandulph encourages King

Philip to forswear what he has sworn to King John (iii. 1).
The long speech of Pandulph in this matter follows directly on
John's defiance of the 'usurp'd authority' of the Pope, which
also echoes the wording of several Homilies – notably, that 'On
Order and Obedience', where 'the usurped power of the
bishop of Rome' is strongly denounced.

This rejection of papal authority is balanced by the assertion of the theory of the 'divine right of kings', whose classical
expression is to be found in the two Homilies, 'On Order and
Obedience' and 'Against Disobedience and Rebellion'. The
influence of the former is particularly strong in *Richard II*,
where John of Gaunt appears from the outset as a champion
of 'divine right'.[10] His words to the Duchess of Gloucester :

> *But since correction lieth in those hands*
> *Which made the fault that we cannot correct,*
> *Put we our quarrel to the will of heaven.* (i. 2)

and again, with even greater clarity :

> *God's is the quarrel; for God's substitute,*
> *His deputy anointed in his sight,*
> *Hath caus'd his death; the which if wrongfully,*
> *Let heaven revenge, for I may never lift*
> *An angry arm against his minister.* (*ibid.*)

are echoed in such sentences of the Homily as : 'It is not lawful for inferiors and subjects in any case to resist or stand
against the superior powers . . . We may not withstand nor in
any ways hurt an anointed king; which is God's lieutenant,
viceregent, and highest minister in that country where he is
king . . . [If he acts tyrannically] We must in such case patiently
suffer all wrongs and injuries, referring the judgement of our
cause only to God.' Even when the Duchess of Gloucester
objects to Gaunt, exclaiming :

> *Call it not patience, Gaunt, it is despair;*
> *In suffering thus thy brother to be slaughtered.*
> (*ibid.*)

she is really criticizing the examples of just men in the past
held up by the Homily as deserving of imitation : 'We read oft
that they patiently suffered all troubles, vexations, slanders,

pangs, and pains, and death itself obediently, without tumult
or resistance.' Further, the ideal of order with which the
Homily opens is precisely that which Ulysses defends in his
famous speech on 'degree' in *Troilus and Cressida* (i. 3) :

> Almighty God hath created and appointed all things, in
> heaven, earth and waters, in a most excellent and perfect
> order . . . And man himself also hath all his parts both
> within and without . . . in a profitable, necessary and
> pleasant order. Every degree of people, in their vocation,
> calling and office, hath appointed to them their duty and
> order . . . Take away kings, princes, rulers, magistrates,
> judges, and such estates of God's order . . . there must
> needs follow all mischief and utter destruction both of
> soul, bodies, goods, and commonwealths.[11]

As for the central position of the King, as emphasized by Laertes
in his conversation with Ophelia (*Hamlet* i. 2), it is stated that
'the whole body of every realm, and all the members and parts
of the same, shall be subject to their head, their king.'

Of yet greater importance in the plays is the latter Homily,
which was added to the second volume after the failure of the
Northern Rising in 1569, and made required reading in
church four times a year. The opening declaration, 'As God
the Creator and Lord of all things appointed his angels and
heavenly creatures in all obedience to serve and to honour his
majesty, so was it his will that man, his chief creature upon the
earth, should live under the obedience of him, his Creator and
Lord,' while reflecting the style of the former Homily, draws
particular attention to the virtue of obedience, as emphasized
by the Archbishop of Canterbury in *Henry V* :

> *Therefore doth heaven divide*
> *The state of man in divers functions,*
> *Setting endeavour in continual motion;*
> *To which is fixed, as an aim or butt,*
> *Obedience.* (i. 2)

In contrast, the hatefulness and horror of rebellion, even in
the name alone, are insisted upon : 'How horrible a sin against
God and man rebellion is, cannot possibly be expressed according to the greatness thereof . . . All sins, I say, against God and

all men heaped together nameth he that nameth rebellion.'

A similar vein appears in *Richard II*, where York accuses Bolingbroke of fault 'in the worst degree', namely, that of 'gross rebellion and detested treason' (ii. 3); in *Henry IV* Part I, where the name of 'rebels, traitors' is characterized as 'hateful' (v. 2); and in *Henry V*, where the King sees in the revolt of Lord Scroop as it were 'another fall of man' (ii. 2). The horror of the sin is particularly dwelt upon by the homilist: 'Surely, no mortal man can express with words, nor conceive in mind, the horrible and most dreadful damnation that such be worthy of, who, disdaining to be the quiet and happy subjects of their good prince, are most worthy to be the miserable captives and vile slaves of that infernal tyrant Satan.' His words are recalled by Shakespeare in the words of Macduff, on discovering Duncan's murder:

> *O horror, horror, horror! Tongue nor heart*
> *Cannot conceive nor name thee! (Macbeth* ii. 3)

as well as in Macbeth's own words, contemplating in that murder 'the deep damnation of his taking off' (i. 7). Camillo's realization, early on in *The Winter's Tale*, that rebellion against 'anointed kings' never prospers, is clearly derived from the following passage in the Homily: 'Turn over and read the histories of all nations; look over the chronicles of our own country; call to mind so many rebellions of old time, and some yet fresh in memory; ye shall not find that God ever prospered any rebellion against their natural and lawful prince.' The character of rebels, as described in the two Parts of *Henry IV*, 'fickle changelings and poor discontents' (Part I v. 1), countenanced 'by boys and beggary' (Part II iv. 1), is likewise represented in the Homily: 'The most rash and hare-brained men, the most greatest unthrifts, that have most lewdly wasted their own goods and lands, those that are over the ears in debt, and such as for thefts, robberies and murders dare not in any well-governed commonwealth where good laws are in force, show their faces . . .' The excuses they make, 'to face the garment of rebellion with some fine colour' (*Henry IV* Part I v. 1), especially by turning 'insurrection to religion' (Part II i. 1), are presented in like manner by Shakespeare and by the homilist: 'They would pretend sundry causes, as the redress

of the commonwealth . . . or reformation of religion . . . they
have made a great show of holy meaning by beginning their
rebellions with a counterfeit service of God . . . they display
and bear about ensigns and banners, which are acceptable
unto the rude ignorant common people.' Lastly, the woeful
consequences of rebellion, as listed by the homilist, 'that they
destroy all places, and undo all men where they come, that the
child yet unborn may rue it, and shall many years hereafter
curse him', are re-echoed in Shakespeare's histories, by the
Bishop of Carlisle in *Richard II* :

> *The woe's to come; the children yet unborn*
> *Shall feel this day as sharp to them as thorn.* (iv. 1)

and by the King (in a rather different context) in *Henry V* :

> *And some are yet ungotten and unborn*
> *That shall have cause to curse the Dauphin's scorn.*
>
> (i. 2)

The theme of human misery and the need for humble self-
knowledge, which is so important an element in Shakespeare's
tragedies, is emphasized from the beginning of the *Homilies*,
in that entitled 'Of the Misery of All Mankind'. Here it is
stated that the aim of the Holy Ghost in the Bible is 'to pull
down man's vainglory and pride' – an aim which also inspires
many of the utterances of Jaques, Hamlet and Lear, Apemantus and Timon; and, conversely, 'to teach us the most commendable virtue of humility, how to know ourselves, and to
remember what we be of ourselves'. This is precisely the lesson
which Lear learns in the midst of his sufferings, and which he
in turn preaches to the suffering Gloucester : 'I will preach to
thee; mark!' (iv. 6). The sermon he goes on to preach follows
the advice of the Homily, to 'consider what we be, whereof we
be, from whence we came, and whither we shall', namely, that
we all 'come into this world and go out of the same in like sort,
that is, as of ourselves, full miserable' : so, too, Lear exclaims :

> *Thou must be patient; we came crying hither;*
> *Thou know'st the first time that we smell the air*
> *We waul and cry . . .*
> *When we are born, we cry that we are come*
> *To this great stage of fools.* (iv. 6)

Of ourselves, the Homily continues, we 'bring forth but weeds, nettles, brambles, briars, cockle, and darnel'. Here, no doubt, is the deep significance of Lear's mad attire,

> *Crown'd with rank fumiter and furrow weeds,*
> *With burdocks, hemlock, nettles, cuckoo-flowers,*
> *Darnel, and all the idle weeds that grow*
> *In our sustaining corn.* (iv. 4)

The consequent insistence on patience, which features prominently in *King Lear*, is derived from the first Homily, 'An Exhortation to the Reading of Holy Scripture'. The Bible, says the homilist, 'teacheth patience in all adversity'; and his words are also echoed in the Duke's famous speech in *As You Like It*: 'Sweet are the uses of adversity' (ii. 1), and parodied by Dromio of Ephesus in *The Comedy of Errors*: 'Nay, 'tis for me to be patient; I am in adversity' (iv. 4).

Particular ethical questions are discussed in such homilies as 'Against Whoredom', 'Against Gluttony and Drunkenness', 'Against Excess of Apparel' and 'Against Idleness'; and these all have their importance for the right understanding of different plays. The first-mentioned has an obvious connection with *Measure for Measure*, especially in its general complaint that 'the outrageous seas of adultery, whoredom, fornication, and uncleanness have not only brast in, but also overflowed almost the whole world'.[12] These very words are echoed by Elbow, who likewise speaks of 'fornication, adultery, and all uncleanliness' (ii. 1). The homilist further laments that 'this vice is grown into such an height, that in a manner among many it is counted no sin at all . . . not rebuked but winked at, not punished but laughed at'. Again his words are echoed, this time by the Duke:

> *In time the rod*
> *Becomes more mock'd than fear'd; so our decrees,*
> *Dead to infliction, to themselves are dead,*
> *And liberty plucks justice by the nose.* (i. 3)

From this Homily, too, the dramatist may well have taken his frequent allusions to 'the deeds and works of darkness', as in *Pericles* (iv. 6) and *King Lear* (iii. 4). In contrast, the description of chastity as 'that treasure which before all other

is most regarded of honest persons, the good fame and name
of man and woman', is re-echoed from play to play: in *The
Comedy of Errors*:

> *I see the jewel best enamelled*
> *Will lose his beauty . . .*
> > *and no man that hath a name*
> *By falsehood and corruption doth it shame.* (ii. 1)

in *Richard II*:

> *The purest treasure mortal times afford*
> *Is spotless reputation: that away*
> *Men are but gilded loam or painted clay.* (i. 1)

in *All's Well That Ends Well*:

> *My chastity's the jewel of our house,*
> *Bequeathed down from many ancestors;*
> *Which were the greatest obloquy i' the world*
> *In me to lose.* (iv. 2)

and, above all, in *Othello* though it is Iago who speaks:

> *Good name in man or woman, dear my lord,*
> *Is the immediate jewel of their souls.* (iii. 3)

The Homily 'Against Gluttony and Drunkenness' has an
obvious relevance, of a general kind, to such characters as Sir
John Falstaff and Sir Toby Belch; but its verbal echoes are
rather to be found in *Richard III* and *Henry V*. The comment of Hastings on 'the momentary grace of mortal men', as
he is led to his execution:

> *Who builds his hope in air of your good looks,*
> *Lives like a drunken sailor on a mast;*
> *Ready with every nod to tumble down*
> *Into the fatal bowels of the deep.* (*Richard III* iii. 4)

recalls the very words of this Homily: 'He doubtless is in great
danger that sleepeth in the midst of the sea, for soon is he overwhelmed with waves. He is like to fall suddenly that sleepeth in
the top of the mast.' Likewise, the learned anecdote about
Alexander told by Fluellen:

> *Alexander, God knows and you know, in his rages and his*
> *furies, and his wraths and his cholers, and his moods and*
> *his displeasures, and his indignations, and also being a*
> *little intoxicates in his prains, did, in his ales and his*
> *angers, look you, kill his best friend, Cleitus.*
>
> (*Henry V* iv. 7)

is evidently derived, not so much from *The Historie of Quintus Curcius, Conteyning the Actes of the Greate Alexander*, as from this Homily: 'The great Alexander, after that he had conquered the whole world, was himself overcome by drunkenness; insomuch that, being drunken, he slew his faithful friend, Clitus.'[13]

The third of these Homilies, 'Against Excess of Apparel', with its criticism of those effeminate men who are 'ever desiring new toys and inventing new fashions', has general echoes in many plays where the dramatist criticizes 'these most brisk and giddy-paced times' (*Twelfth Night* ii. 4); but above all in *All's Well That Ends Well*, where the King speaks feelingly against

> *Younger spirits, whose apprehensive senses*
> *All but new things disdain; whose judgments are*
> *Mere fathers of their garments; whose constancies*
> *Expire before their fashions.* (i. 2)

In this play the typical representative of these 'younger spirits' is, of course, Parolles, whose soul is said to be 'his clothes' (ii. 5). Another such spirit is Falconbridge, 'the young baron of England', who is merely mentioned in *The Merchant of Venice* to provide Portia with a target for her wit:

> *He is a proper man's picture, but alas, who can converse*
> *with a dumb-show? How oddly he is suited! I think he*
> *bought his doublet in Italy, his round hose in France, his*
> *bonnet in Germany, and his behaviour everywhere.* (i. 2)

It is interesting to note how her comments give detailed illustration to the following anecdote told by the homilist: 'A certain man that would picture every countryman in his accustomed apparel, when he had painted other nations, he pictured the Englishman all naked, and gave him cloth under his arm, and bade him make it himself as he thought best, for he changed his fashion so often, that he knew not how to make it.' Above all, Hamlet's disapproval of women's use of cosmetics in the case of Ophelia is apparently derived from this Homily, though it was also a commonplace in medieval sermons[14] – and there are parallels in contemporary sermons: 'Who can paint her face, and curl her hair, and change it into an unnatural colour, but therein doth work reproof to her Maker who made her hair, as though she could make herself more comely than God hath appointed the measure of her beauty? What do these women but go about to reform that which God hath made, not knowing that all things natural are the work of God, and things disguised and unnatural are the works of the devil?'

Lastly, the Homily 'Against Idleness' serves to illustrate the characterization of Prince Hal in contrast to Falstaff in *Henry IV* Part I. In particular, his soliloquy at the end of the first Falstaff scene, where he sets 'the unyok'd humour of your idleness' against his own resolution of 'redeeming time' (i. 2), largely echoes the unfavourable description in the Homily of 'the serving men of this realm', 'who spend their time in much idleness of life, nothing regarding the opportunity of their time'. In the foregoing scene, Falstaff pleads that ' 'tis no sin for a man to labour in his vocation' – words which have been attributed to II *Thessalonians* iii. 10 and the Catechism, but which perhaps come closer to the phrasing of this Homily: 'Everyone ought . . . in some kind of labour to exercise himself, according as the vocation, whereunto God hath called him, shall require.' There is also one precise echo of the Homily, word for word, in the Clown's declaration in *All's Well That Ends Well* – another play on the theme of idleness – that 'service is no heritage' (i. 3), meaning that the mere fact of being a servant does not provide for old age or posterity.

VII

Smith and Hooker

CONSIDERING THE abundance of homiletic material in the plays of Shakespeare, one might naturally expect him to have drawn upon other sermons of his age in the same manner. The official *Homilies* were, of course, read out in church Sunday after Sunday and would thus have exercised a continual influence on the mind of Shakespeare from his boyhood. Other sermons he would have heard only in passing and later in life; and these would have affected him mainly through their repetition of certain Scriptural texts and homiletic common-places. The sermons that were most likely to have impressed him were those delivered on important occasions at Paul's Cross; and of these the text has in many cases survived in pub-lished form. One such sermon, at least, that of William Barlow on the execution of the Earl of Essex in 1601, seems to have left its imprint on the composition of *Hamlet*.[1] Like Hamlet, the Earl is said to have been 'beloved of the commons' and 'followed and honoured by men of all sorts'. Like Hamlet, his aim is said to have been 'to remove such evils as the common-wealth is burdened with'. Like Horatio in praying for Hamlet, his final prayer is given as a petition to God for the angels to 'receive my soul and convey it to thy joys in heaven'. Even without such verbal parallels, the circumstances of the sermon make it probable that Shakespeare and his company would have been among Barlow's audience. But its contents have a political rather than a homiletic interest.

There is, however, one preacher of the day whose sermons

offer more parallels than most to Shakespeare's language, and who may well have attracted the dramatist's interest. This was Henry Smith, who was giving his eloquent sermons at St Clement Danes in the Strand about the very time when Shakespeare was spending his 'apprentice years' in London.[2] On his premature death in 1591, Smith received an enthusiastic eulogy from the pen of the 'university wit', Thomas Nash, in a well-known passage of *Pierce Penniless*:

> Silver-tongued Smith, whose well-tuned style hath made thy death the general tears of the Muses, quaintly couldst thou devize heavenly ditties to Apollo's lute, and teach stately verse to trip it as smoothly as if Ovid and thou had but one soul. Hence alone did it proceed that thou wert such a plausible pulpit man, that before thou enteredst into the rough ways of theology, thou refinedst, preparedst, and purifiedst thy mind with sweet poetry. If a simple man's censure may be admitted to speak in such an open theatre of opinions, I never saw abundant reading better mixed with delight, or sentences which no man can challenge of profane affectation sounding more melodious to the ear, or piercing more deep to the heart.

It may have been through Nash, his fellow-dramatist, who even features in *Love's Labour's Lost* in the character of Moth, that Shakespeare was introduced to the living sermons of Smith at St Clement Danes.[3] Or else he might have become acquainted soon after with the printed *Sermons*, which were published in 1593 by Richard Field, his fellow-townsman from Stratford and the printer of his two long poems about this very time.[4] Certainly, the printed *Sermons* contain a remarkable number of verbal parallelisms and illustrations of a more general nature that seem to anticipate many things in the plays. This has been explained as a deliberate attempt by the preacher to compete with the dramatists of his time; but the dramatists, and Shakespeare in particular, may well have repaid the compliment by borrowing images and turns of phrase from the preacher.[5]

To begin with, the preacher was not above employing theatrical metaphors in his sermons, such as might well have impressed men of the theatre in his audience. The theme that

'All the world's a stage', which resounds in Shakespeare's plays from *As You Like It* to *Macbeth* and *King Lear*, receives vivid elaboration in his sermon entitled 'The Magistrate's Scripture':

> While we play our pageants upon this stage of short continuance, every man hath a part, some longer, and some shorter, and while the actors are at it, suddenly death steps upon the stage like a hawk which separates one of the doves from the flight; he shoots his dart; where it lights, there falls one of the actors dead before them, and makes all the rest aghast, they muse and mourn, and bury him, and then to the sport again.

Other themes that are echoed particularly in the comedies are no less vividly portrayed in these sermons. The ideal of the perfect woman, as later described by Orlando in his verses on Rosalind (*As You Like It* iii. 2) and by Benedick in his requirements for a wife (*Much Ado About Nothing* ii. 3), is used to represent the good Christian: 'As a painter would draw a beautiful picture which should be fairer than all women in the world, he would mark the special grace of every one, and make one beauty of all: so we must make up a Christian.' The metaphor of joining is drawn upon to illustrate advice on marriage, in much the same way that Jaques advises Touchstone on his marital affairs in *As You Like It* (iii. 3): 'As boards, well joined at the first, fit closer ever after; but if they square at the first, they warp more and more; so they which are well joined, are well married.'

Among the comedies, it is perhaps *The Merchant of Venice* which has the largest number of echoes, some fainter, some clearer, from the sermons. The theme of Shylock's usury is naturally foreshadowed to some extent in the sermon devoted to an 'Examination of Usury'. Smith states very clearly that 'a man cannot love and be a usurer'; and he goes on to associate usury with the Jewish people: 'Now there be no such usurers upon earth as the Jews, which were forbidden to be usurers.' He further anticipates Antonio's argument against taking 'a breed for barren metal', when he points out that God 'never said unto money, Increase and multiply, because it is a dead thing, which hath no seed, and therefore is not fit to engender'.

On the other hand, the situation of Antonio, the merchant, waiting for his ships to return, is foreshadowed in 'The Banquet of Job's Children' : 'Job showeth in what fear he stood of his sons so long as their feasts lasted, even as a merchant doth till his ship come home.' The same image, with an opposite state of mind, recurs in 'The Heavenly Thrift', where the preacher describes how 'the ship sinketh upon the sea, while the merchant sporteth upon the land'. The general theme of appearance and reality – fair show obscuring foul substance – which is repeated by Antonio, concerning Shylock (i. 3), and by Bassanio, concerning the caskets of gold and silver (iii. 2), is emphasized many times by Smith with some verbal parallelism to the words of Shakespeare :

Hath it not the show of error, to broach a religion which was never heard of before ?
There is no sin, but hath some show of virtue.
Every heresy seemeth truth, every evil seems good.
Under the colour of goodness evil is always lurking.

The theme of God's mercy, as celebrated by Portia in her central speech (iv. 1), is developed by Smith along similarly Scriptural lines – first, in his use of the rain-image from *Ecclesiasticus* xxxv. 19, 'God's mercies are resembled to rain'; and secondly, in his general commendation of this virtue : 'Many sweet things are in the word of God, but the name of *mercy* is the sweetest word in all the Scriptures.' Finally, the imagery of music, which dominates the final act of Shakespeare's play, is twice used by Smith in a similar context :

Love is the marriage virtue, which sings music to their whole life.
There is a comfort of all the members when the heart is in tune . . . It sounds like a melody in the ears of God.

It is only natural that verbal and thematic foreshadowings of *Hamlet*, the most homiletic of the plays, should be abundant in the sermons.[6] An interesting discussion of the whole question of ghosts – 'the old question often debated among the simple people, once deluded, whether the souls of men departed walk after death and appear unto men, exhorting them to this or that' – occurs in 'The Pilgrim's Wish', though it seems to have escaped the attention of most commentators of the play. On the one hand, Smith mentions the opinion held 'in time of popery', whereby ghosts 'were taken for the souls of them which were dead' – as Hamlet instinctively assumes on his first encounter with his father's ghost (i. 5). On the other hand, the preacher gives his own view, to which Hamlet later inclines (ii. 2), that 'the devil can change himself into the likeness of a man'. Two homiletic commonplaces that are given prominence in the play are likewise developed in the sermons. The inevitable denunciation of woman's painting in 'A Dissuasion from Pride', recalls the similar denunciation in the Homily 'Against Excess of Apparel' and foreshadows Hamlet's words to Ophelia (iii. 1): 'This is their work, so soon as they rise, to put a pedlar's shop upon their backs, and colour their faces, and prick their ruffs, and frisle their hair. . . . They disguise themselves that God might not know them, nay they disguise their bodies so, till they know not themselves.' Secondly the medieval-classical theme of *'Ubi sunt?'* Smith himself may have borrowed out of a passage in Persons' *Christian Directory* mentioned in a previous chapter: 'Where is Alexander that conquered all the world? . . . Where are they which founded this goodly city, which possessed these fair houses, and walked these pleasant fields? . . . Is not earth turned to earth, and shall not our sun set like theirs when the night comes?' The parallel theme of death, as developed by Hamlet in his famous soliloquy (iii. 1), is anticipated by Smith in a variety of verbal echoes. He calls this life 'a sea of troubles'. He remarks of death that 'if it were but a sleep, no man would fear it at all'. He characterizes the frailty of the human body by saying, 'A pin is able to kill us.' He speaks of our life on earth as a 'pilgrimage', and of our possessions as a 'fardle of vanities'. As for the theme of conscience, troubling a sinner like Claudius, he has these interesting words in 'The Betraying of Christ': 'There is a warning conscience, and a gnawing conscience. The warning conscience cometh before sin; the gnawing conscience followeth after sin. The warning conscience is often lulled asleep; but the gnawing conscience waketh her again. If there be any hell in this world, they which feel the worm of conscience gnawing upon their hearts may truly say that they have felt the torments of hell.'

This analysis of conscience finds apt illustrations, not only in the case of Claudius, but also in those of Macbeth and Othello. In its sequel, moreover, Smith goes on to develop his meaning with reference to the Elizabethan stage, in terms that must have appealed to the dramatist's imagination.

> Who can express that man's horror but himself? Nay, what horrors are they which he cannot express himself? Sorrows are met in his soul as at a feast: fear, thought and anguish divide his soul between them. All the furies of hell leap upon his heart like a stage. Thought calleth to Fear; Fear whistleth to Horror; Horror beckoneth to Despair, and saith: Come and help me to torment this sinner. One saith that she cometh from this sin; and another saith that she cometh from that sin; so he goeth through a thousand deaths and cannot die. Irons are laid upon his body like a prisoner. All his lights are put out at once; he hath no soul fit to be comforted. Thus he lieth as it were upon the rack, and saith that he bears the world upon his shoulders.

Few passages from Elizabethan literature throw so much light on the basic meaning of Shakespeare's tragedies as this one does. Even verbally, it looks forward to Macbeth's 'I have supp'd full with horrors' (v. 5) and the witches' mutual questionings, 'Where hast thou been, sister? . . . Sister, where art thou?' (i. 3), to Macbeth's 'Out, out, brief candle!' (v. 5) and Othello's 'Put out the light' (v. 2), and to Lear's sufferings 'upon the rack of this tough world' (v. 3).

In the same sermon, on 'The Betraying of Christ', we find implicit support for the Folio reading of 'base Judean' in the last scene of *Othello*, whereby the hero's murder of Desdemona is compared to Judas's betrayal of Christ. Thus Smith says of Judas: 'He repented, like one which slayeth his friend in his rage, and sorroweth when it is past . . . But to show that he did not repent well, when he had committed one sin, he added another to it; for when he had murdered his master, he murdered himself too.' He also goes on to foreshadow Emilia's words of pity and indignation for 'the sweetest innocent' (v. 2): 'When the innocents are betrayed, nay when the innocentest is betrayed, it seemeth more than sin, because never any betrayed innocent Christ but Judas.' Other illustrations of *Othello* occur in 'The Way to Walk In'. Here Smith speaks of envy in a manner that anticipates Iago's 'green-eyed monster' (iii. 3) and Othello's subsequent 'Nothing canst thou to damnation add greater than that' (*ibid.*): 'If thou hast envy, and art an adversary, thou resemblest the devil; for thou canst not come nearer the devil any way, than to be envious . . . Let us slaughter this monster.' It is curious that a paragraph or so later on the preacher refers to 'the black Moor'. He also gives a warning in the same sermon against drunkenness, as making 'no difference between a man and a beast', which is recalled by Cassio in his post-drunken remorse (ii. 3). Finally, Othello's 'If after every tempest come such calms' has two verbal parallels in another sermon, 'The Trial of the Righteous': 'You must go through a sea of troubles, and then you shall come to a haven of rest. As the calm was greater after the tempest than it was before, so my joy shall be sweeter after tears than it was before.'

Macbeth, as we have noticed, also echoes the general themes of horror and a guilty conscience developed in 'The Betraying of Christ' – in accord with the implicit self-comparison of Macbeth to Judas in his words, ' 'twere well it were done quickly' (i. 7). Another Scriptural comparison might be to Hazael, of whom Smith remarks that he 'blushed before he sinned, and was impudent after'. The atmosphere of 'thick night' conjured up by Lady Macbeth, with the image of 'the blanket of the dark' (i. 5), recalls the self-deception of the sinner as portrayed by Smith in 'The Calling of Jonah': 'How should God know it? Should he be able to see through the dark? The thick clouds are a covering to him, that he may not see.' The impulse first of Macbeth, and later of Lady Macbeth, to wash their hands clean of their sin, is indeed rooted in several texts of Scripture; but it is likewise foreshadowed more than once in these sermons. 'If the black Moor could be clean, here is water enough to wash him.' 'As if we were night-black ravens, which cannot be washed with all the soap of the Gospel.' 'No water can wash the leprosy of sin, but the blood of the Lamb.' The symbolism of the knocking at the gate, as later defined by Thomas De Quincey, is confirmed by two brief statements of Smith: 'Death knocks at his door.' 'His conscience within bleeding, God at the door of his heart knocking.' Finally, the strong homiletic content of Macbeth's 'Tomorrow' speech (v. 5) is underlined by three interesting parallels in the sermons : 'All his lights are put out ot once; he hath no soul fit to be comforted.' 'Our fathers, marvelling to see how suddenly men are and are not, compared life . . . to a player which speaketh his part upon the stage, and straight he giveth place to another.' 'If any of you go away no better than you came, you are not like hearers, but like ciphers, which supply a place, but signify nothing.'

As for *King Lear*, which is hardly inferior to *Hamlet* in homiletic content, the parallels in the sermons, though fewer in number, are no less significant. The old king's indignation against his 'thankless child' (i. 4) echoes Smith's 'Alarum from Heaven' : 'They shall find no such cross or curse as graceless or unruled children.' His consequent curses echo the preacher's warning : 'Behold the heavens frown upon you for your sins, and the earth denieth her fruit and is become barren, because of your unthankfulness.' The main lesson of the play, as preached by Lear and by Edgar to the blind Gloucester (iv. 6), is inevitably echoed by Smith from various places of Scripture : 'As every one had a day to come into this world : so he shall have a day to go out of this world.' 'Man was not born at his own will, and therefore may not die at his own pleasure.' Edgar's lament over 'World, world, O world !' (iv. 1), moreover, recalls Smith's exclamation : 'O world, unworthy to be beloved !' Similarly, Lear's experience of 'the rack of this tough world' (v. 3) echoes, as we have noticed, 'The Betrayal of Christ' : 'Thus he lieth as it were upon the rack and saith that he bears the world upon his shoulders.' Finally, the apocalyptic element in *King Lear*, which is voiced by Kent and Edgar in the last scene, and which looks forward to Prospero's speech in *The Tempest*, is aptly summed up by Smith in 'The Godly Man's Request' : 'These little worlds are destroyed first, and at last the great world shall be destroyed too.'

The abundance of such parallels places Henry Smith apart from the other preachers of his time in relation to the plays of Shakespeare. Whether they serve to prove, at least in their totality, a direct influence on the plays or not, they afford valuable illustrations of the religious context in which Shakespeare developed and enriched his themes. In addition to Smith,

there is only one other Anglican writer who may be claimed as
an important 'source' for the thematic material of the plays,
the great theologian, Richard Hooker, who published the first
four books of his *Laws of Ecclesiastical Polity* in 1594. In comparison with the *Homilies* and Smith's *Sermons*, this work has
but few verbal echoes in the plays; and the few that may be
noted are evidently proverbial or commonplace expressions.
Yet the main lines of Hooker's theological position are surprisingly parallel to those discernible in the plays.[7] It is
generally recognized that Shakespeare was traditional and
conservative in sympathy; and within the Church of England
Hooker was the great champion of traditional thought, in the
main stream of Augustinian and Thomist theology, as opposed
to the extreme Protestant position championed by the Puritans
of his time. Whether Shakespeare was, in fact, influenced by
Hooker or not, may never perhaps be proved one way or the
other. There is no objective evidence that points even to a
possible connection between the two men. The circle within
which Hooker moved was a very restricted one: after his
Mastership of the Temple he retired in 1591 to Boscombe in
Wiltshire, and later in 1595 to Bishopsbourne in Kent, where
he died in 1600. As for his great work, it was acclaimed by a
very limited audience, and remained unchallenged by the
Puritans until the anonymous *Christian Letter* appeared in
1599.[8] But there is one small item of interest: that the divine
who undertook the defence of Hooker in this matter was
William Covell, who had earlier (in 1595) added the famous
marginal note to his *Polimanteia*: 'All praiseworthy. Lucrecia.
Sweet Shakspeare. Eloquent Gaveston. Wanton Adonis.'[9]

With regard to the theological system of Hooker, particularly as expounded in Book I of the *Laws*, there are several
important passages in which it comes remarkably close to the
thought of Shakespeare's plays, giving expression to ideas that
are more latent than explicit in them. From the very opening
words of this Book Hooker states a psychological truth, which
is as it were the starting-point of his own treatise and which
finds abundant illustration in the plays from *Hamlet* (in
Laertes's insurrection) to *Coriolanus* (in the demagogy of the
Tribunes):

He that goeth about to persuade a multitude that they are not so well governed as they ought to be, shall never want attentive and favourable hearers. (I. 1)

He goes on to preface his rational defence of the laws concerning the established Church by an eloquent acknowledgement of the inadequacy of man's reason with regard to things divine – in words that have more than one echo in *Hamlet*:

Dangerous it were for the feeble brain of man to wade far into the doings of the most high; whom although to know be life, and joy to make mention of his name; yet our soundest knowledge is to know that we know him not as indeed he is, neither can we know him : and our safest eloquence concerning him is our silence. (II. 2)

Herein we may find the reasoned basis of what has been called Shakespeare's 'reverent agnosticism',[10] and of the pregnant silence with which *Hamlet* ends and *King Lear* begins. The simple contrast, too, which Hooker adds in explanation, 'He is above and we upon earth', is likewise suggested in Claudius's reference to 'him who is above' (iii. 3). Even with regard to things on earth, he emphasizes man's ignorance,

The least thing in the world hath in it more than the wisest are able to reach unto. (III. 2)

in words that are echoed by Hamlet in his often quoted reply to Horatio:

There are more things in heaven and earth, Horatio,
Than are dreamt of in your philosophy. (i. 5)

Subsequently, Hooker speaks in a similar vein of, 'somewhat above the capacity of reason, somewhat divine and heavenly, which with hidden exaltation it rather surmiseth than conceiveth' (XI. 4). So, too, Hamlet finds the appearance of the ghost shaking his disposition 'with thoughts beyond the reaches' of his soul (i. 4). On the other hand, Hooker only draws attention to the limitations of man's reason in order to indicate the positive capability of 'that divine power of the soul', as he terms it (VII. 1). He points out that 'By reason man attaineth unto the knowledge of things that are and are not sensible.' (*ibid.*) Yet Hamlet still follows him, both in his exclamations: 'How noble in reason! how infinite in faculty! . . . how like an angel in apprehension!' (ii. 2), and in his calmer reflection on 'that capability and godlike reason' (iv. 4). At the same time, Hooker recognizes that in practice the use of reason is impeded by the prevalence of custom and prejudice among men; and it is against this, rather than against an undue exaltation of reason, that he argues:

> Custom inuring the mind by long practice, and so leaving there a sensible impression, prevaileth more than reasonable persuasion what way soever. (VII. 6)

His words are again echoed by Hamlet in his allusion to 'that monster custom, who all sense doth eat of habits evil' (following Theobald's emendation) (iii. 4).

The main emphasis of Hooker, therefore, in his refutation of the Puritans, is on the light of Reason, by which the divinely given law of Nature is made manifest to the human mind. This light had been considerably obscured by the Protestant reformers: by Luther, in his exaltation of Faith over Reason, and of the Bible over human interpretations; and by Calvin, in his exaltation of Grace over Nature, and of divine Predestination over human Free Will. Hence whereas their lead had been zealously followed by the English Puritans, Hooker looked back to that synthesis of Faith and Reason which he found in the twin volumes of Scripture and Nature and in their further elaboration by the great scholastic thinkers of the Middle Ages. Thus he complains in Book III: 'The name of the light of Nature is made hateful with men; the star of Reason and learning, and all other such like helps, beginneth no otherwise to be thought of than if it were an unlucky comet; or as if God had so accursed it, that it should never shine or give light in things concerning our duty any way towards Him, but be esteemed as that star in Revelation called Wormwood' (VIII. 4). His optimistic approach to Nature is mainly developed in Book I, where it is expressed in the pithy, scholastic statement: 'All things that are, are good' (V. 1). He looks, in much the same way as Pope in the *Essay on Man*, 'through Nature to Nature's God' without dwelling, like the reformers, on the corruption of sin: 'Forasmuch as the works of Nature are no less exact, than if she did both behold and study how to express some absolute shape or mirror always present before her; yea, such her dexterity and skill appeareth, that no intellectual creature in the world were able by capacity to do that which Nature doth without capacity and knowledge; it cannot be but Nature hath some director of infinite knowledge to guide her in all her ways. Who the guide of Nature, but only the God of Nature? "In Him we live, and move, and are." Those things which Nature is said to do, are by divine art performed, using Nature as an instrument; nor is there any such art or knowledge divine in Nature herself working, but in the Guide of Nature's work' (III. 4). This passage has, indeed, no precise echoes in the plays; but it serves at once to illustrate and to set in a wider context the various allusions in later plays, such as *King Lear* and *The Winter's Tale*, to 'goddess Nature' and 'great creating Nature'. In particular, the distinction between the greater world and the 'little world of man', which is also common in these plays, while being a commonplace of the age, also echoes the statement of Hooker: 'Man is not only the noblest creature in the world, but even a very world in himself.'

With such an emphasis on Reason and Nature, it is natural for Hooker to draw attention to the magnificent order in the universe, in much the same terms as the Homilies, 'Of Order and Obedience' and 'For Rogation Week'. He speaks of the divine law at work in the world, according to the analogy of human laws, and asks with some eloquence :

If Nature should intermit her course, and leave altogether, though it were but for a while, the observation of her own laws; if those principal and mother elements of the world, whereof all things in this lower world are made, should lose the qualities which now they have; if the frame of that heavenly arch erected over our heads should loosen and dissolve itself; if celestial spheres should forget their wonted motions, and by irregular volubility turn themselves any way as it might happen; if the prince of the lights of heaven, which now as a giant doth run his unwearied course, should as it were through a languishing faintness begin to stand and to rest himself; if the moon should wander from her

beaten way, the times and seasons of the year blend themselves by disordered and confused mixture, the winds
breathe out their last gasp, the clouds yield no rain, the
earth be defeated of heavenly influence, the fruits of the
earth pine away as children at the withered breasts of their
mother no longer able to yield them relief; what would become of man himself, whom these things now do all serve?

The general similarity of this passage to the 'degree' speech of
Ulysses in *Troilus and Cressida* (i. 3) has been noted by
several scholars, as well as the verbal parallel between 'blend
themselves by disordered and confused mixture' and Shakespeare's 'when the planets in evil mixture to disorder
wander'.[11] There is also an interesting verbal echo in the first
scene of *Antony and Cleopatra*, where Antony's speech contains the implication of universal chaos as the outcome of his
illicit amour:

> *Let Rome in Tiber melt, and the wide arch*
> *Of the rang'd empire fall!* (i. 1)

The importance of this theme in the total scheme of the
dramatist's thought is evident from the frequency with which
it recurs throughout his plays: in the fragment of *Sir Thomas
More* attributed to him, in *Henry IV* Part II (iii. 1), in
Hamlet (iv. 5), in *King Lear* (iv. 2), in *Coriolanus* (iii. 1), as
well as in the Ulysses speech.[12]

The common experience of the destructive impact of evil on
the world of Nature, which seems to justify the pessimism of
Luther and Calvin in view of sinful humanity, is carefully
explained by Hooker – according to the tradition of scholastic
thought – in terms of Will and Appetite. Of one thing, he says,

we must have special care, as being a matter of no small
moment; and that is, how the Will, properly and strictly
taken, as it is of things which are referred unto the end that
man desireth, differeth greatly from that inferior natural
desire which we call Appetite. The object of Appetite is
whatsoever sensible good may be wished for; the object of
Will is that good which Reason doth lead us to seek. Affections, as joy, and grief, and fear, and anger, with such like,
being as it were the sundry fashions and forms of Appetite,

can neither rise at the conceit of a thing indifferent, nor yet choose but rise at the sight of some things. Wherefore it is not altogether in our power, whether we will be stirred with affections or no : whereas actions which issue from the disposition of the Will are in the power thereof to be performed or stayed. (VII. 3)

From this distinction he goes on to speak about the freedom of the Will in its choice of evil, not as evil, but as apparent good.

There is in the Will of man naturally that freedom, whereby it is apt to take or refuse any particular object whatsoever being presented unto it. Whereupon it followeth, that there is no particular object so good, but it may have the show of some difficulty or unpleasant quality annexed to it, in respect whereof the Will may shrink and decline it; contrariwise (for so things are blended) there is no particular evil which hath not some appearance of goodness whereby to insinuate itself. For evil as evil cannot be desired : if that be desired which is evil, the cause is the goodness which is or seemeth to be joined with it. Goodness doth not move by being, but by being apparent; and therefore many things are neglected which are most precious, only because the value of them lieth hid . . . Reason therefore may rightly discern the thing which is good, and yet the Will of man not incline itself thereunto, as oft as the prejudice of sensible experience doth oversway. (VII. 6.)

Finally, turning to the actual choice of evil, Hooker continues in the following section :

Nor let any man think that this doth make any thing for the just excuse of iniquity. For there was never sin committed, wherein a less good was not preferred before a greater, and that wilfully; which cannot be done without the singular disgrace of Nature, and the utter disturbance of that divine order, whereby the pre-eminence of chiefest acceptation is by the best things worthily challenged. There is not that good which concerneth us, but it hath evidence enough for itself, if Reason were diligent to search it out. Through neglect thereof, abused we are with the show of that which is not; sometimes the subtilty of Satan inveigling us as it did

Eve; sometimes the hastiness of our Wills preventing the more considerate advice of sound Reason, as in the Apostles, when they no sooner saw what they liked not, but they forthwith were desirous of fire from heaven; sometimes the very custom of evil making the heart obdurate against whatsoever instructions to the contrary. (VII. 7.)

The relevance of these three passages to Shakespeare's plays, particularly to the cantrasting themes of reality and appearance, fate and freedom, will and appetite, will be readily evident – though whether or not they are 'influences' may remain a matter of doubt.[13] They serve to explain the rational choice of Bassanio before the three caskets, as he reflects on the deception of 'outward shows' and 'the seeming truth which cunning times put on to entrap the wisest' (*Merchant of Venice* iii. 2). On the other hand, they provide an intellectual context for Macbeth's irrational yielding to the temptation of the witches :

> *This supernatural soliciting*
> *Cannot be ill, cannot be good; if ill,*
> *Why hath it given me earnest of success,*
> *Commencing in a truth? I am Thane of Cawdor:*
> *If good, why do I yield to that suggestion*
> *Whose horrid image doth unfix my hair*
> *And make my seated heart knock at my ribs,*
> *Against the use of nature? ...*
> *My thought, whose murder yet is but fantastical,*
> *Shakes so my single state of man, that function*
> *Is smother'd in surmise, and nothing is*
> *But what is not.* (i. 3)

Subsequently, Macbeth realizes his self-deception, but instead of turning back he only hardens his heart in 'the custom of evil' :

> *My strange and self-abuse*
> *Is the initiate fear that wants hard use.* (iii. 4)

Most clearly of all is the teaching of these passages reflected in *Troilus and Cressida*, both in the Greek council where Ulysses utters his warning:

> *Then everything includes itself in power,*
> *Power into will, will into appetite.* (i. 3)

and in the subsequent council of the Trojans where Hector likewise warns Paris and Troilus:

> *The reasons you allege do more conduce*
> *To the hot passion of distemper'd blood*
> *Than to make up a free determination*
> *'Twixt right and wrong; for pleasure and revenge*
> *Have ears more deaf than adders to the voice*
> *Of any true decision.* (ii. 2)

Hector goes on to speak, with a verbal echo of Hooker, of the 'law of nature' which may be 'corrupted through affection' and resisted through 'partial indulgence' to 'benumbed wills', and of the need 'to curb those raging appetites' by appropriate laws 'in each well order'd nation'. Yet in the outcome, for all the rightness of his reasons, Hector gives way to the affections of Paris and Troilus, as it were illustrating Hooker's observation that the Will of man may allow itself to be overswayed by 'the prejudice of sensible experience'.

On the political level, it may well have been the ideas of Hooker, if not the actual reading of his *Laws*, that led Shakespeare to adopt an increasingly critical attitude to the theory of 'divine right' from *Richard II* onwards. Among Anglican writers of the sixteenth century, Hooker stood out for his rational theory of popular 'consent', based on the political philosophy of the schoolmen, in contrast to the official Tudor doctrine of 'divine right' and 'passive obedience' as taught, somewhat hysterically, by the *Homilies*. His discussion of the nature of civil power and its origin in human society is noted by the Tory writer, Abednego Seller, in his interesting *History of Passive Obedience since the Reformation* (1689), as the only discordant opinion in the general Anglican teaching on this point – because he 'follows the schoolmen too strictly'.

> To fathers within their private families Nature hath given a supreme power; for which cause we see throughout the world even from the foundation thereof, all men have ever

been taken as lords and lawful kings in their own houses. Howbeit over a grand multitude having no such dependency upon any one, and consisting of so many families as every politic society in the world doth, impossible it is that any should have complete lawful power, but by consent of men, or immediate appointment of God; because not having the natural superiority of fathers, their power must needs be either usurped, and then unlawful; or if lawful, then either granted or consented unto by them over whom they exercise the same, or else given extraordinarily by God, unto whom all the world is subject. (X. 4.)

There is, indeed, in Shakespeare's plays no direct echo of this important passage – no more than of the other passage in the *Conference on the Next Succession* which supports the popular voice in the election of a king; but the criticism of the official doctrine implied in both passages would have afforded the dramatist a theoretical support for the increasing ambiguity of his attitude. On the one hand, it is true, he tends to support the established monarchical order of the commonwealth and to regard treason and rebellion with horror. But in this tendency he looks rather to a political and moral ideal, than to the real world in which the ideal is so often belied by 'seeming truth'.

Even in *Richard II* it is difficult for the audience to take sides in the dispute between Mowbray and Bolingbroke, as it is difficult to judge on which side the truth lies; and the same difficulty extends to the subsequent dispute between Bolingbroke and Richard himself. York taxes Bolingbroke with 'gross rebellion and detested treason' (ii. 3); but he soon acquiesces in the situation, and thereafter defends Bolingbroke, now Henry IV, from the 'foul treason' of his own son Aumerle (v. 2). On the other hand, it is while Richard is king and a professed upholder of the doctrine of 'divine right' that he is shown to be, humanly speaking, in the wrong; whereas, once he is deposed, he is presented in a more sympathetic light and a more truly Scriptural frame of mind. In fact, such was the ambiguity of the play to Shakespeare's own contemporaries that it could be interpreted as an incentive to the Queen's deposition, or at least that of her councillors, when it was revived in 1601 by the followers of Essex just before his abortive rebellion. In other plays, such as *Richard III* and *Macbeth*, the rule of a tyrant is not allowed to pass unopposed, according to the explicit teaching of the *Homilies*, but it is successfully overcome by force of arms. As for *Julius Caesar*, the fatal error of Brutus is shown to consist not so much in his deposition of an assured tyrant, as in his anticipation of a possible tyrant: 'Then, lest he may, prevent!' (ii. 1). In *Hamlet* the prince's dilemma arises out of his apparent duty 'to set things right', not so much because this involves taking revenge on the *king* who has been lawfully elected to succeed his father, but merely because it involves the taking of *revenge*, and revenge of any kind is contrary to the same divine 'canon' which forbids self-slaughter (i. 2). There is one duty imposed from without by the ghost of the past; and there is a contrary duty imposed from within by his Christian conscience. It is Claudius himself who declares, in Tudor fashion, that

> *There's such divinity doth hedge a king,*
> *That treason can but peep to what it would,*
> *Acts little of his will.* (iv. 5)

But his words are belied by the outcome of the play, when he is stabbed by the envenomed point he has prepared for Hamlet (v. 2). Above all, in *King Lear* the theory of 'passive obedience', no less than the army of Cornwall and Edmund, is countered by the armada which Cordelia brings over from France for the relief of her afflicted father. The outcome is, indeed, defeat for the invaders; but the sympathies of both dramatist and audience are clearly with Cordelia, when she exclaims disconsolately:

> *We are not the first*
> *Who, with best meaning, have incurr'd the worst.*
>
> (v. 3.)

VIII

Parsons and Puritans

THE PLAYS of Shakespeare, in their capacity as 'abstracts and brief chronicles of the time' (*Hamlet* ii. 2), bear witness not only in their language to the new forms of worship and doctrine, but also in their characterization to the new clergy of the Anglican Church. None of them, it is true, have their setting in Elizabethan England : they are all remote, both in place and in time, from the immediate surroundings of Shakespeare's London. But their remoteness belongs rather to the main plots, which are invariably derived from sources in continental literature or ancient chronicle; whereas the sub-plots, with their rich scenes of common life, may be regarded as living pictures of contemporary life and manners. Thus the 'humour of the constable' in *Much Ado About Nothing* is said (by John Aubrey) to have been taken from Shakespeare's observation of real life in a Buckinghamshire village on the road from London to Stratford.[1] The characters of Don Armado and Holofernes in *Love's Labour's Lost* are evidently drawn from an individual braggart and an individual pedant, even though scholars may dispute as to their precise identification.[2] The rehearsal of the play by Bottom and his friends in *A Midsummer Night's Dream* serves to place the Athenian wood in Shakespeare's own Warwickshire.[3] It is, no doubt, the same wood, the Forest of Arden, which reappears in *As You Like It*, where Touchstone's remark, 'Here we have no temple but the wood' (iii. 3), may possibly contain a reference to

Temple Grafton.[4] The whole sub-plot of *Twelfth Night*, centring on the character of Malvolio, has been shown to have its historical setting in an incident that took place at the court of Queen Elizabeth (the lady Olivia).[5]

In the same way, we find four of the comedies containing in their respective sub-plots the character – or caricature – of an Elizabethan parson. In *Love's Labour's Lost* we have Sir Nathaniel; in *The Merry Wives of Windsor*, Sir Hugh Evans; in *As You Like It*, Sir Oliver Martext; and in *Twelfth Night*, the Clown's impersonation of Sir Topas. Generally speaking, these parsons are represented as sincere men, conscious of their religious profession; yet they are all more or less buffoons, and are treated with little respect by the other characters. This contrast is made explicit by Costard in *Love's Labour's Lost*, where he describes the parson as 'an honest man' and 'a marvellous good neighbour', yet also as 'a foolish mild man' (v. 2). The role of Sir Nathaniel is mainly that of an uncritical and somewhat ridiculous admirer of the pedant, Holofernes, whom he praises in affectedly pious terms :

> *Very reverend sport, truly; and done in the testimony of a good conscience ... Sir, you have done this in the fear of God, very religiously.* (iv. 2)

> *I praise God for you, sir; your reasons at dinner have been sharp and sententious; pleasant without scurrility, witty without affection, audacious without impudency, learned without opinion, and strange without heresy.* (v. 1)

There is even something Puritan in his appeal to the 'testimony of a good conscience', such as we find in the writings of Thomas Cartwright and the authors of the *Admonition*.[6] His nemesis comes in the final scene, when he takes the incongruous part – 'a little o'erparted' – of Alexander among the Nine Worthies and incurs quite undeserved ridicule from the spectators.

The character of Sir Hugh Evans in *The Merry Wives of Windsor* is more fully drawn, and even more comic. He, too, is a simple, upright man, deeply conscious of his vocation – so conscious, in fact, that he is apt to use religious words and phrases in the most incongruous situations. He is particularly free with expletives and adjurations that are colourful, but hardly creditable to his cloth :

> *Got deliver to a joyful resurrections!* (i. 1)
>
> *Pless you from His mercy sake!* (iii. 1)
>
> *Got's will, and his passion of my heart!* (iii. 1)

As such expressions indicate, he is the opposite of mild, even if he is a buffoon. He is an irascible Welshman, who allows his anger to involve him in an undignified duel with the French Doctor Caius. In the midst of his anger, moreover, he indulges in language that can scarcely be called religious :

> *Pless my soul! how full of chollors I am, and trempling of mind! I shall be glad if he have deceived me. How melancholies I am! I will knog his urinals about his knave's costard when I have goot opportunities for the 'ork: pless my soul!* (iii. 1)

He goes on to sing a love ditty, into which he inserts a line from the metrical version of *Psalm* 137 : 'When as I sat in Pabylon'. His opponent, the no less irascible French Doctor, adds to his indignity by abusing him with such epithets as 'scurvy jackanape priest' (i. 4), 'de coward Jack-priest of the world' (ii. 3), and 'scurvy jack-dog priest' (*ibid.*). The undignified part he plays in the little comedy of the duel is followed by the equally undignified part of a satyr which he plays in the concluding scene of Falstaff's discomfiture. At the end, so far from winning the good opinions of the others for his pains, he is only dismissed by Mrs Ford as 'the Welsh devil' (v. 3) and by Falstaff himself as 'one that makes fritters of English (v. 5). In spite of his religious function, there seems to be nothing sacred about him; and, like Sir Nathaniel, he merely ends up as a pathetic figure of fun.

Sir Oliver Martext appears in only one scene of *As You Like It* (iii. 3); and then he says very little. Yet the few words he does say, the words that are said to him and about him by the others, and his very name, sufficiently indicate the comic aspect of his character and the satirical intention of the dramatist. The peculiar name was evidently suggested by that of Martin Marprelate, whose attacks on the episcopacy in the late eighties had been answered by several of the 'university wits'. In that controversy, the prefix mar- had been commonly bandied about, both by Marprelate and by his opponents; and Thomas Cooper, in his *Admonition to the People of England* (1589), speaks of 'not only Mar-prelate, but Mar-prince, Mar-state, Mar-law, Mar-magistrate and all together'. The particular form of Mar-text may have been suggested to the dramatist's mind by the words of Bassanio :

> *In religion,*
> *What damned error, but some sober brow*
> *Will bless it and approve it with a text,*
> *Hiding the grossness with fair ornament?*
> (*Merchant of Venice* iii. 2)

Sir Oliver is introduced as 'the vicar of the next village'; and he comes into the forest to perform the wedding ceremony for Touchstone and Audrey. From the first, he insists on an inessential formality :

> *Is there none here to give the woman? . . . Truly, she must be given, or the marriage is not lawful.*

He then listens in stony silence, while Jaques urges Touchstone :

> *Get you to church, and have a good priest that can tell you what marriage is: this fellow will but join you together as they join wainscot.*

This opinion of Jaques is secretly seconded by Touchstone himself in an aside to the audience :

> *I am not in the mind but I were better to be married of him than of another; for he is not like to marry me well, and not being well married, it will be a good excuse for me hereafter to leave my wife.*

In the outcome, again without apparently having deserved it, he is covered with ridicule by the departing jester; and his only response is a wooden assertion of his religious calling, which wins him no sympathy from the audience :

> *'Tis no matter: ne'er a fantastical knave of them all shall flout me out of my calling.*

These parting words of his are interestingly echoed at two points in an anonymous *Dialogue* which appeared at the time of the Marprelate controversy.[7] The Anglican minister is made to refer contemptuously to 'these fantastical Puritans', and at the end, when he is put to silence by the Puritan, he defiantly declares :

> *You say your pleasure, but I care not what you say, that's the best of it.*

The same kind of self-conscious dignity and sanctimonious utterance we find parodied in the Clown's impersonation of Sir Topas in *Twelfth Night*, when he visits the unfortunate Malvolio in prison (iv. 2). He begins in the manner prescribed by the 'Visitation of the Sick' in the *Book of Common Prayer*, declaiming : 'What ho ! I say. Peace in this prison !' He then continues in a tone of religious unction, with an affectation of Biblical erudition :

> *Madman, thou errest; I say there is no darkness but ignorance, in which thou art more puzzled than the Egyptians in their fog.*

In these words, there may well have been an intentional irony on Shakespeare's part; since their reference to the 'Egyptiacal darkness' puzzling the Puritanical Malvolio was a commonplace in the writings of Puritans like Cartwright and Travers.[8] Finally, on his return to the dark room, the Clown adopts a severe tone of moral exhortation :

> *Malvolio, Malvolio, thy wits the heavens restore! Endeavour thyself to sleep, and leave thy vain bibble-babble.*

It has been suggested that this scene in general, and these words in particular, may owe something to the account of certain exorcisms performed by John Darrel and described by him in his *True Narration* (1600).[9] The children who were the objects of his exorcisms are described as using 'much light behaviour and vain gestures, sundry also filthy scurrilous speeches, but whispering them for the most part among themselves, so as they were no let to that holy exercise we there had in hand. Sometimes also they spake blasphemy, calling the word preached, bible bable, he will never have done prating, prittle prattle'. Martin Marprelate, too, in his *Mineral and Metaphysical Schoolpoints* (1589), alludes to a criticism of the Puritans that their long prayers 'before and after their sermons are nothing else but "beeble-babble, beeble-babble".' Darrel himself was a Puritan preacher; and it may be that the Clown is referring to such preachers in his prefatory remark : 'I would I were the first that ever dissembled in such a gown'. For the gown was generally worn, without a surplice, by Calvinist ministers – the 'black gown of a big heart', as it is called by the other Clown in *All's Well That Ends Well* (i. 3). In this case, there is something ironical in the pitting of a Puritan minister against Malvolio, who is 'a kind of Puritan'.

The critical attitude towards the Elizabethan clergy which seems to be implied in these four characters is amply justified by contemporary documents from the Protestant, no less than from the Catholic side.[10] One of the results of the Reformation in England had been the appropriation of many Church benefices by lay patrons, who were not always particular in their choice of suitable candidates for the livings; and in the early years of Elizabeth's reign the number of such candidates was insufficient to replace the 'popish' Marian priests. For the sake of material profit, the patrons were often willing to entrust the benefices in their gift to illiterate men, 'weavers, pedlars and glovers', who would gladly accept them for a fraction of their revenue. To this situation William Harrison, in his *Description of England* (1576), attributes what he calls 'the general contempt of the ministry', namely that 'the greatest part of the more excellent wits choose rather to employ their studies unto physic and the laws, utterly giving over the study of the Scriptures, for fear lest they should in time not get their bread by the same'. In his *Sermons* Bishop Jewel likewise complains that benefices have been so pillaged by the laity that 'all shun and flee the ministry' and 'even in the properest market towns benefices are so simple that no man can live upon them, and therefore no man will take them'. The prevalence of 'dumb dogs' in the Anglican ministry was, in fact, one of the main points of Puritan criticism against the establishment – in Cartwright's words, 'such as gave but one leap out of the shop into the church, as suddenly are changed out of a serving-man's coat into a minister's cloak, making for the most part the ministry their last refuge'.[11] Nor could Whitgift, defending the establishment, gainsay him : 'It is true that covetous patrons of benefices be a great plague to this church, and one of the principal causes of rude and ignorant ministers.'[12] Even towards the end of Elizabeth's reign, after various attempts had been made to remedy the situation, Richard Hooker still speaks of the parish clergy as drawn from 'the scum and refuse of the whole land', as in the time of Jeroboam. It is quite possible that this state of affairs is signified by the Fool in *King Lear* in his cryptic prophecy, which seems pointless unless it points to Shakespeare's England :

> *When priests are more in word than matter.* . . .
> *No heretics burn'd, but wenches' suitors* . . .
> *Then shall the realm of Albion*
> *Come to great confusion.* (iii. 2)[13]

Abstractly speaking, it might be maintained that these characters of parsons refer no less to the 'Sir John lack-Latins' of Marian times, whose ignorance was commonly derided by the Protestants, than to the 'new clergy' of the Elizabethan Church. But by the nineties, when Shakespeare was writing his comedies, the old Marian priests had long since passed away; and in these characters he was presumably satirizing a type of parson familiar to his audience. In any case, the self-consciousness of their religiosity, combined with their inability to command the respect of the other characters, suggests that they may well have given 'but one leap out of the shop into the church'. In all of them, too, there is a Puritanical flavour, even though they belonged to a type of ignorant clergy criticized by the Puritan leaders. Sir Nathaniel appeals to 'the testimony of a good conscience'; Sir Hugh sings snatches of metrical psalms; Sir Oliver is nominally associated with Martin Marprelate; and Sir Topas, or rather the Clown masquerading as Sir Topas, dissembles in a Puritan gown. This need cause no great surprise, seeing that a large proportion of the lower clergy during Elizabeth's reign was Puritan at least in sympathy – apart from those members of the Marian clergy who had temporized with the religious changes.

Turning, then, from these more or less Puritanical parsons to the Puritans, as they were known to Shakespeare's audience in the nineties, one may distinguish in his plays – as in real life – two different kinds of Puritan according to different kinds of motive. On the one hand, we have the sincere but over-zealous type, inclined to fanaticism as well as to solemnity of manner. This is the type referred to by the Clown in *All's Well That Ends Well* as 'young Charbon', whether on account of his red-hot zeal (Thomas Cooper compares Martin Mar-prelate to a 'flaming firebrand'),[14] or because of his readiness to eat flesh on Fridays ('chair bonne') in opposition to the fish-eating Papists, such as 'old Poysam the papist' (i. 3). The latter reason may be illustrated by the remark of Demetrius in John Udall's dialogue, *Diotrephes* (1588): 'I am a Pro-testant, for I love to eat flesh on the Friday.' The fiery zeal of the Puritans, impatient of past tradition, may well be cari-catured in Laertes, whose hot-headed insurrection in Act IV of *Hamlet* involves the neglect of antiquity and ignorance of custom (iv. 5). Similarly, in *Timon of Athens* reference is made by Timon's servant to 'those that under hot ardent zeal would set whole realms on fire' (iii. 3). They are identified by Dr Johnson with the Elizabethan Puritans, who 'were then set upon a project of new-modelling the ecclesiastical and civil government according to Scripture rules and examples'. The solemn manner cultivated by the same Puritans more readily lent itself to caricature on the stage, as in Ben Jonson's por-trayal of Ananias in *The Alchemist*. It was, no doubt, with reference to this manner in Malvolio – as well as to his general attitude of censoriousness – that Maria remarks of him: 'Sometimes he is a kind of Puritan' (ii. 3). A more general description of the type occurs in the opening scene of *The Merchant of Venice*, where Gratiano warns Antonio:

> *There are a sort of men whose visages*
> *Do cream and mantle like a standing pond,*
> *And do a wilful stillness entertain,*
> *With purpose to be dress'd in an opinion*
> *Of wisdom, gravity and profound conceit,*
> *As who should say, 'I am Sir Oracle,*
> *And when I ope my lips let no dog bark!'* (i. 1)

These are precisely the men portrayed by Whitgift, when, in his *Answer* to the *Admonition* (1572), he compares the English Puritans to the continental Anabaptists: 'They earnestly cried out against pride, gluttony, &c. They spake much of mortification; they pretended great gravity; they sighed much; they seldom or never laughed; they were very austere in reprehending; they spake gloriously; to be short, they were hypocrites, thereby to win authority to their heresy among the simple and ignorant people.'

Towards these sorts of men Shakespeare would hardly have felt at all kindly disposed. They were, in fact, the principal opponents of the London stage, which they professed to regard as a hot-bed of popery, idolatry, whoredom and all immorality. The literary attack on stage-plays, as expressed in Stephen Gosson's *School of Abuse* (1579) and in Philip Stubbes's *The Anatomy of Abuses* (1583), was followed up by practical measures against the theatres on the part of the City authorities, who were largely Puritan in sympathy. In return, the dramatists were able to launch a counter-attack against the Puritans, when the support of the 'university wits', Lyly, Nash and Greene, was enlisted by the Church authorities against the pamphlets of Martin Marprelate, who has been identified as a near neighbour of Shakespeare in Warwickshire, Job Throckmorton.[15] Such was the situation of the London theatre at the time of Shakespeare's arrival; and though he took no active part in this counter-attack, he was influenced by it in various ways – in the first place, by the Harvey–Nash controversy, which was an offshoot of the Marprelate controversy, and which is echoed in *Love's Labour's Lost*.[16] Unlike Jonson and Middleton, he does not come out into the open against the Puritans, partly because he refuses to give a contemporary setting to his plays, and partly because of his general reluctance to take sides in view of the universality of human nature. Yet when he does mention them, his tone is generally unfavourable. In addition to the points cited above, there is mention of a Puritan at the sheep-shearing feast in *The Winter's Tale*, who 'sings psalms to horn-pipes' (iv. 3). The allusion here is perhaps to the high nasal tone affected by the Puritans in reciting the Psalms, with a hint at their general disapproval of singing and dancing; or else to their custom of chanting metrical versions of the Psalms to inappropriate popular tunes, such as – to give the example cited by Mistress

Ford in *The Merry Wives of Windsor* – 'the Hundredth
Psalm to the tune of Greensleeves' (ii. 1).[17] The same custom
of singing Psalms is also alluded to by Falstaff in *Henry IV
Part I*, where he speaks particularly of the Puritan weavers
who had emigrated from the Low Countries to East Anglia:
'I would I were a weaver: I could sing psalms or anything'
(ii. 4).

On the other hand, there was a less sincere type of Puritan,
who adopted – or at least, was widely believed to adopt – a
Pharisaic attitude as a cloak for worldly ambition and avarice,
and merely made use of religion, by appealing to texts mainly
from the Old Testament, to justify his practices of usury and
oppression. It is this type which was the main target for the
dramatists and satirists of the age, though it is frequently mixed
up with the former type. Thus Marston in his second *Satire*
(1598) points out 'yonder sober man, that same devout meal-
mouth'd precisian' (as the Puritans were called especially at
the universities),[18] and exposes him as 'a vile sober damned
politician', who 'bites the needy in deepest usury'. In his play
Eastward Ho (1605), which he wrote in collaboration with
Chapman and Jonson, he also refers to such Puritans as 'the
smoothest and slickest knaves in a country'. This is exactly the
kind of 'stage Puritan' ridiculed in the plays of Jonson and
Middleton.[19] And this is also the kind pilloried in several of
Shakespeare's major characters, not always openly, but quite
unmistakably – at least, to an Elizabethan audience.

The most obvious of these characters is Malvolio in *Twelfth
Night*, who is pointed out by Maria as 'a kind of Puritan' (ii.
3). It is true that she goes on to qualify her statement by adding: 'The devil a Puritan that he is, or anything constantly,
but a time-pleaser.' But her qualification is itself qualified by
certain contemporary overtones of the words she uses. The
opening phrase, besides its apparent correction of what she has
just said, has a further association with the cant phrase of the
time, 'The devil is a Puritan' – which is later recalled by the
bawd in *Pericles* where he says of Marina: 'She would make a
Puritan of the devil, if he would cheapen a kiss of her' (iv. 6).[20]
As for the epithet of 'time-pleaser', it was commonly on the
lips of Elizabethan Puritans with reference to their Anglican
adversaries – usually in the parallel forms of 'time-server' and

'men-pleaser', which we find (for example) in the anonymous *Second Admonition* and in the writings of Cartwright against Whitgift.[21] Thus, as we have already noticed in connection with Sir Topas and his baiting of Malvolio, there is in the latter at once something distinctively Puritan and something no less distinctively attacked by the Puritans. On the one hand, Malvolio is not a Puritan in the religious sense of the word, not even as a religious hypocrite. But he is 'a kind of Puritan' in the self-regarding pomposity of his manner, as it were priding himself on being one of the 'elect', and in his censorious reprehension of others for indulging in undue merriment. It is with reference to the former quality that Maria characterizes him, in the same context, as

> *an affectioned ass that cons state without book, and utters it by great swarths; the best persuaded of himself; so crammed, as he thinks, with excellencies, that it is his ground of faith that all that look on him love him.* (ii. 3)

This is exactly how Whitgift characterizes the Puritans in his *Answer* to the *Admonition* (1572): 'This name *Puritan* is very aptly given to these men, not because they be pure . . . but because they think themselves to be more pure than others . . . as though they only had the word of God and were of the Church . . . arrogant spirits . . . that think themselves of all men best learned, and disdain to learn of any.' As for the latter quality, it is to this that Sir Toby objects with the historic demand: 'Dost thou think, because thou art virtuous, there shall be no more cakes and ale?' In general, the Puritans were criticized for their austerity in reprehending; and in John Udall's *Diotrephes* the innkeeper, Pandochus, is made to complain of the Puritan: 'A gentleman cannot come all this evening, in any place where he is, but he is finding fault with him for one thing or another.' The particular reference to 'cakes and ale' may well have been suggested by the (probable) identification of Malvolio with the solemn Comptroller of the Queen's Household, Sir William Knollys, whose father, Sir Francis, had been a staunch defender of the Puritans, and whose country seat was near Banbury, famous for its cakes and its ale.[22]

Oddly enough, even in Sir Toby – the confirmed adversary

of Malvolio – there is a touch of Puritan doctrine : in his tipsy remark, 'Give me faith, say I' (i. 5), which seems to imply the characteristic Protestant tenet of justification by faith alone. The early emphasis of English Protestantism on this point is chiefly illustrated by Shakespeare in his great comic creation, Sir John Falstaff, from the moment of his first appearance in *Henry IV* Part I. Of course, there is nothing of the 'stage Puritan' in Falstaff; but he is none the less a living parody of the earlier Elizabethan Puritans, like John Foxe, who held that 'those once called cannot be lost' and that 'any who thought otherwise believed in salvation by works'.[23] The practical reason for such a parody is that, as has been noted in a previous chapter, Falstaff's role in the play was originally suggested by the historical figure of the Lollard leader, Sir John Oldcastle, in whom Foxe had recognized a forerunner of the Reformation.[24] Thus, in spite of his lax behaviour, as a 'reverend Vice' (ii. 4), he is ready with a remarkable store of pious expressions. From the first he defends his practice of purse-taking with an appeal to Scripture :

> *Why, Hal, 'tis my vocation, Hal: 'tis no sin for a man to labour in his vocation.* (i. 2.)[25]

Later on, too, he adduces Scriptural justification for his sins of the flesh :

> *Dost thou hear, Hal? Thou knowest in the state of innocency Adam fell; and what should poor Jack Falstaff do in the days of villainy? Thou seest I have more flesh than another man, and therefore more frailty.* (iii. 3)

At the same time, he occasionally assumes the role of 'Monsieur Remorse' and resolves to 'give over this life' (i. 2). As he feels himself growing old and withered, he declares on a sudden impulse :

> *Well, I'll repent, and that suddenly while I am in some liking: I shall be out of heart shortly, and then I shall have no strength to repent. An I have not forgotten what the inside of a church is made of, I am a peppercorn, a brewer's horse: the inside of a church! Company, villainous company, hath been the spoil of me.* (iii. 3)

Nevertheless, even amid his sins, he speaks of himself, in Puritan terminology, as 'a saint', in contrast to 'the wicked' (i. 2) and 'the sons of darkness' (ii. 4); and in his dying moments he raves, like a fanatical Puritan, about 'the whore of Babylon' (*Henry V* ii. 3). His most explicit reference to the doctrine of justification by faith alone, parallel to that of Sir Toby, is when he says of Poins :

> *If men were to be saved by merit, what hole in hell were hot enough for him?* (i. 2)

– where his words have an application no less to his own case, and his own wishful thinking.

The most obviously Puritan character in the plays is Lord Angelo in *Measure for Measure* – even though the setting is in Catholic Vienna. Though the word 'Puritan' is never used of him, as it is of Malvolio, he is characterized as 'precise' (i. 3), an epithet used in Elizabethan times almost exclusively of the Puritans, who were called 'these precise fellows', 'our precise apostles', and 'these precise and hot preachers'.[26] Ben Jonson likewise speaks, a few years later in *Volpone* (1607), of 'a precise, pure, illuminate brother' (i. 1). By reason of his preciseness, Angelo – according to the Duke's description –

> *Stands at a guard with envy; scarce confesses*
> *That his blood flows, or that his appetite*
> *Is more to bread than stone.* (i. 3)

He is – in Lucio's words –

> *a man whose blood*
> *Is very snow-broth; one who never feels*
> *The wanton stings and motions of the sense,*
> *But doth rebate and blunt his natural edge*
> *With profits of the mind, study and fast.* (i. 4)

The Puritans of the time did indeed seem, in the words of William Covell, to 'impropriate Conscience, Holiness, Innocency and Integrity' only to themselves, and to assume a 'singular affection' of uprightness.[27] So, too, Angelo is recognized by the Duke from the beginning as one of 'our seemers'; and Isabella comes to realize from her experience of him that, though he has spoken of himself as 'a saint' (ii. 2), he is in fact no more than an 'outward-sainted deputy' (iii. 1). In him is illustrated the truth that pride comes before a fall – a fall into the very sin which he most condemns in others, and which he strives to cover with 'false seeming' (ii. 4) as a moral hypocrite. It is, moreover, with reference to his false seeming as described by Isabella, that Claudio applies to him the unusual epithet, 'the prenzy Angelo' – a word which has been explained as a rare corruption of 'precise'.[28] The same epithet is further echoed by his sister :

> *O, 'tis the cunning livery of hell,*
> *The damned'st body to invest and cover*
> *In prenzy guards!* (iii. 1)

The particular severity of Lord Angelo is manifested, above all, in his manner of upholding the 'rigour of the statute' (i. 4) against all sins of the flesh. It is true that in this he does but follow the commission of the Duke to enforce the 'strict statutes and most biting laws' of Vienna, lest 'evil deeds have their permissive pass' owing to the leniency of those in office (i. 3). Yet in his severity he goes beyond the Duke's commission; and in his personal bearing he fails to 'be as holy as severe' (iii. 2) – though he protests to Escalus, in response to the latter's plea for Claudio :

> *You may not so extenuate his offence*
> *For I have had such faults; but rather tell me,*
> *When I that censure him do so offend,*
> *Let mine own judgment pattern out my death.*
>
> (ii. 1)

In other words, he fails to observe the prescription of Christ in just such a case : 'Let him that is among you without sin, cast the first stone at her' (*John* viii. 7). Now it is interesting to notice that this very passage from *John* viii was urged by Whitgift against Cartwright during their celebrated controversy in the seventies. Whereas Whitgift had appealed to 'the lenity of the Gospel' over 'the severity of the law', Cartwright denied (with Calvin) that 'the sentence of Our Saviour Christ in the eight of John brought any grace to adulterers, as touching the civil punishment'.[29] He denied indeed that the magistrate had any right to save the life of offenders, or that the civil law of Christian countries had any right to set aside the judicial law of Moses which made adultery, no less than idolatry, punishable by death. On this point Cartwright was quite adamant, maintaining that 'Every transgression of the law, be it never so little of itself and in the own nature, is damnable': that 'There are certain laws amongst the judicials [of Moses], which cannot be changed . . . the laws which command that a stubborn idolater, blasphemer, murderer, incestuous person and suchlike, should be put to death': and that 'If this be bloody and extreme, I am content to be so counted with the Holy Ghost'. Thus his attitude, in clinging to the law of the Old Testament, is precisely echoed by that of Angelo; in contrast to the protestation of Whitgift that he is merely bringing back the intolerable 'bondage of the law' upon Christian people.

Another sin of which Angelo is shown to stand guilty, and which further relates him to the Puritans of the time (at least, as they were represented by their enemies), is that of his hardhearted avarice in deserting Mariana when he heard how she had lost 'the portion and sinew of her fortune, her marriagedowry' (iii. 1). This is how Matthew Sutcliffe criticizes the Puritans in his *Answer to a Certain Libel* (1592): 'I know none more hard-hearted than the Puritans . . . As for pettifoggers and scribes, they do skin the poor, and help them not', and again: 'What else should we look for at their hands, seeing in racking of rents, extremity of dealing, usury and unlawful practices of gain, and Turkish and inhuman cruelty, divers of these zealators of Puritanism pass both Turks and heathen.' It is interesting to note that Malvolio, too, incurs a similar charge, in that the captain who has given assistance to Viola is said – quite irrelevantly to the action of the play – to be 'in durance at Malvolio's suit' (*Twelfth Night* v. 1). A third instance of such hardness of heart in enforcing the law occurs in *The Merchant of Venice*, where Shylock is abused as a 'stony, inhuman wretch' and compared unfavourably with 'stubborn Turks and Tartars' at the opening of the trialscene (iv. 1).

In this third instance, the parallel between Shylock the Jew and the Puritans of Shakespeare's time is by no means fortuitous. So many, indeed, are the parallels which recur throughout the play that it might even be maintained that in the eyes of an Elizabethan audience Shylock would have come to appear more Puritan than Jew.[30] In the first place, Shylock's practice of usury seems to have been followed by many Elizabethan Puritans, who were particularly influential in the City of London. In his *Discourse upon Usury* (1572), Thomas Wilson criticizes them particularly on this point: 'The dissembling gospeller, under the colour of religion, overthroweth all religion, and bearing good men in hand that he loveth plainness, useth covertly all deceit that may be, and for private gain undoeth the common welfare of man. And touching this sin of usury, none do more openly offend in this behalf than do these counterfeit professors of this pure religion.' Sutcliffe, too, in his above-mentioned *Answer*, reprehends 'these counterfeit hypocrites, that shaking off their ministry, and disdaining the base account of it, trade in usury, merchandise, farms and other suchlike occupations, giving over themselves to serve Mammon', and he even accuses the Puritan leader, Thomas Cartwright, of usurious practices. Secondly, Shylock's justification of himself by appealing to the Bible reflects a habit of the Puritans in this and in all other matters, considering that (as Cartwright tells Whitgift) 'whatsoever is commanded of the Lord unto the church is contained in the word of God'. This is why Antonio makes the sarcastic comment: 'The devil may cite Scripture to his purpose' (i. 3); and Bassanio remarks on a later occasion :

> *In religion,*
> *What damned error, but some sober brow*
> *Will bless it and approve it with a text,*
> *Hiding the grossness with fair ornament?* (iii. 2)

Likewise, Whitgift in his *Defence of the Answer* (1574) retorts against Cartwright that heretics have the word of God 'evermore in their mouth, and always talk of it'. Thirdly, Shylock's rigid emphasis on the law – like that of Angelo in *Measure for Measure* – is exactly paralleled by that of Cartwright in his controversy with Whitgift. Against the Puritan leader, Whitgift declares that his opinion 'smelleth of Judaism', and demands with indignation : 'What remaineth but to say that Christ is not yet come?' Similarly, the anonymous author of *A Defence of the Ecclesiastical Regiment* (1574) supports Whitgift by saying: 'I see not what can be intended by this new devised discipline, but only restitution of the veil, and clogging men's consciences with such Jewish observation, from the which we are enfranchised by the Gospel.'

Moreover, Shylock's contempt for the 'shallow foppery' of the Christians in contrast to his own 'sober house', and his commendation of a 'thrifty mind' (ii. 5), would have reminded an Elizabethan audience of the Puritan emphasis on the virtues of sobriety and thrift. His hypocrisy, too, which makes Antonio compare him to 'a villain with a smiling cheek' and 'a goodly apple rotten at the heart' (i. 3), may be matched by Bancroft's characterization of the Puritans in his *Survey of the Pretended Holy Discipline*: 'Many sepulchres are gorgeous to the eyes, and yet inwardly have nothing in them but bones and corruption . . . Men may often times be deceived with shews and probabilities, as always heretofore many have been.' In the same *Survey* there is also an interesting parallel to Shylock's famous refusal to eat, drink or pray with Christians (i. 3): 'Seeing our church, our government, our ministry, our service, our sacraments, are thus and thus . . . therefore they will not pray with us, they will not communicate with us, they will not submit themselves to our church . . . they will have nothing to do with us.' The same characteristic is reiterated at greater length by Whitgift in his *Answer to an Admonition*: 'These men separate themselves from our congregation, and will not communicate with us neither in prayers, hearing the word, nor sacraments; they contemn and despise all those that be not of their sect, as polluted and not worthy to be saluted or kept company with; and therefore some of them, meeting their old acquaintance, being godly preachers, have not only refused to salute them, but spit in their faces, wishing the plague of God to light upon them.' Lastly, just as Shylock is repeatedly called a devil, especially by Lancelot (ii. 2) and by his opponents in the trial-scene (iv. 1), so the Puritans – as we have noticed – were often called devils by their enemies. The very words of Lancelot, characterizing Shylock as 'the devil incarnal' (ii. 2), echo the anonymous anti-Martinist tract, *Martin's Month's Mind*, which speaks of the Puritan Martinists as 'very devils incarnate, sent out to deceive and disturb the world'.

Yet despite all this anti-Puritanism which seems to pervade the comedies, right up to *Measure for Measure*, there are a few scholars who have discerned a form of Puritanism in the later plays, from *Hamlet* onwards, particularly in view of their emphasis on original sin and human corruption, as well as their tone of revulsion from sexual vice.[31] It is, in the first place, noteworthy – and the dramatist draws our attention repeatedly to the fact – that both Hamlet and his friend Horatio come from school in Wittenberg, the cradle of the German Reformation (i. 2); and there is surely something Lutheran in the former's brooding emphasis on the corruption of human nature :

> *I am myself indifferent honest; but yet I could accuse me of such things that it were better my mother had not borne me. I am very proud, revengeful, ambitious; with more offences at my beck than I have thoughts to put them in, imagination to give them shape, or time to act them in. What should such fellows as I do crawling between heaven and earth? We are arrant knaves, all; believe none of us.* (iii. 1)

This emphasis reached a frenzied crescendo in the curses of Lear and Timon against mankind. Lear indeed exclaims in his madness, 'None does offend, none, I say none' (iv. 6); but in their context his words sound the very opposite of their logical meaning, and are rather to be interpreted in the light of Timon's declaration :

> *There's nothing level in our cursed natures*
> *But direct villainy.* (iv. 3)

All this seems to prepare the way for the more sober, moralistic 'puritanism' of the last plays. In *Pericles* Marina resists all temptations against her chastity, until the bawd exclaims in wonder : 'She would make a Puritan of the devil' (iv. 6). In *The Winter's Tale* Florizel insists that his desires for Perdita 'run not before mine honour', and in the same place Perdita, unlike Ophelia, refuses to be painted with artificial beauty (iv. 3). In *The Tempest* Prospero warns Ferdinand not to break the virginal knot of Miranda before the marriage rite has been duly performed; to which Ferdinand replies that no suggestion of the blood shall ever 'melt mine honour into lust' (iv. 1). For this reason Prospero is seen as a 'puritanical father', and the play as a whole interpreted as an 'expression of the Renaissance imagination under pressure from British puritanism'.[32]

This trend in the last plays is further connected with certain biographical details, which seem to indicate a link with Puritanism in Shakespeare's later years. There is, in the first place, his association with Dr John Hall, who married his eldest daughter Susanna in 1607, and who is often thought to have been a Puritan. The evidence for this opinion is partly the sympathy shown by Hall for Thomas Wilson, the 'puritan' vicar of Stratford, in his dispute with the town corporation during the years following Shakespeare's death, and partly the statement made by James Cooke in 1657 that 'such as hated him for his religion often made use of him'.[33] Yet whatever his sympathies may have been – and the above-mentioned evidence is far from being conclusive – he was evidently a conforming Anglican, diligent in the execution of his duties both as sidesman and as churchwarden (which he was in 1628–9). It was perhaps on account of this diligence that he incurred the dislike of some parishioners, who still 'made use of him'. It may also have been at Hall's request that Shakespeare entertained a visiting preacher at New Place during the Christmas season of 1614, and a quart of sack and another quart of claret were provided by the town council for his entertainment. At the same time, there is evidence that Susanna herself was a Catholic recusant; for her name appears on a list of recusants for 1606, in the aftermath of the Gunpowder Plot, and shortly before her marriage with Dr Hall.[34] The list had been drawn up in accordance with a regulation of the same year aimed explicitly against all 'persons popishly affected'. Her husband, too, for all his zeal as a parishioner of Holy Trinity Church, seems to have been favourably disposed towards Catholics. At least, he numbered many of them among his regular patients, including one 'Father Browne, a Romish priest', and he was appointed trustee in the will of a Catholic, Richard Lane, in 1613.[35]

In any case, the element of 'puritanism' discerned in the

later plays of Shakespeare has little connection with the historical Puritan movement of the Elizabethan Age, with its emphasis on justification by faith alone, its insistence on the written word of the Bible, its rejection of episcopal authority, and its hatred of the Church of Rome as 'the Whore of Babylon'. If anything, it is a moral puritanism, derived from the dramatist's long acquaintance with human frailty, together with his absorption of that homiletic tradition which goes back to and beyond the Parson of Chaucer's *Canterbury Tales.*

IX

Henry VIII and Elizabeth

AFTER HAVING surveyed the impact first of Catholic tradition, then of the Protestant Reformation, on Shakespeare's plays, we may pause to consider what attitude he reveals in them towards the religious changes which had affected him so deeply, along with all his fellow-countrymen. These changes were for him, as for the majority of his contemporaries, on the level not so much of ideas, as of personalities; for the Reformation in England had been brought about not so much by popular acceptance from below, as by official imposition from above. From the time of Henry VIII the people were obliged, if they wished to live at peace, to adapt their religion – at least in the externals of religious worship – to the fluctuating policy of the Crown. In the first place, the breach with Rome had been effected by Henry VIII, with the assistance of Thomas Cromwell, in his unprecedented claim to be Supreme Head of the Church in England, which was decreed by the Act of Supremacy in 1534. Subsequently, the Protestant religion was officially introduced into the country by Edward VI, under the regency of the Duke of Somerset, and was eventually established – after the temporary reunion with Rome under Mary – by Elizabeth, with the collaboration of William Cecil and Nicholas Bacon, at her first Parliament of 1559. What made these religious changes possible in England at that time was, above all, the centralized nature of the Tudor monarchy, in general, and the personalities of the individual monarchs, Henry VIII and Elizabeth, together with their chief ministers, Cromwell and Cecil.

At first sight, it seems that Shakespeare has very little to say about either of these monarchs, or of their ministers, right up to the last of his plays. It even seems that he is deliberately avoiding the fundamental issue of his time, no doubt because of the danger involved in any meddling in affairs of state.[1] In common with all the dramatists of the age, he had to observe extreme caution in touching on political matters, considering the strictness of the Elizabethan censorship. Hence in his series of English history plays he progresses as far as the reign of Richard III and the advent of Henry Tudor; but there he prudently breaks off – 'thus far and no farther'. In his comedies, which keep pace with the histories, he wanders from one European country to another, as though in exile – Italy, France, Belgium, though the Forest of Arden in *As You Like It* does not seem far from his native Warwickshire. But he carefully refrains from crossing the narrow seas to England, though the English character of many of his foreign scenes is barely disguised.[2] In the tragedies and final romances he seems to stray even farther afield from contemporary England, until in *The Tempest* he quits his fictitious magic island, apparently one of the Bermudas transported to the Mediterranean, and bids farewell to the stage in the Epilogue. Then, and only then, he comes out – or someone else using his name, with several scenes written by him, comes out – with a play on sixteenth-century England entitled *The Famous History of the Life of King Henry the Eighth*.

Even so, this play was not composed and produced till well on into the reign of the Stuart King, James I, at a convenient remove from the Tudor period, when Shakespeare himself had retired to Stratford, at a convenient distance from the City of London. There are, moreover, serious doubts as to whether the play as a whole belongs to him, though many parts of it are evidently from his hand. From the time such doubts were first raised by James Spedding in 1850, many scholars have been unwilling to attribute the whole play to Shakespeare, and have agreed to divide it between him and a collaborator, possibly John Fletcher (who may also have collaborated with him in *Two Noble Kinsmen*).[3] How much of the play is Shakespeare's, and how much Fletcher's, and which of the two was responsible for its general plan and its completion –

these are matters which must remain forever uncertain. With this uncertainty at the back of our minds, we have to approach the play and enquire into the manner in which the dramatist presents the character of Henry VIII and his divorce from Queen Katharine, which was the event precipitating the breach with Rome in 1534.

From the outset we are left in no doubt as to the central subject of the play, which is the tragedy of this very divorce. It is to this event that our attention is drawn by the opening words of the Prologue :

> *I come no more to make you laugh: things now,*
> *That bear a weighty and a serious brow,*
> *Sad, high, and working, full of state and woe,*
> *Such noble scenes as draw the eye to flow,*
> *We now present.*

The first scene, which is evidently in Shakespeare's hand, presents the triumph of Wolsey at the Field of the Cloth of Gold, together with comments on his pride and vanity. One by one he proceeds to pluck down his enemies from their places of eminence, first the noble Duke of Buckingham, and then the Queen herself. It is he who

> *dives into the king's soul, and there scatters*
> *Dangers, doubts, wringing of the conscience,*
> *Fears and despairs; and all these for his marriage.*
>
> (ii. 2)

It is also under his auspices, as it were, that the King first meets Anne Bullen at York Place and falls in love with her. The upshot of these proceedings is the state trial of Katharine, who takes the opportunity to accuse Wolsey openly of being her enemy and of having 'blown this coal betwixt my lord and me' (ii. 4). But in bringing dishonour on her, Wolsey only hastens his own downfall, as he becomes involved in what Henry angrily calls 'this dilatory sloth and tricks of Rome' (*ibid.*). He is summarily dismissed by the King on a charge of misusing public funds, and realizes when it is too late the vanity of trusting in princes.

Had I but served my God with half the zeal
I served my king, he would not in mine age
Have left me naked to mine enemies. (iii. 2)

In contrast to Wolsey's end, that of Katharine is irradiated with harmony and peace, which is also somehow reflected on her former enemy as she thinks of him with charity and learns how, after all, he 'found the happiness of being little' (iv. 2). She is blessed with a vision of angels, such as commonly attend the concluding scenes of Shakespeare's romances in varying forms, and she pronounces the blessing of heaven on her daughter, Mary. In this climax we may recognize her as the last of a long line of Shakespearian heroines, reaching back through Hermione and Imogen to Cordelia and Desdemona – all noble ladies who have been unjustly treated, but have borne their sufferings with fortitude and patience. In her ending, the opening words of the Prologue are fulfilled; and with her departure, as Dr Johnson remarked in a famous note on the play, the genius of Shakespeare goes out as well.[4]

In all this development, it may be asked, how does the character of Henry himself appear? The simple answer is that it hardly appears at all. From the beginning the King speaks with an authoritative tone of voice, as one who is accustomed to command and be obeyed; but – rather like Lear in his opening scene – he is easily swayed this way and that, now by the suggestions of flattery, now by the whims of caprice. As the German scholar Gervinus has observed: 'His dependence upon flatterers, together with his jealous desire to rule alone; the ease with which he is deceived, together with his resentful bitterness when he sees himself deluded, and his deceitful dissimulation in suppressing malice and revenge; his caprice, together with his impetuosity; his unwieldy, clumsy appearance, together with a certain mental refinement; his lack of feeling, together with isolated traits of good nature; his sensuality under the transparent mask of religion and conscience; his manner, condescending even to vulgarity – all these are so many delicate contrasts, in which the player has to hit the fine line of contact.'[5] This apparent complexity of his character, however, is not so much in himself, as in the variety of characters and situations around him. On the one hand, in response to Katharine's supplication he reduces the taxation of his subjects; and on the other, in view of the evidence adduced by the Surveyor at the desire of Wolsey, he has the Duke of Buckingham arrested on a charge of treason. While he outwardly shows courtesy to his Queen, Katharine, he readily falls in love with Anne Bullen at the party given by Wolsey, exclaiming in almost Augustinian terms: 'O beauty, till now I never knew thee!' (i. 4).[6] It is, significantly, only after this meeting that we first hear rumours of his marriage with his brother's wife having 'crept too near his conscience'; and they are promptly countered by the cynical remark of Suffolk: 'No, his conscience has crept too near another lady' (ii. 2). At Katharine's trial, the speech made by the King after her dignified departure smacks rather too much of 'conscience' to be sincere. To use the words of the Queen in *Hamlet*, he 'doth protest too much' (iii. 2); and the hollowness of his words is revealed in a concluding aside, which betrays a concern not for truth and justice, but for his own selfish lust. Having come to this point, he finds it convenient to deal with Wolsey as Wolsey has had him deal with others; and he causes his downfall by the manifestation of his anger.

In the fifth Act, however, the play makes a complete *volte-face*; and the atmosphere of tragedy rolls away, with no accompanying change of character. The King is indeed affected with sadness at the news of his poor queen's death, but he gives no sign of remorse over the part he has played in her downfall. He goes on to take the side of Cranmer, who has been accused of heresy by Gardiner and other members of the Council. Finally, he is crowned with happiness in the birth of a princess to his new queen, Anne Bullen, and at the christening ceremony of the infant he listens with delight to Cranmer's glowing words of prophecy about her. This is all quite out of harmony with the preceding acts, as shadow suddenly turns to light, tragedy ends in comedy, and tears are exchanged for laughter, without any justification in terms of character. After the injustice he has done to Katharine, through Wolsey, Henry is unrepentant but happy with Anne Bullen and the new-born princess Elizabeth. Nor is there a breath of the tragedy so soon to befall Anne herself and the succeeding wives of the much-to-be-married king. In the other characters, one after another – Buckingham, Katharine, even Wolsey – there appears a disposition of repentance or forgiveness; but in the King himself, who is principally responsible for their ruin, there is no sign of either disposition. One can only suspect that this final act was left in the hands – for whatever reason – of an inferior dramatist, who was insufficiently aware of the master plan – whatever it may have been – and was chiefly intent on bringing the tragic events to a happy outcome, on the superficial model of Shakespeare's previous tragi-comedies.

In any case, the character of Henry remains shadowy in the play that bears his name; whereas the main character who wins our sympathy is that of Katharine, who has to endure the injustice and the tragedy of divorce from her royal husband. The further implications of this divorce in English history are kept in concealment, even as the further fortunes of Anne Bullen and the princess Mary are passed over in silence. On the surface, there is some feeling of admiration for the royal dignity of Henry's bearing; but it is without any accompanying feeling of enthusiasm for his personality. At a deeper level, however, there are some significant strands of thought and characterization which link the play of *Henry VIII* with those that precede it, and which point by way of comparison to the more intimate feelings of the dramatist concerning this monarch. It is a major characteristic of Shakespeare that he is always repeating himself in play after play under changing characters and situations, writing 'still all one, ever the same' (*Sonnet* 76). None of his plays is an island to itself, unconnected with the others. As T. S. Eliot has well remarked : 'We do not understand Shakespeare from a single reading, and certainly not from a single play. There is a relation between the various plays of Shakespeare, taken in order.'[7] The very fact, too, that *Henry VIII* stands at the end of his dramatic career, dealing with so delicate a subject, requires that it be interpreted in the light of its fore-runners – or it will be misunderstood. In them, perhaps, the figure of Henry, so shadowy in the play that bears his name, may become more substantial – no longer a stage puppet dressed in royal robes, but a tragic human being who has exercised an enduring fascination over the mind of Shakespeare.

The most evident parallel to the action of *Henry VIII* is to be found in *The Winter's Tale*, where the events that take place in Leontes's Sicilia bear a striking resemblance to those in Henry's England. First of all, it is noteworthy that Shakespeare reverses the relationship between Bohemia and Sicilia as given in his source, Greene's romance *Pandosto*, so as to bring out the parallel relationship between the European continent and England, another 'three-cornered island'. Like *Henry VIII*, the play opens with a description of the 'embracement' of two great kings, 'as over a vast'. Shortly afterwards, however, the jealousy of Leontes is aroused against the friendly King of Bohemia, Polixenes, and his own Queen, Hermione – corresponding roughly to Henry's attachment of the noble Duke of Buckingham for treason and his subsequent doubts as to the validity of his marriage with Katharine. Moreover, just as Henry turns for advice to Cardinal Wolsey, hailing him as 'the quiet of my wounded conscience' (ii. 2), so Leontes seeks the counsel of Camillo, whom he calls 'priest-like' in cleansing his bosom (i. 2) – though Wolsey, it is true, is less deserving of the royal trust than Camillo. Later, both the one and the other fall from the royal favour, though for different reasons. The action of *The Winter's Tale*, like that of *Henry VIII*, now leads up to the state trial of Hermione, who (like Katharine) defends herself with dignity, in a manner befitting 'a great king's daughter', and laments (in words that recall those of Katharine) her fall from the 'good grace' of her royal husband (iii. 2). In the event, while Katharine makes her 'appeal unto the Pope', the outcome of which is passed over in silence, Hermione refers herself to the oracle of Apollo, and she is duly vindicated. At this point, it is interesting to notice how the oracle is delivered at Delphos, amid the offering of a 'ceremonious, solemn and unearthly' sacrifice (iii. 1), as it were the pagan counterpart – noted in a previous chapter – of a solemn High Mass as it might have been offered by the Pope in St Peter's, Rome.[8]

From this point onwards, there is a noticeable divergence between the two plays, as in one the dramatist is limited by historical fact, while in the other he is free to follow his imagination and to fulfil his private wishes. Accordingly, whereas Katharine withdraws from her trial to spend her last days in confinement at Kimbolton, leaving Henry to marry another woman, Hermione swoons in a dead faint and Leontes is 'smitten to the noble heart' (iii. 2). There follow sixteen long years of repentance, during which his lost daughter Perdita (who thus corresponds to the princess Mary) grows to maidenhood in the land of Bohemia and is courted by Prince Florizel, son of that very Polixenes against whom Leontes had entertained unjust suspicions. Together they return to Sicilia, where they are warmly welcomed by the penitent Leontes, who tells the Prince:

> *You have a holy father,*
> *A graceful gentleman, against whose person,*
> *So sacred as it is, I have done sin.* (v. 1)

These rather surprising words suggest an interpretation which might seem far-fetched but for all the other circumstances in the play connecting it with *Henry VIII*.[9] A thorough-going pursuit of the political analogy would perhaps identify Florizel with Philip of Spain, who married Queen Mary, while his father Polixenes would be the Emperor Charles V, the nephew of Katharine. But in these words Polixenes, the 'man of many guests', seems rather to be compared to the 'holy father', the Pope of Rome, whose dwelling is across the sea from Sicilia-England, and 'against whose person, so sacred as it is', Leontes-Henry has committed the sin of schism. In this case, the return of Perdita with Florizel may signify the accession of Mary Tudor to the throne and her association with Cardinal Pole, as Papal Legate, in reuniting England with Rome – or at least the known intention of Henry himself to bring this about towards the end of his reign. Certainly, the final scene of reconciliation is full of Catholic implications: the statue of Hermione, 'newly performed by that rare Italian master, Julio Romano', who is significant both for his name and for his actual association with the Vatican; the kneeling of Perdita before it, as if before a statue of the Virgin Mary, to 'implore her blessing'; and the apparent miracle by which 'dear life redeems' Hermione from death (v. 3). Finally, the living words of Hermione are, interestingly enough, addressed not to Leontes, but to Perdita, upon whom she invokes the graces of the gods – even as Katharine pronounces the blessing of 'the dews of heaven' upon her daughter Mary.[10]

This interpretation, with all it implies, derives additional support from comparison with another play of the same period, *Cymbeline*. Here, too, we find the theme of jealousy, in the wager-plot, which is somewhat unnaturally foisted into the British play from Boccaccio's *Decameron* (II. 9). In this plot Posthumus Leonatus, who shares part of his name with Leontes (possibly with reference to the heraldic lion of England), is banished to Rome, where he listens too readily to Iachimo's lying report about his British wife, Imogen. This theme is subsidiary to the main action of the play, which concerns the aged king of Britain, Cymbeline, in his relations with Imogen, who is his daughter by his former queen. From the beginning of the play we sense an atmosphere of restraint, even of fear, in the general lament: 'You do not meet a man but frowns' (i. 1); since the King is infatuated with his second wife, 'the wicked queen' (v. 5), and has begun to behave like a tyrant. He subjects Imogen to confinement, on her refusal to wed the Queen's worthless son, Cloten; he banishes Posthumus to Rome, on learning of his previous union with Imogen; and he renounces the wonted tribute to Rome, on the Queen's persuasion (as we are told later). All these elements point, if not to the play of *Henry VIII*, at least to historical facts of his reign beyond the scope of the play. There are other elements which point to the play itself. If Cymbeline's treatment of Imogen recalls Leontes's treatment of Hermione, as when he furiously calls her, 'O disloyal thing!' and 'O thou vile one!' (i. 1), her dignified bearing and her charitable refusal of revenge associate her, not only with Hermione, but also with Katharine, whose meekness in suffering is described by Henry himself as 'saint-like' (ii. 4).[11]

It is in this context, while Posthumus is in Rome, that Iachimo comes from him to Imogen and describes her husband as one who

> *sits among men like a descended god;*
> *He hath a kind of honour sets him off,*
> *More than a mortal seeming . . .*
> *a sir so rare,*
> *Which you know cannot err.* (i. 6)

Here, too, are surprising words, which seem to bear no relation to the real circumstances of Posthumus, but which form an interesting parallel to those of Leontes about Polixenes discussed above.[12] Even more clearly, they seem to have reference – by some hidden analogy – to the Pope of Rome, whom Shakespeare calls 'his holiness' in *Henry VIII* (ii. 4) and in *Measure for Measure* (iii. 2), and who is held to be immune from error when teaching *ex cathedra* (from the Chair of Peter) on matters of faith and morals. In either case, the person so described is presented as dwelling on the mainland, which in *Cymbeline* is precisely identified as Rome. He also stands in a special relation to the heroine, whose character recalls that of Katharine in *Henry VIII*. This interpretation is further borne out by the sequel of the play which, like *The Winter's Tale*, diverges from the historical facts of Henry's reign to present what may be the wishful thinking of the dramatist. The turning-point, as in *The Winter's Tale*, is a pastoral episode where Imogen, disguised as Fidele, or 'faithful one', finds refuge in Wales and is welcomed by Belarius and the two princes as 'an earthly paragon' (iii. 6) – recalling Henry's praise of Katharine as 'before the primest creature that's paragon'd o' the world' (ii. 4).[13] In the happy outcome, Imogen is restored both to her father Cymbeline and to her husband Posthumus, who has returned from Rome with the Roman army; and while husband and wife embrace, as it were 'upon a rock', the father exclaims: 'My tears that fall prove holy water on thee!' (v. 5).[14] The wicked queen, at whose persuasion the tribute to Rome had been withheld, now ends her own life, 'with horror, madly dying', like another Lady Macbeth; while the King is represented – contrary to the chronicle – as deciding, though victor in battle, to 'submit to Caesar and to the Roman empire'. He goes on to express the wish, in a context of religious devotion, that 'a Roman and a British ensign wave friendly together'.

From *Cymbeline* the transition is not difficult to *King Lear*, where we are presented with another legendary king of Britain and with a certain parallel in the opening situation. Just as Cymbeline listens to his wicked queen and vents his anger first on Imogen, whom he places in confinement, then on Posthumus, whom he banishes to Rome; so Lear listens to the flattering words of his two wicked daughters and falls into a rage first with his truthful daughter, whom he disinherits, then with the faithful Kent, whom he banishes. Even in his anger, however, Lear, like Cymbeline and Henry, retains that in his countenance which Kent 'would fain call master', namely 'authority' (i. 4), and he remains, in his own words, 'every inch a king' (iv. 6). Only in him, as in Cymbeline and Henry, 'majesty falls to folly' (i. 1), as he fails to discern truth from 'plighted cunning' and falls into consequent indignation and madness. Here again, as in his other romances, Shakespeare departs from the realm of historical fact (in its analogous form) and turns to that of wishful thinking. For whereas Henry never once in the play shows any sign of self-reflection or repentance, Lear learns through his sufferings to know himself and his past injustice to Cordelia, and so comes to be reconciled with her. Here, too, Cordelia recalls the character of Katharine, in her queenly bearing and her tender charity; while, as daughter of the King, she corresponds to the princess Mary, who married a foreign prince and brought about the historical reconciliation of England with Rome. The continuation of this historical analogy might well have suggested to the dramatist's mind the tragic outcome of the play – in contravention of his sources: in that the reconciliation brought about by Mary was soon afterwards broken with the accession of her sister Elizabeth.

Turning next to Othello, we still find the same line of development continuing into 'the dark backward and abysm of time', as though indicating a deep-rooted fascination in the character of Henry VIII and the events of his reign. The resemblances, as usual, cluster round the figure of the heroine, Desdemona, who is described by Cassio as 'a maid that paragons description and wild fame' (ii. 1). She, too, is one who has to endure unjust suffering at the hands of a passionate husband; and though she is subjected to no formal trial like Hermione and Katharine, there is at least the foreshadowing of a trial in Othello's insistence on the need of objective proof of her guilt and in his self-deceiving idea of retributive justice. In her subsequent disgrace she finds solace, like Katharine, in a song; and the atmosphere of that scene, in which she converses with Emilia, is reproduced in the scene of Katharine conversing with Griffith and Patience. As for Othello himself, he is

presented from the beginning as endowed with a royal character, 'the noble Moor' who fetches his life and being 'from men
of royal siege' (i. 2); and, like Henry, he retains this royalty of
nature to the end. Even in his manner of frowning, when blood
and passion have collied his 'best judgment' (ii. 3) and
instead of speaking he gnaws his 'nether lip' (v. 2), he recalls
Henry's characteristic expression of anger both against Wolsey
(iii. 2) and against Gardiner (v. 3). The agent of his jealousy,
Iago, is likewise comparable to Wolsey, both in the way he
suggests doubts in the mind of his master so as to make him
'perplexed in the extreme' (v. 2), and in his pretence of
defending the heroine only to whet his master's passion. The
theme of jealousy is, of course, unrepresented in *Henry VIII*;
but it furnishes an important link with *The Winter's Tale*,
where the attitude of Leontes to Hermione is to some extent
patterned on that of Othello to Desdemona, and also with
Cymbeline, where the prime mover of the wager-plot,
Iachimo, derives his very name from Iago. The tragic outcome is also different from the ending of *Henry VIII*, in that,
whereas the news of Katharine's death has little impact on
Henry's conscience or even on his consciousness, the sudden
realization of what he has done to Desdemona makes Othello
burst out in an agony of despair: 'My wife! my wife! what
wife? I have no wife!' (v. 2). His reaction may be interpreted
as yet another 'might have been' in Shakespeare's conjectural
meditations on the royal divorce.

If in *Othello* we are reminded of the majesty and nobility, as
well as the tragic gullibility, of Henry's character, in *Macbeth*
our attention is drawn rather to the tyrannical rule of his later
years which fall outside the scope of *Henry VIII*. Here we are
afforded a glimpse of the previous order under the holy king
Duncan, who is recognized by Macbeth himself as having
'borne his faculties so meek' and been 'so clear in his great
office' (i. 7). The usurpation of his royal office by Macbeth
may be interpreted, according to the present line of conjecture,
as analogous to Henry's usurpation of spiritual authority
over the Church in England with the assistance of his 'cruel
ministers' (v. 7). This analogy is supported by the religious
terms in which the murder of Duncan is described, first by
Macduff:

> *Most sacrilegious murder hath broke ope*
> *The Lord's anointed temple, and stole thence*
> *The life o' the building.* (ii. 3)

and soon afterwards by Macbeth himself :

> *His gashed stabs looked like a breach in nature*
> *For ruin's wasteful entrance. (ibid.)*

In both descriptions there is a probable allusion to Cromwell's ruthless spoliation of the monasteries, which had become by Shakespeare's time 'bare ruin'd choirs, where late the sweet birds sang' (*Sonnet* 73). The whole atmosphere of the play, as of the concluding years of Henry's reign, is one of terror and spiritual oppression, a veritable 'blanket of the dark' – as John Buchan recognized in choosing the title for his novel on the suppression of the monasteries.[15] The frowns in the opening scene of *Cymbeline* are here transformed into the dark uncertainties of fear, as Ross says to Lady Macduff :

> *But cruel are the times, when we are traitors*
> *And do not know ourselves, when we hold rumour*
> *From what we fear, yet know not what we fear,*
> *But float upon a wild and violent sea*
> *Each way and move.* (iv. 2)

As the fear is progressively realized, the tone of speech rises to one of helpless lamentation over 'our poor country', as described again in the words of Ross :

> *Almost afraid to know itself. It cannot*
> *Be called our mother, but our grave; where nothing*
> *But who knows nothing, is once seen to smile;*
> *Where sighs and groans and shrieks that rend the air*
> *Are made, not marked; where violent sorrow seems*
> *A modern ecstasy.* (iv. 3)

This description applies only too well to the England of Henry VIII, from the very time he assumed the spiritual power and began to punish with the utmost severity those like Sir Thomas More who would not give their assent to his action. Concerning the death of More, Erasmus commented : 'Every man bewaileth the death of Sir Thomas More, even they who are adversaries unto him for religion . . . How many souls hath that axe wounded, which cut off More's head?'[16] Further, Stapleton in his *Life of Sir Thomas More* adds that 'the king's thirst for blood, once gratified, grew apace'.[17]

The parallel between Macbeth's Scotland and Henry's England is also confirmed by some similarities in detail with the romances noticed above : with *Cymbeline*, where the end of the 'wicked queen' dying 'most cruel to herself' (v. 5) recalls the suicide of Lady Macbeth 'with self and violent hands' (v. 7); and with *The Winter's Tale*, where the restoration of 'grace' to Leontes from Bohemia corresponds to that which comes from England with Malcolm and sets him on the Scottish throne.

There is a similar contrast between the old order of legitimate rule and the present misrule of avarice and ambition in *Hamlet*. Outwardly, the change appears to have been effected by constitutional means, and the new order has the approval of the Privy Council; just as in England the wishes of Henry were followed, first by his Council, then by the Parliament which was convened to determine measures of reformation.[18] But all is based on the hidden crimes of adultery and murder; just as in England Henry's usurpation of the spiritual power followed on his adultery with Anne Bullen and involved him in the judicial murder of those who held to the Catholic position. The confusion produced by this usurpation, and the armed preparations it occasioned for dealing with any uprising, may be echoed in the mysterious 'post-haste and romage in the land' with which the play begins. In the character of Claudius there are not a few points of resemblance between him and Henry. Despite Hamlet's instinctive dislike of him, there is a certain dignity in his bearing both at the meeting of his Privy Council and in the moment of danger when he calmly appeals to the 'divinity' that 'doth hedge a king' (iv. 5). At the same time, there is something bluff and hearty in his manner, which recalls the Tudor monarch. In spite of his villainy, he is – like Henry – a man of conscience; though in this he differs from Henry, that 'conscience' is for him not a mere word of excuse, but one of self-accusation – and it is this that makes him, unlike Henry, a truly human character. On the other hand, the dilemma of Hamlet is precisely that of

Catholic Englishmen in face of the King's assumption of spiritual supremacy : either to say nothing and thereby associate themselves with the country's guilt, by helping to 'film the ulcerous place' (iii. 4); or to take up arms against their guilty rulers, as scourges and ministers of heaven, and thereby plunge the country into civil strife. The pitiful wanderings of Ophelia's mind, with her snatches of medieval song and prayer, may well reflect the lamentable condition of religion in Henry's reign.[19] On a lower level, the characterization of Osric in the final scene points, through that of Cloten in *Cymbeline* (iv. 1), to the satirical description of the English court in *Henry VIII* with its newly imported fashions from France (i. 3).

The background of lamentation, which is almost entirely absent from *Henry VIII*, but which grows in volume as we move backward through *Cymbeline* and *Macbeth*, comes to the fore in several of the English history plays which have other points of analogy with the reign of Henry VIII. In *Richard III*, which anticipates *Macbeth* in many ways, Richard of Gloucester usurps the royal power by his ambitious cunning, and is thus the prototype as well of Iago as of Macbeth, and of Henry and Wolsey combined – though there is nothing royal about his character. In the background of the play is the chorus of lamenting women, who seem to come as it were out of a Greek tragedy. Their lamentations are punctuated by those of Richard's successive victims, such as Lord Hastings, who exclaims in his downfall : 'Woe, woe for England !' and adds, as though in anticipation of Wolsey :

> *O momentary grace of mortal men,*
> *Which we more hunt for than the grace of God!*
> (iii. 4)

The subsequent play of *Richard II* – also, like *Richard III*, entitled a 'tragedy' – has a similar background of lamentation, which is directed not merely to the contemporary state of England in terms of the play itself, but prophetically to the undefined future. While others, such as the Bishop of Carlisle, look through the usurpation of Bolingbroke to the horrors of civil strife, John of Gaunt refers in his famous speech of prophecy to the 'shameful conquest' England has made of itself by travesties of legal form, 'with inky blots and rotten parchment bonds' (ii. 1). The deposition of Richard, unworthy though he may have been of his sacred office, is represented by his poor Queen as 'a second fall of cursed man' in the symbolic setting of a garden (iii. 4).

It is, however, chiefly in *King John* that the reference to Henry VIII's reign becomes most pointed. The words of Ross quoted above are echoed by the Bastard, speaking of the common people of England :

> *I find the people strangely fantasied,*
> *Possessed with rumours, full of idle dreams,*
> *Not knowing what they fear, but full of fear.*
>
> (iv. 2)

The complaint of John of Gaunt is also taken up by the Bastard, and linked with the opening words of *Cymbeline*, when he says on discovering the dead body of Prince Arthur :

> *From forth this morsel of dead royalty,*
> *The life, the right and truth of all this realm*
> *Is fled to heaven; and England now is left*
> *To tug and scamble and to part by the teeth*
> *The unowed interest of proud-swelling state . . .*
> *And heaven itself doth frown upon the land.* (iv. 3)

Yet for all his complaining, it is the Bastard who, in anticipation of Cromwell, abets the King in his religious policy, by 'shaking the bags of hoarding abbots' (iii. 3) and 'ransacking the church' (iii. 4). As for John himself, he is unmistakably presented in this play, as in its Protestant sources, as a precursor of Henry VIII. This is how John had already been hailed, in John Bale's morality play of *Kynge Johan* and in John Foxe's *Book of Martyrs*, largely for his opposition to the Pope; and this was also the theme of the anonymous Elizabethan play, *The Troublesome Reign of King John*, which was probably Shakespeare's immediate source.[20] The opposition of John to the Pope, particularly when he bids defiance to the Papal Legate, Cardinal Pandulph, is represented in terms that are quite anachronistic for the thirteenth century, but accurate enough in the case of Henry VIII :

Tell him this tale; and from the mouth of England
Add thus much more: that no Italian priest
Shall tithe or toll in our dominions;
But as we under heaven are supreme head,
So under him that great supremacy,
Where we do reign, we will alone uphold,
Without the assistance of a mortal hand. (iii. 1)

But so far from appearing as a Protestant hero or English patriot, John is portrayed from the outset as a usurper who has seized what rightfully belongs to Prince Arthur, and who goes on to consolidate his position by ordering the death of Arthur. In this John foreshadows Claudius, who has likewise stepped in between Hamlet and the throne of his father. He also resembles Claudius in the uneasiness of his conscience, wherein 'hostility and civil tumult reign' (iv. 2); though in his too much protesting he looks forward not so much to Claudius as to Henry.

The above-mentioned lamentations in the English history plays are all, no doubt, justified by their several contexts, as they arise out of the tragic events of England's past; but the dramatist seems to feel the past not merely as past, but as continuing into the present. This is why the lamentations fit in so well with the various references which point, whether directly or indirectly, to particular events and situations in the reign of Henry VIII. They derive additional significance from that other chorus of lament for the present and regret for the past which resounds no less in the comedies than in the histories and tragedies. In play after play, through the mouthpiece of one character after another, the dramatist seems to shake his head over 'these naughty times' (*The Merchant of Venice* iii. 2) and 'the foul body of th' infected world' (*As You Like It* ii. 7), while looking back with scarcely disguised nostalgia to 'old fashions' (*The Taming of the Shrew* iii. 1), 'old custom' (*As You Like It* ii. 1) and 'the constant service of the antique world' (*ibid.* ii. 3). In his own person, too, he states his unequivocal preference in *Sonnet* 67 for 'days long since, before these last so bad'. For him the turning-point in the history of his time seems to have been the destruction of the monasteries, to which he looks back so often and so tenderly in his comedies – as has been amply documented in a previous chapter.[21] Such abbey ruins are mentioned, not only in the above-quoted *Sonnet* 73, but also in two such early plays as *The Comedy of Errors* (v. 1) and *Titus Andronicus* (v. 1). The ruinous state of the country, following on the ruin of the abbeys, is also perhaps hinted at in the early comedy of *Two Gentlemen of Verona* – in two remarks that have a wider relevance than that suggested by their immediate context : that of Proteus :

> *Indeed, a sheep doth very often stray,*
> *An if the shepherd be a while away.* (i. 1)

and that of Valentine :

> *Leave not the mansion so long tenantless,*
> *Lest, growing ruinous, the building fall*
> *And leave no memory of what it was.* (v. 4)

Turning from Henry VIII to his daughter Elizabeth, we may make a similar kind of enquiry concerning Shakespeare's presentation of her in his plays. As with the father, so with the daughter, we may take our beginning in the end; since the most impressive statement of the dramatist's attitude seems to come in the concluding scene of his last play, *Henry VIII* – in Cranmer's words of prophecy concerning the infant princess. In particular, he declares that 'truth shall nurse her; holy and heavenly thoughts still counsel her', and that in her reign 'God shall be truly known' (v. 5). Here we have a clear statement, not only of approval of Queen Elizabeth herself, but also of endorsement of her religious policy in favour of the Protestant religion. Only, as I have indicated above, there is some doubt as to which dramatist put these words into Cranmer's mouth. It is not merely that they occur in the final act after Shakespeare's genius has departed in company with Katharine, but also that they occur in a scene which is regarded as dubiously Shakespearian on literary and stylistic grounds. All the same, the favourable attitude to Elizabeth apparent in this speech seems to be supported by a few mentions of her in earlier plays. She is mentioned explicitly in the Chorus to Act V of *Henry V* as 'our gracious empress'; and there is a clear reference to her in *A Midsummer Night's Dream* as the 'fair vestal throned by the west', the 'imperial votaress', who succeeded in avoiding the 'bolt of Cupid' and 'passed on, in maiden meditation fancy-free' (ii. 1). She is also identified with the lady Olivia in *Twelfth Night*, whose mourning is significantly ascribed, not (as in the source) to her bereavement of a husband, but (as would have been the case of Elizabeth, after the death of Edward VI) to 'a brother's dead love' (i. 1). The contemporary background of the play is, moreover, probably identified as a state visit paid by Don Virginio Orsino, Duke of Brachiano, to the court of Queen Elizabeth.[22] It is further possible that she may be the incomparable Phoenix in Shakespeare's metaphysical poem, *The Phoenix and the Turtle*, which is said (according to one well-documented interpretation) to lament the tragic end of the relationship between the Queen and the Earl of Essex (the Turtle).[23] These references to Elizabeth, whether open or cryptic, seem to chime with Cranmer's prophecy concerning her – whether written by Shakespeare himself or not – and with the well-known anecdote about him recorded by Nicholas Rowe : 'Queen Elizabeth had several of his plays acted before her, and without doubt gave him many gracious marks of her favour . . . She was so well pleased with that admirable character of Falstaff in the two parts of Henry the Fourth, that she commanded him to continue it for one play more, and to show him in love. This is said to be the occasion of his writing the *Merry Wives of Windsor*. How well she was obeyed, the play itself is an admirable proof.'[24]

On the other hand, it must be admitted that such references are remarkably few, and indirect, in an age that was addicted to extravagant flattery of the ageing Queen. What is more, her death in 1603 was passed over by Shakespeare in complete silence – a silence that was noticed and deplored by a contemporary poet, Henry Chettle, in his *England's Mourning Garment* (1603) (where Melicert is evidently a pastoral name for Shakespeare) :

> *Nor doth the silver-tongued Melicert*
> *Drop from his honied muse one sable tear*
> *To mourn her death that graced his desert,*
> *And to his lays opened her royal ear.*

Shepherd, remember our Elizabeth,
And sing her rape, done by that Tarquin, Death.[25]

It has been suggested, in explanation of this silence, that Shakespeare had been deeply offended by Elizabeth's treatment of Essex, the intimate friend of his patron, Southampton. And there may have been other reasons, too. In any case, there are signs – especially in the history plays – that these few open references in favour of the Queen are belied by the underlying attitude of the dramatist.

In the first place, Shakespeare's treatment of his historical and dramatic material in *King John* indicates that he had in mind the events not just of the remote medieval past, but also – as we have seen – of the sixteenth-century present, and within this present, not just of Henry VIII's reign, but also of that of Elizabeth.[26] For example, the dispute between the English and French kings over the possession of Angiers is described in terms of the more recent dispute over the possession of Calais, which was settled by the Treaty of Cateau-Cambrésis in 1559. The rebellion of the English barons against King John is likewise described in terms of the more recent rebellion of the Northern Earls against Queen Elizabeth in 1569. The sentence of excommunication pronounced by the Papal Legate, Cardinal Pandulph, against King John is clearly modelled on the Papal Bull of 1570 by which Pope Pius V excommunicated Queen Elizabeth, enjoining all her subjects 'that they shall not once dare to obey her, or any of her directions, laws, or commandments, binding under the same curse those who do anything to the contrary'. The French 'armado of scattered sail', which is scattered on its way to England 'by a roaring tempest on the flood' (iii. 4), is an obvious allusion to the Spanish Armada of 1588. Above all, the imprisonment and death of Prince Arthur, which is the main point of interest in the play, is closely parallel to the imprisonment and execution of Mary Queen of Scots in 1587. This historical parallel had already been urged by John Leslie, Bishop of Ross and Mary's most loyal supporter, in maintaining her right to the English succession; but what the play concentrates upon – without historical justification – are the circumstances of her tragic death.[27] In Mary rested the main hope of the Catholic cause in England; and all through her long imprisonment in England she was a continual embarrassment to Elizabeth, who wished her out of the way, yet was reluctant to decree her execution for fear not only of the precedent it might give, but also of the reprisals it might incur. Her royal hand was, however, forced in 1586 by the 'discovery' of the Babington Plot, and she was persuaded to put her signature to the death-warrant against Mary. Her private instructions to William Davison on this occasion, to have Mary not formally executed, but secretly assassinated, are mirrored in those of King John to Hubert concerning the death of Arthur (iii. 3); and her subsequent displeasure with Davison for neglecting her instructions is likewise mirrored in John's subsequent anger against Hubert (iv. 2).[28] Lastly, the Bastard's lament over the dead body of Arthur:

> From forth this morsel of dead royalty,
> The life, the right and truth of all this realm
> Is fled to heaven. (iv. 3)

interestingly echoes the Latin epitaph which was set up for a time above Mary's tomb in Peterborough cathedral, as recorded in Camden's *Annales*: 'A strange and unusual monument this is, wherein the living are included with the dead; for, with the sacred ashes of this blessed Mary, know that the majesty of all kings and princes lieth here, violated and prostrate.'[29]

This play of *King John*, with its remarkable mirroring of contemporary events, may serve in turn to unlock the hidden meaning of other plays. For the similarities listed above are not limited to this one play, but re-echo again and again from one to another – as though there were certain events in his time which Shakespeare was unable to forget, least of all in moments of dramatic composition. The rebellion of the Northern Earls, which took place during his boyhood and was not without repercussions on the town of Stratford, is reflected in both Parts of *Henry IV*: first, in the rebellion of Hotspur and the Percys, and secondly, in that led by Archbishop Scroop, whose ecclesiastical prestige 'turns insurrection to religion' (i. 1). There is a certain parallel between the latter and the above-mentioned Bishop of Ross, who was regarded by Cecil as 'the principal instrument of this late rebellion'.[30] The historical analogy is even hinted at by the Earl of Warwick in *Henry IV* Part II, though in general terms :

> *There is a history in all men's lives,*
> *Figuring the nature of the times deceas'd.* (iii. 1)

The cause of the rebels is not entirely condemned, but presented to some extent in a sympathetic light, partly owing to the fact that their leader is respected even by his enemies as

> *To us the imagin'd voice of God himself,*
> *The very opener and intelligencer*
> *Between the grace, the sanctities of heaven,*
> *And our dull workings.* (iv. 2)

Only there is apparent disapproval of the forceful assertion of right to the detriment of peace and order. On the other hand, when an armada reappears in two of the tragedies, *Macbeth* and *King Lear*, it is presented with undisguised sympathy – though its identification with the Spanish Armada is more disguised. In the former play the expedition sent from England to restore a just rule to Scotland is successful, and suitable punishment is meted out to 'the cruel ministers of this dead butcher and his fiend-like queen' (v. 7). In *King Lear*, however, the power sent from France 'into this scattered kingdom' (iii. 1) is not successful; but it is justified, in Cordelia's words, 'with best meaning' (v. 3).

As for the execution of Mary Stuart, it is not only central to *King John*, but it continues to re-echo through the histories and the tragedies. Thus the murder of the two princes by royal command in *Richard III* is described by the murderer himself as

> *The most arch deed of piteous massacre*
> *That ever yet this land was guilty of.* (iv. 3)

At the beginning of *Richard II* Bolingbroke accuses Mowbray of having plotted the Duke of Gloucester's death,

> *Sluic'd out his innocent soul through streams of blood;*
> *Which blood, like sacrificing Abel's, cries*
> *Even from the tongueless caverns of the earth.* (i. 1)

Later on, Gaunt more directly accuses the King himself of complicity in the deed, which he calls 'spilling Edward's blood' ii. 1). Finally, when Richard eventually pays the penalty at the orders of Bolingbroke, now Henry IV, the latter – like John in dealing with Hubert – disclaims the responsibility, but vows :

> *I'll make a voyage to the Holy Land,*
> *To wash this blood off from my guilty hand.* (v. 6)

In the tragedies this theme of the murder of innocents recurs in *Macbeth*, with the murder of Lady Macduff and her children by royal command (iv. 2), and in *King Lear*, with the hanging of Cordelia at the orders of Edmund (v. 3). The association with Mary Stuart has also been discerned in Macbeth's murder of Duncan, who is at once his kinsman and his guest – even as Mary was at once the cousin and the 'guest', if under confinement, of Elizabeth.[31] The odd remark of Lady Macbeth, that she herself would have done the deed, only she saw how Duncan 'resembled my father as he slept' (ii. 2), may have reference to the family resemblance between Elizabeth's father, Henry VIII, and her cousin, Mary Stuart. The further incident of Lady Macbeth's sleep-walking has a general parallel with Elizabeth's final sickness, which was accompanied by fearful dreams and imaginations, according to the eye-witness account of Lady Southwell.[32]

It would thus appear that Shakespeare associated her in his dramatic imagination with such characters as King John and Bolingbroke, Richard III and Edmund, Macbeth and his 'fiend-like queen' – mainly in view of her complicity with the execution of Mary Stuart. Nor is this all. There is yet another line of analogy deriving from another history play, *Richard III*.[33] In his character as a 'Machiavel', which he openly flaunts in *Henry VI* Part III (iii. 2), Richard would have reminded many in an Elizabethan audience of the hated Earl of Leicester; and, in fact, Leicester had been accused, in the anonymous Catholic pamphlet, *Leicester's Commonwealth* (1584), of Machiavellian methods and compared to Richard himself.[34] In particular, when Richard woos Queen Elizabeth, the widow of Edward IV, for her daughter's hand, many would have recognized the parallel with Leicester's notorious courtship of the reigning Queen Elizabeth, which had been connected in the public mind with the mysterious death of his wife, Amy Robsart. This is explicitly pointed out in the pamphlet: 'Do you not remember the story of K. Richard the Third, who at such time as he thought best for the establishing of his title: to marry his own neice, that afterward was married to King Henry the Seventh, how he caused secretly to be given abroad that his own wife was dead, whom all the world knew to be then alive and in good health, but yet soon afterward she was seen dead indeed.' Further, when Margaret characterizes the widow of Edward IV as 'poor shadow, painted queen', and when Richard dismisses her after the wooing as 'relenting fool, and shallow changing woman' (iv. 4), it is possible to detect a reference to the reigning Queen, whose painting was well known, especially towards the end of her life, and whose continual vacillations were frequently the despair of her advisors.

This is also a point in the widely recognized comparison of the Queen to Richard II, who is the most self-regarding of Shakespeare's kings both in his royal splendour and in his downfall. The incident in the deposition-scene, where the deposed king calls for a glass but dashes it to the ground, calling it a 'flattering glass' (iv. 1), may be compared with Lady Southwell's account of an episode in the Queen's last sickness – though the latter took place after the play's composition: 'Afterwards, in the melancholy of her sickness, she desired to see a true looking-glass, which in twenty years before she had not seen, but only such a one which of purpose was made to deceive her sight; which glass being brought her, she fell presently exclaiming at all those which had so much commended her, and took it so offensively, that all those which had before flattered her durst not come in her sight.'[35] The parallel between Elizabeth and Richard, however, as it was canvassed in such pamphlets as the above-mentioned *Leicester's Commonwealth* and another anonymous work entitled *A Declaration of the True Causes* (1592), was mainly concerned with her undue reliance on unworthy counsellors, such as Leicester himself and Sir William Cecil. They are the 'caterpillars of the commonwealth', of whom Bolingbroke speaks (ii. 3); and the allegory implied in his words is developed at length by the Gardener:

> *Why should we in the compass of a pale*
> *Keep law and form and due proportion,*
> *Showing, as in a model, our firm estate,*
> *When our sea-walled garden, the whole land,*
> *Is full of weeds, her fairest flowers chok'd up,*
> *Her fruit-trees all unprun'd, her hedges ruin'd,*
> *Her knots disorder'd, and her wholesome herbs*
> *Swarming with caterpillars?* (iii. 4)

It is interesting to notice that the same image of a garden is applied in *Leicester's Commonwealth* to the two universities: 'Consider the fruit of the garden, and thereby you may judge of the gardener's diligence.' Even more precisely, the poor Queen's indignant demand of the Gardener:

> *What Eve, what serpent, hath suggested thee*
> *To make a second fall of cursed man?* (*ibid.*)

echoes the words of another pamphlet, *A Treatise of Treasons* (1572), probably by John Leslie, who compares the evil counsellors of Elizabeth, Cecil and Bacon, to the serpent that tempted Eve: 'As the first serpent tempted with ambition the first maiden Eve, to eat of the forbidden apple, by telling her that she should thereby be made like unto God by knowing good and ill: even so did these serpents tempt this virgin by a like motion.' It was with such ideas in his mind that the Earl of Essex undertook his ill-fated rising in 1601, intending – as Barlow explained in his Sermon at the execution – not to do injury to the Queen, but 'to remove such evils as the commonwealth is burdened with'. For this reason some of his followers commissioned a special performance of *Richard II*, including the deposition scene, for the eve of the rising; and it was on this occasion that the Queen herself recognized the parallel in her angry words to William Lambarde: 'I am Richard II, know ye not that?'[36]

In view of this image of a garden, and its contemporary application to the realm, one may find a deeper meaning in Hamlet's complaint about Denmark, that it is 'an unweeded garden' (i. 2). Not only has his father failed, in the words of the Homily on Matrimony, 'to weed out little by little the noisome weeds of uncomely manners' out of Gertrude's mind; but the weeds have been deliberately sown by the evil counsel of Claudius – and Polonius. For it is significant that this complaint occurs to Hamlet's mind just after the meeting of the Danish Privy Council, at which the new king has expressed his thanks to Polonius among others for his wise cooperation, and further added his high praise in his words to Laertes:

> *The head is not more native to the heart,*
> *The hand more instrumental to the mouth,*
> *Than is the throne of Denmark to thy father.*
>
> *(ibid.)*[37]

Not only could Elizabeth have aptly spoken such words of praise about Sir William Cecil; but there are many other elements in the play which lend themselves to this identification. The very name of Polonius, invented by the dramatist, may be a Latinized form of Cecil's title, Burghley, pronounced in the Welsh manner (as Cecil was of Welsh origin). The King's trust in him as 'a man faithful and honourable' (ii. 2) seems to echo the praise of Cecil in *Leicester's Commonwealth* for 'his great wisdom, zeal and singular fidelity to the realm'. His advice to Laertes, stuffed with precepts of worldly wisdom (i. 3), has its parallel in the precepts left by Cecil for his son – though other, more precise parallels have been noted in Lyly's *Euphues*.[38] His pompous assumption 'of wisdom and of reach' (ii. 1), combined with his apparent folly, reflects the characterization of Cecil in *A Declaration of the True Causes*: 'It is a world to see . . . how for his labour he hath purchased among fools the reputation of wisdom, albeit he hath lost among wise men the esteem of honesty.' His admission that often 'with devotion's visage and pious action we do sugar o'er the devil himself' (iii. 1) likewise recalls the 'hypocritical cloak of devotion', mentioned in the same pamphlet, which Cecil assumed for a time during the days of Queen Mary. A further parallel may be found with the character of Ulysses in *Troilus and Cressida*, where Ulysses stands not only for the abstract ideal of 'degree' (i. 3), but also for the shady political means by which it is maintained. His words on this point might well have been echoed by Cecil:

The providence that's in a watchful state
Knows almost every grain of Plutus' gold,
Finds bottom in the uncomprehensive deeps,
Keeps place with thought, and almost, like the gods,
Does thoughts unveil in their dumb cradles.
There is a mystery – with whom relation
Durst never meddle – in the soul of state,
Which hath an operation more divine
Than breath or pen can give expressure to. (iii. 3)

The comparison between Ulysses and Cecil had indeed already been made in the *Treatise of Treasons*, which also draws an elaborate parallel between the Trojan War and the religious controversy in England.

Thus the discontent which the Catholics of England inevitably felt concerning the government of the realm was directed – like that of Essex in 1601 – rather against her 'cruel ministers' and flattering advisers than against the Queen herself. It is on them that the above-mentioned *Treatise* lays the principal blame for the establishment in England of what he calls 'a Machiavellian State and Regiment: where Religion is put behind in the second and last place; where the civil Policy, I mean, is preferred before it, and not limited by any rules of Religion, but the Religion framed to serve the time and policy'. Shakespeare, too, seems to echo this sentiment, when he says in *Timon of Athens* through the mouth of a stranger:

> *Men must learn now with pity to dispense;*
> *For policy sits above conscience.* (iii. 2.)

With regard to the Queen herself, the tone of Catholic writings is usually respectful, as in Persons' dedication of his *Brief Discourse* (1580) 'to the Queen's most excellent majesty': 'Jesus Christ, in abundance of mercy, bless your Majesty, to whom (as he knoweth) I wish as much good as to mine own soul: persuading myself that all good Catholics in England do the same.' Even in the hour of their execution it was common for priests, such as Edmund Campion and Robert Southwell, to pray aloud for the Queen's prosperity.[39] But their loyalty was put to a severe strain during the long years of persecution; and one or two Catholic authors, such as

Nicholas Sanders and Richard Bristow, penned words against her which they afterwards regretted having used. The strongest words, however, were those written by William Allen in his unpublished *Admonition*, drawn up on the eve of the Spanish Armada in 1588 and intended for publication in the event of success. He openly describes the Queen as 'an incestuous bastard, begotten and born in sin of an infamous courtesan . . . an infamous, depraved, accursed, excommunicate heretic; the very shame of her sex and princely name; the chief spectacle of sin and abomination in this our age; and the only poison, calamity, and destruction of our noble church and country'.[40] Such words might well have been echoed in the hearts of many English Catholics, who could hardly go on pretending that the Queen was ignorant of their unjust sufferings. They may also correspond to Shakespeare's own sentiments – especially if we interpret the lamentations in *Macbeth* for 'our poor country' in terms of the 'lamentable and general cries and complaints of the oppressed multitude' mentioned in *A Declaration of the True Causes*. Yet in his attitude there remained no less ambivalence towards the daughter than towards her father. Even if he hated Elizabeth, he could not help – like Pope Sixtus V himself – admiring her. In this respect it is not unlikely that his final portrait of her is to be found, not in Cranmer's speech of prophetic praise, but in the brilliant characterization of Cleopatra, 'the enchanting queen . . . cunning past man's thought' (i. 2), who succeeds so completely in seducing Antony from his path of duty and his ties with Rome.[41]

In and through all these glimpses of Henry VIII and Elizabeth, as they seem to haunt the histories and tragedies of Shakespeare, we may sense a certain passion moving the dramatist from the depths of his being. For what he has to say, at the deepest level, in his plays is derived not merely from his ever fertile artistic invention, but from the real situation of his age – in which he himself was far from being a disinterested spectator. As Robert Southwell aptly remarks in his Preface to *Mary Magdalen's Funeral Tears* (1591), 'I know that no man can express a passion that he feeleth not, nor doth the pen deliver but what it copieth out of the mind.' This passion, which he feels in his heart, and strives to utter in his plays, is denied open expression; but for this very reason, just as 'fire that's closest kept burns most of all' (*Two Gentlemen of Verona* i. 2), it accumulates a greater force. His feeling is that of the sad queen in *Richard II*, who is 'pressed to death for want of speaking' (iii. 4), or of Constance in *King John*:

> *O that my tongue were in the thunder's mouth!*
> *Then with a passion would I shake the world.* (iii. 4)

What he cannot express openly, in a cruel and dangerous time, 'when we are traitors and do not know ourselves' (*Macbeth* iv. 2), he is forced to convey indirectly by means of hints and analogies. Like Launce in *Two Gentlemen of Verona*, he has a secret which he will not let us get from him 'but by parable' (ii. 5). Like the Duke in *Measure for Measure*, his 'givings-out are of an infinite distance from his true-meant design' (i. 4). Like Lennox in *Macbeth*, he implies a hidden meaning in his 'former speeches' (iii. 6). He is also like Hamlet, who feels his heart breaking within him, but must hold his tongue; who would like to 'drown the stage with tears and cleave the general ear with horrid speech' (ii. 2); but who takes an indirect course, so as to 'catch the conscience', not only of the king, but also of the people, by presenting in his plays the dramatized reality of what has happened and is happening in his country. What Hamlet says to Gertrude, Shakespeare in turn says to England :

> *Let me wring your heart; for so I shall,*
> *If it be made of penetrable stuff,*
> *If damned custom have not brass'd it so*
> *That it be proof and bulwark against sense.* (iii. 4)

Finally, like the dying Hamlet, he is concerned by the thought of 'what a wounded name, things standing thus unknown, shall live behind me' (v. 2) – if he fails to cry out against the injustice and oppression that have marked the passing away of the old faith from England.

It is this same cry which is heard, at a deeper level and in a more poignant manner, in *King Lear*, which is perhaps for this fundamental reason Shakespeare's masterpiece. While the old king bears a certain resemblance to Henry VIII, as noted above, the very fact that he is 'every inch a king' makes him stand for

> *This royal throne of kings, this scepter'd isle,*
> *This earth of majesty, this seat of Mars.*
> (*Richard II* ii. 1)

But after having rejected the old faith, personified in Cordelia, who is exiled to France, he comes to suffer the bitter consequences of this rejection. At first, he yields to passionate indignation against his unnatural daughters, in whom are personified the heretics and politicians, whose flattering words have deceived him. But later, through his sufferings and his sympathy with others like himself, 'poor naked wretches' like Edgar, who may stand for the hunted priests, he gradually learns – and perhaps Shakespeare, too, learns from him – to calm his passion and to 'bear free and patient thoughts' (iv. 6). This newly acquired calm of mind is, in fact, the spirit pervading the final plays, in which the dramatist is seeking – by implication – not revenge on his persecutors, but reconciliation with their descendants. Yet this is not entirely a new desire on his part. Already in *A Midsummer Night's Dream* he implies a strong distaste for religious conflict, 'when truth kills truth, O devilish-holy fray!' (iii. 2). Now in the final plays this becomes his predominant theme; as Lear's reconciliation with Cordelia is re-echoed in that of Pericles with Marina, that of Cymbeline with Imogen (and through her with Rome), and that of Leontes with Hermione and Perdita – all insisting, as it were, in the same direction.

Following this line of development, we may find it quite fitting for the dramatist to pass from *The Tempest*, with its ideal of a 'brave new world' where the sins of the past are forgiven and forgotten (v. 1), to the last history play of *Henry VIII*, where the real characters of Henry and Katharine finally emerge from among the shadows of his poetic imagination. Only with them there also emerges the formidable contrast between the ideal and the actual world; with the result that, while there is dramatic effectiveness (as the Prologue has promised) in the noble end of Katharine, there is no convincing substitute in the last act for Henry's lack of reconciliation with her or with Rome. Perhaps it was there that Shakespeare left the play; and it was completed by a lesser dramatist like Fletcher, who saw the need of a reconciliation scene, but felt no artistic repugnance to the simple substitution of Anne Bullen for Katharine and of Elizabeth for Mary. For himself, he was perhaps content to find the solution in his personal life : in his return home to Stratford, after having broken his staff and drowned his book (*The Tempest* v. 1); in his reunion with his wife and his daughter Susanna, recently wedded to Dr John Hall; and ultimately in his death as a 'papist', according to the testimony given by Richard Davies towards the end of the century.[42] To this faith, personified in the character of the 'gracious queen' Hermione, he may have intended the words of Perdita at the end of *The Winter's Tale* as a personal expression of welcome :

> *Dear queen, that ended when I but began,*
> *Give me that hand of yours to kiss.* (v. 3)

X

Elizabethan Atheism

TOWARDS THE end of the Elizabethan Age the spread of
atheism – or what is called 'atheism' – is noted with increasing
alarm by many writers. In his *Christ's Tears over Jerusalem*
(1593), Thomas Nash makes an earnest plea to 'university
men that are called to preach at the cross and the court':
'Arm yourselves against nothing but atheism, meddle not so
much with sects and foreign opinions, but let atheism be the
only string you beat on; for there is no sect now in England so
scattered as atheism.' He explains his meaning by distinguishing between two types of atheist, the 'inward' and the 'outward'. The former type – like Malvolio in *Twelfth Night*, who
is described by Maria as 'a kind of Puritan', yet 'a time-
pleaser' – 'makes conscience and the Spirit of God a long side-
cloak for all his oppressions and policies. A holy look he will put
on when he meaneth to do mischief, and have Scripture in his
mouth even while he is cutting his neighbour's throat.' His
type may perhaps be recognized in Richard of Gloucester, in
Shylock, and even in Iago. By reason of his 'hood of religion'
he gives occasion to others to blaspheme the name of God and
to lead irreligious lives. The other, or 'outward', type, resulting
from the former, 'establisheth reason as his God and will not
be persuaded that God (the true God) is, except he make him
privy to all the secrecies of his beginning and government'.
Further, it is not only the 'inward' atheist, or hypocritical
Puritan, who prejudices the cause of true religion in England,
but also the convinced Puritan whose fanatical zeal (in Nash's

opinion) brings religion into ridicule. Against such Puritan preachers he raises his voice on more than one occasion : 'It is only ridiculous dull preachers (who leap out of a library of catechisms into the loftiest pulpits) that have revived this scornful sect of atheists . . . Such is the division of God's ambassadors here amongst us, so many cow-baby bawlers and heavy-gated lumberers into the ministry are stumbled, under this College or that Hall's commendation, that a great number had rather hear a jarring black-sant than one of their bald sermons.'

This evil of atheism had been noted by Robert Persons in the Preface to his *Book of the Christian Exercise* (1582); and he later inserted two additional chapters into the newly entitled *Christian Directory* (1585), proving 'that there is a God' and 'that the service which God requireth of man in this present life is religion, with the particular confirmation of the Christian religion above all other in the world'. The impact of these particular chapters on Elizabethan readers is attested – over and above the frequency of their editions – by the fact that the preacher, Henry Smith, freely borrowed from them (without acknowledgement) in his treatise *God's Arrow Against Atheists* (1953). Nash also gave them his warm commendation in the above-mentioned work : 'In the Resolution [Persons' book] most notably is this tractate enlarged. He which peruseth that and yet is Diagorized, will never be Christianized.' Evidently, Persons is arguing against those who deny the very existence of God; and Nash implies as much in his reference to Diagoras, the ancient Athenian philosopher, who was known to Renaissance writers as 'the Atheist'. But the term was generally used to include those who, with the Epicureans, rejected or cast doubt on the providence of God, as well as those who practically lived without thought of God or religion.[1]

Elsewhere, in his *Brief Discourse containing certain reasons why Catholics refuse to go to Church* (1580), Persons gives an interesting reason for the growth of atheism, which is not mentioned by Nash. Pointing out the evil of enforced conformity to the new religion, whereby many thousands of Englishmen are led into continual violation of their consciences, he declares : 'Many, being Catholics in heart, by going to Protestant churches, must needs be brought either to flat atheism, that is, to leave off all conscience and to care for no religion at all (as many thousand seem to be resolved to do), or else to live in continual torment of mind.' On the one hand, he continues, they are prohibited by law from observing the traditional religion, while, on the other, they are presented with the continual spectacle of 'schisms and sects, wherein they hear nothing but wrangling and contradictions in matters of controversies'. Hence, he concludes, they are brought to 'a certain contempt and careless insensibility in these affairs'.[2] This last point is, as we have noted, touched on by Nash; and also by Hooker in the fifth Book of his *Laws of Ecclesiastical Polity* (1597), speaking of Christians and atheists: 'With our contentions their irreligious humour is also much strengthened. Nothing pleaseth them better than these manifold oppositions upon the matter of religion, as for that they have hereby the more opportunity to learn on one side how the other may be oppugned, and so to weaken the credit of all unto themselves.'

Here then, is an important aspect of the religious situation in Elizabethan England, which is not without impact on the drama of Shakespeare. There are, in fact, not a few scholars who regard this impact as fundamental to the outlook of Shakespeare, making him, either reluctantly or willingly, the great agnostic and forerunner of the 'national apostasy' of England from the Christian faith.[3] Some have been shocked by the undercurrent of obscenity and profanity in his plays, and have discerned in his view of life, if not a positive atheism, at least a prevailing scepticism which prompted him to overlook religious matters in favour of the affairs of the present life. At best, they see him endeavouring 'to give philosophical consolation to mankind, to inculcate submission to inevitable circumstances, and to encourage scientific investigation into the nature of things'.[4] Others have presented him as a victim of the situation described by Persons, and as the representative spirit of an age when, 'with all their strongly Catholic sympathies, the faith of many tottered on the verge of utter ruin'.[5] Their deduction is, no doubt, drawn from the contrast between Shakespeare's Catholic upbringing and the apparent absence of a Catholic or religious spirit in the plays. They see only the pervading secularism of the plays, even in relation to death;

and they cannot help connecting it with the infidelity that was rampant in the Bohemian circles of London society at that time.[6] But vague impressions are misleading. It is necessary to determine more precisely the *extent* to which atheistic, or agnostic, tendencies are observable in the plays, and the *manner* in which they appear in the total context. These tendencies are of various kinds; and it is important to distinguish these various kinds, one by one, and to consider how they are represented in the plays.

The most obvious form of 'atheism' in Elizabethan literature may be found in the impact of classical paganism, which came through the Italian Renaissance, and provided an occasion for many poets and scholars to abandon – or to modify – their Christian beliefs and values. The ancient classics of Greece and Rome were, indeed, for the most part proposed merely as literary models; and pagan gods and goddesses were regarded as no more than personifications of human values – Venus for Beauty, Cupid for Love, Bacchus for Ecstasy, and so on. Such an attitude was rather an artistic or literary fashion than a religious cult, even if artists and poets of a more religious bent came to represent the Father as Jupiter, the Son as Apollo, and Heaven as Olympus. But there were others, such as the Italian humanist, Lorenzo Valla, who deliberately embraced classical paganism in opposition to traditional Christianity, and who adored the pagan gods as symbols of human values. In place of the Christian ethic, there was an increasing tendency for humanists – even those who had made no conscious rejection of the Christian faith – to accept either the Epicurean ethic, which encouraged the enjoyment of the present life within the limits imposed by a 'hedonistic calculus', or that of the Stoics, who taught a sternly moralistic but fatalistic attitude to life. In Elizabethan England, the former ethic was for the most part repudiated as atheistic; and it was common to mention 'Epicures' and 'atheists' in the same breath. But the latter was widely accepted as in keeping with the moral teaching of Christianity; though it increasingly tended towards a secularization of morals and a separation of moral from religious life.[7]

In the plays of Shakespeare the influence of the Renaissance is, of course, everywhere to be seen. Though lacking the advantages – and disadvantages – of a university education, he was hardly less familiar with Ovid and Seneca, Plautus and Terence, than were the 'university wits' who ruled the stage at the time of his arrival in London. His two major poems, *Venus and Adonis* and *The Rape of Lucrece*, the former derived from the *Metamorphoses* and the latter from the *Fasti*, show how well he followed Tranio's advice to Lucentio in *The Taming of the Shrew* :

> *Let's be no stoics, nor no stocks, I pray;*
> *Or so devote to Aristotle's checks,*
> *As Ovid be an outcast quite abjur'd.* (i. 1)

Indeed, in the opinion of his contemporary, Francis Meres, 'the sweet witty soul of Ovid lives in mellifluous and honey-tongued Shakespeare, witness his Venus and Adonis, his Lucrece, his sugared Sonnets among his private friends, etc.'. Among his plays, too, there are abundant references to classical mythology and literature, particularly in *A Midsummer Night's Dream*, where the setting of pagan Athens enshrines a thematic contrast between 'Dian's bud' and 'Cupid's flower' (iv. 1). It is even tempting to see in the early comedies indications of an 'Epicurean' period in Shakespeare's career, culminating in the very unclassical figure of Falstaff, who may be related to Priapus or 'plumpy Bacchus' (*Antony and Cleopatra* ii. 7). The subsequent Roman plays and great tragedies might then be interpreted in terms of the so-called 'Senecan Stoicism of Shakespeare', as exemplified in Brutus, Horatio and possibly Othello.[8] Finally, it may be noted that the plays from *King Lear* onwards are almost continuously pagan in setting and sentiment, even where – as in *The Tempest* – a Christian background would seem to be in order. The last plays, in particular, culminate in a series of pagan theophanies – that of Diana in *Pericles* (v. 1), of Jupiter in *Cymbeline* (v. 4), the oracle of Apollo in *The Winter's Tale* (iii. 2), and the masque of spirits representing Iris, Ceres and Juno in *The Tempest* (iv. 1).

None of these classical allusions, however, can be proved to be anything more than the literary ornamentation fashionable in the Renaissance, or to have any more religious significance than they have, for instance, in the poetry of Chaucer. At

most, they may be interpreted as fitting in with the Renaissance tradition of 'Ovid moralized', such as we find, for
instance, in Arthur Golding. Rather, one feels a noticeable
difference in the early comedies between the classical allusions
on the surface, inserted – as in *A Midsummer Night's Dream* –
largely for the sake of 'local colour', and the religious themes
underlying them, inspired by Holy Scripture and Christian
tradition. These two elements, pagan and Christian, are by no
means – as some critics have suggested – on the same level or
equally implemented to the dramatist's purpose.[9] Rather, the
former is merely employed as ornament, whereas the latter is
followed as model and inspiration. The former glitters on the
surface of the plays, whereas the latter dwells and moves about
in their depths. The former, it may be added, tends to appear
in the 'aristocratic' main plots of the comedies, where the feeling is often superficial; whereas the latter is more often than
not to be found in the 'democratic' sub-plots, which are closer
to ordinary life. The Christian element, it is true, often includes
matter that seems irreverent to a Puritan mind; but the
irreverence is that not of a Renaissance cynic, but of a medieval believer, whose attitude to the 'sacred' was not so much
solemn as familiar.

As for the 'epicureanism' of the comedies, it disappears on
closer examination. The theme of romantic love is here treated
not so much in the manner of the Renaissance, which preferred
a Jonsonian 'comedy of humours', as in that of the Middle
Ages, which looked to comedy in general, both human and
divine.[10] The ideal of true love, which is presented as having
its natural culmination in marriage, is not at all 'epicurean',
but sharply contrasted both with the bestiality of lust (as in
Venus and Adonis 799–804) and with the illusions of mere
fancy, or 'love-in-idleness' (*A Midsummer Night's Dream* ii.
1; cf. *The Merchant of Venice* iii. 2). On a lower level, the
figure of Falstaff and all he represents in the way of self-
indulgence – while admittedly appealing to something deep in
the dramatist, and in his audience – is finally rejected by
Prince Hal on his attaining the maturity of kingship, and presumably by the dramatist, too.[11] For there is an unmistakable
symbolism in this rejection. Falstaff – as the King now declares
– is but a dream, or rather, an archetypal figure in a dream;

and now that the King has woken up and ascended the throne, it is natural for the dream, even its very memory, to disappear. Only at the end of Shakespeare's dramatic career, in *The Tempest*, he reappears as it were in the form of Caliban, now unwillingly subservient to Prospero, but eventually resolving to 'be wise hereafter, and seek for grace' (v. i). On the other hand, the 'stoicism' of the tragic period is mainly limited to a few characters and to a certain vein of thought which may be said to reach its term in *King Lear*. It has been maintained that this latter play touches the depths of agnosticism 'within the confines of a grim, pagan universe'; but if it does so, it does so only to rise again.[12] For, as we have noticed time and again, in the last plays despair gives place to hope, and the darkness of death to the light of life; and though this all takes place in a pagan setting, like that of *King Lear*, the undercurrent of thought is both religious and Christian. The precise theological significance of these plays, however, must be reserved to the final chapter.

Another aspect of Renaissance thought, the important revival of Neo-Platonism by the Florentine thinkers, Marsilio Ficino and Pico della Mirandola, came to take on certain 'atheist' associations in Elizabethan England. In itself it was a deeply religious movement: Platonic thought had long possessed intimate connections with Christian theology, and Ficino, as a Catholic priest, sought to renew those connections after the temporary dominance of Aristotle in the West. His efforts and those of Pico were welcomed by the early English humanists, John Colet, Thomas Grocyn and Thomas More; and the subsequent expression of Neo-Platonic thought in Castiglione's *The Courtier*, whose English translation by Sir Thomas Hoby was published in 1561, was no less welcomed at the court of Queen Elizabeth – particularly by Sir Philip Sidney.[13] In the second half of the sixteenth century, however, a heterodox strain appeared in the pantheistic and magical ideas of the ex-Dominican friar, Giordano Bruno.[14] Banished from Italy for his 'atheism', he came to England in 1583 and was hospitably entertained by Sir Philip Sidney. His exposition of his 'new philosophy' at Oxford that year only involved him in ridicule; but this did not prevent him from disseminating his ideas both at court and elsewhere during the two years of his sojourn in the country. The precise extent of his influence is uncertain; but while in England he wrote two books, *Spaccio della bestia trionfante* (1584) and *De gli eroici furori* (1585), both of which he dedicated to Sidney, with much fulsome praise of Queen Elizabeth in the latter. It is not clear how far he was regarded as an atheist by English contemporaries; though later, in the eighteenth century, he is mentioned by Dr Joseph Warton as 'the famous atheist'.

At all events, there are some indications of his influence on Shakespeare in the early comedy of *Love's Labour's Lost*.[15] In the first place, the character of Berowne reflects him at one or two points. The very name may be an echo of Bruno, no less than of Biron, the French Huguenot leader, with whom it is more commonly associated. This echo is supported by a number of interesting parallels. Berowne's fluctuating attitude towards women, alternately despising and idealizing them, is thought to reflect a similar contrast in Bruno's writings between a Petrarchan and an anti-Petrarchan vein. His emphasis on 'ladies' eyes' and his particular comparison of them to stars may be found in Bruno's *De gli eroici furori*, especially in the prefatory sonnet in praise of the ladies of England. His long speech on love in Act IV, celebrating the music of the spheres and the voice of the gods, which 'makes heaven drowsy with the harmony' (iv. 3), is possibly derived from a passage in the *Spaccio della bestia trionfante*, where the gods speak the praises of Love in one of the constellations. Even the opening proposal of 'a little academe' (i. 1) may have been suggested by the Platonic academies of Italy to which Bruno makes reference. Moreover, the comic characters of Don Armado and Holofernes may represent between them the two types of pedantry criticized by Bruno in the *Spaccio*: the truculence and ambition of Catholic Spain, and the pedantic ignorance of the Protestant grammarians at Oxford. These parallels, however, indicate not so much the influence of Bruno on Shakespeare, as his utilization by Shakespeare for a satirical purpose.

The influence of Bruno has also been traced to the esoteric circle of savants and litterateurs grouped round Sir Walter Raleigh, which may have been the object of Shakespeare's satire in *Love's Labour's Lost*.[16] This circle, later called 'the school of night' from an obscure mention in the play (iv. 3), included at various times the poets Christopher Marlowe, George Chapman and Matthew Roydon, the mathematician John Hariot, the astrologer John Dee, and the 'wizard' Earl of Northumberland. Its interest in Pythagorean ideas is attributed to the influence of Bruno; and its general aspiration towards higher, and even 'forbidden' knowledge, in Faustian fashion, gave some credibility to the contemporary charges of atheism and contempt of religion made against several of its members. The best known contemporary accusation made against this group is that of Robert Persons in his Latin reply to the Proclamation of 1591 against the Catholics: 'Of Sir Walter Raleigh's school of Atheism by the way, and of the conjuror that is master thereof, and of the diligence used to get young gentlemen of this school, wherein both Moses and Our Saviour, the Old and the New Testament, are jested at, and the scholars taught among other things to spell God backwards.'[17] This accusation was subsequently borne out a year or two later by information submitted to the Privy Council concerning two members of the group, Marlowe and Hariot (the 'conjuror' mentioned by Persons). According to the statement of a government informer, Ralph Baines, it was Marlowe's opinion that 'Moses was but a juggler and that one Hariot, being Sir W. Raleigh's man, can do more than he', and that 'the first beginning of religion was only to keep men in awe'.[18] This statement concurs with Greene's admonition to Marlowe in *A Groatsworth of Wit* (1592), urging him to abandon his 'diabolical atheism', and recalling with regret how he too had said, 'like the fool in his heart, There is no God'. Shortly afterwards, in 1594, Raleigh was himself subjected to an inquisition concerning the charge of atheism in his home county of Dorset; but nothing was proved against him, though the rumour remained attached to him.[19] The truth of the matter may well be that given later by Francis Osborne in his *Miscellany of Sundry Essays* (1659), that he 'was the first that ventured to tack about, and sailed aloof from the beaten track of the Schools', and so he 'was ever after branded with the title of an atheist, though a known assertor of God and Providence'.

Whatever may have been the precise religious opinions of

this group, or of its individual members, there has never been any suggestion that Shakespeare himself was associated with it for any period. If anything, he seems to have belonged to an opposite school of thought. About this time, Gabriel Harvey refers in his *Pierce's Supererogation* (1593) to the existence of two groups of litterateurs: those who upheld academic education in the arts, and those who advocated the priority of living experience.[20] It may have been on behalf of the latter group that Shakespeare composed his *Love's Labour's Lost*, with its veiled ridicule of the former group – though the identifications of Don Armado as Raleigh, and Holofernes as Chapman and/or Harvey, must necessarily remain uncertain. Chapman, in particular, has long been regarded as a strong candidate for the 'rival poet' of the *Sonnets*; and two implicit attacks on him and his obscure poem, *The Shadow of Night* (1594), have been detected in *Love's Labour's Lost*: first, the words of the Princess:

> *Beauty is bought by judgment of the eye,*
> *Not uttered by base sale of chapmen's tongues.*

> (ii. 1)

and secondly, the King's response to Berowne's paradoxical praise of his 'dark lady':

> *O paradox! black is the badge of hell,*
> *The hue of dungeons and the school of night.*

> (iv. 3)

One might add that the notorious conceit of Chapman,

> *No pen can anything eternal write,*
> *That is not steep'd in humour of the Night.*

seems to be taken up and twisted in an opposite direction by the words of Berowne:

> *Never durst poet touch a pen to write,*
> *Unless his ink were tempered with Love's sighs.*

> (iv. 3)[21]

If Shakespeare indeed cherished an aversion to Chapman, who was never accused of 'atheism' – though there is a certain rationalism and even determinism in his thought[22] – what may be said of his attitude to Marlowe, who was in some ways

Chapman's predecessor, and who did come under this accusation? The literary influence of Marlowe is clearly discernible in Shakespeare's early history plays; and in *As You Like It* there is an open reminiscence of the 'dead shepherd' (iii. 5), in a tone of affectionate regret. But the influence has all too often been overstated and misunderstood. The bombastic speeches of Tamburlaine, in particular, moved Shakespeare rather to parody – whether in the mouths of villains like Richard of Gloucester in *Henry VI* Part III :

> *How sweet a thing it is to wear a crown,*
> *Within whose circuit is Elysium,*
> *And all that poets feign of bliss and joy!* (i. 2)

or in those of buffoons like Pistol in *Henry IV* Part II :

> *Shall pack-horses,*
> *And hollow pamper'd jades of Asia,*
> *Which cannot go but thirty miles a day,*
> *Compare with Caesars and with Cannibals?* (ii. 4)

Marlowe has also been identified – anticipating Chapman – as the 'rival poet', in view of Shakespeare's reference to the 'proud full sail of his great verse' in *Sonnet* 86.[23] In any case, his milieu, whether courtly or theatrical, was different from that of Shakespeare. It is perhaps significant that in the same pamphlet in which he warns his friend against atheism, Greene also utters the famous warning against 'an upstart crow, beautified with our feathers', who is 'in his own conceit the only Shake-scene in a country'. In this, the first contemporary reference to him, Shakespeare is presented as an unwelcome outsider to the fraternity of 'university wits'.

The particular form of 'atheism' attributed to Marlowe by Greene was that derived from the writings of the Florentine, Nicholas Machiavelli. As Greene asked his friend, 'Is it pestilent Machiavellian policy that thou hast studied? O peevish folly! What are his rules but mere confused mocqueries, able to extirpate in small time the generations of mankind?' Not that Machiavelli himself openly denied God; but in advocating the subjection of all religious motives to the good of the state, he was regarded as a practical atheist. All his followers, too, the so-called 'politiques', were called 'atheists' in this practical sense.[24] His ideas had first been applied in England by Thomas Cromwell, who admitted as much to Reginald Pole; and those who followed him in establishing the 'via media' of Queen Elizabeth, Sir William Cecil, Sir Nicholas Bacon and the Earl of Leicester, were all accused of being Machiavellians.[25] In a remarkable political pamphlet, attributed to John Leslie, the supporter of Mary Queen of Scots, *A Treatise of Treasons* (1572), Elizabethan England as a whole is described as a model Machiavellian state, under the guidance of Cecil and Bacon: 'And that is it, that I call a Machiavellian state and regiment: where religion is put behind in the second and last place: where the civil policy, I mean, is preferred before it, and not limited by any rules of religion, but the religion framed to serve the time and policy . . .' Later, the same charge was made against the Earl of Leicester in another anonymous pamphlet, popularly known as *Leicester's Commonwealth* (1584). Sir Walter Raleigh himself was a known admirer of Machiavelli, at least in the field of practical politics, or 'secondary causes'; and on occasion he exhibited the ruthlessness encouraged by the Florentine.[26] There is a letter of his to Sir Robert Cecil, urging him to do away with the Earl of Essex: 'Lose not your advantage: if you do I read your destiny' – the very advice which Shakespeare puts into the mouth of Antonio in *The Tempest* (ii. 1).[27] Such men are the 'atheists of our time', criticized by the author of *A Conference about the Next Succession*, for pretending to be 'great politiques' by affirming that 'religion ought not to be so greatly respected in a prince or by a prince'.

Marlowe himself had evidently imbibed the ideas of Machiavelli while a student at Cambridge; and they subsequently entered very deeply into the inspiration of his plays – with a characteristically Elizabethan combination of fascination and rejection.[28] In all his major heroes there is the same bold defiance of tradition and convention, echoing both the refusal of their author 'to be afeared of bugbears and hobgoblins' and the prior boldness of Machiavelli. On the other hand, they are all undoubtedly villains, however brazen they may be about it, and their ending – especially that of Faustus – is despair unrelieved by prayer. In *The Jew of Malta* Machiavelli himself springs on to the stage for the Prologue, with the impudent proclamation:

> *I count religion but a childish toy,*
> *And hold there is no sin but ignorance.*

It was thus in Marlowe's footsteps that Shakespeare was following, as he developed the character of Richard of Gloucester in *Henry VI* Part III:

> *I can add colours to the chameleon,*
> *Change shapes with Proteus for, advantages,*
> *And set the murd'rous Machiavel to school.* (iii. 2)

Only, whereas there remains some ambiguity in Marlowe's attitude right up to his tragic end, there is – by way of exception – no room for ambiguity in that of Shakespeare from the beginning. The general attitude of Shakespeare may be gathered from his customary manner of alluding to policy and politicians – words which in his time tended to have Machiavellian connotations. Policy is described as 'base and rotten' in *Henry IV* Part I (i. 3), as 'devilish' in *Henry IV* Part II (iv. 1), as 'that mongrel cur' in *Troilus and Cressida* (v. 4), as sitting 'above conscience' in *Timon of Athens* (iii. 2). Likewise, politicians are characterized as 'vile' in *Henry IV* Part I (i. 3), as 'crafty, swearing rascals' in *Troilus and Cressida* (v. 4), as ready to 'circumvent God' in *Hamlet* (v. 1), and as 'scurvy' in *King Lear* (iv. 6). A combined denunciation of 'policy' and 'politicians' comes naturally to the mind of Sir Andrew Aguecheek in *Twelfth Night*, in terms that echo the common feeling of the age: 'Policy I hate: I had as lief be a Brownist as a politician' (iii. 2).

Among the characters in his plays, moreover, there is an impressive line of villains who can be described as more or less 'Machiavellian' – that is, generally speaking, prompted by the lust for power and prepared to employ the worst means to attain it.[29] Whereas in Marlowe's plays hero and villain tend to be combined in one character, as Tamburlaine, Barabas, and Faustus, in those of Shakespeare there is usually a clear separation of roles. Richard of Gloucester, as noted above, comes closest to the Marlovian pattern of hero-villain; but this is possible because in the history plays, until the emergence of

Prince Hal as Henry V, there is no clearly identifiable hero apart from England.[30] When we turn to the contemporary play of *Titus Andronicus*, we find in Aaron the Moor a villain of the same type as Richard, ambitious to 'mount aloft' with his imperial mistress Tamora (ii. 1), and at the same time stooping to 'acts of black night, abominable deeds' (v. 1). But he is presented in no heroic manner, and is rather contrasted throughout the play with the hero, Titus. In the later history plays, we meet with half-hearted Machiavellians, such as King John and Bolingbroke, who are prepared to commit murder to attain their political ambitions, but who suffer the pangs of conscience thereafter. They are followed by Claudius in *Hamlet* and, to some extent, by Macbeth.

A more thorough-going, or (in his own words) 'plain-dealing villain' (i. 3) is Don John in *Much Ado About Nothing*. He is prompted as much by envy of his brother's prosperity as by personal or political ambition. It is said of him that his 'spirits toil in frame of villanies' (iv. 1), and that 'he is compos'd and fram'd of treachery' (v. 1). But in the context of a comedy his role is comparatively insignificant, his treachery is discovered by 'shallow fools' (v. 1), and he vanishes into the outer darkness. Yet he is the precursor of a more effective villain, in whom is combined the envy of Don John, the lustful ambition of Aaron the Moor, and the artistic delight in evil of Richard of Gloucester – Iago. In him we have Shakespeare's full-length portrait of a Machiavellian and an 'atheist' (in the common Elizabethan sense of the word).[31] He follows Othello only 'for my peculiar end' (i. 1); he is moved merely by envy and hatred; he is inspired in all his scheming by 'hell and night' (i. 3); and he comes to be identified as it were with the 'divinity of hell' (ii. 3). Even so, he is not the central character of the play. His role is but secondary to that of his victim, Othello; and when his envy and hatred have done their worst, in Desdemona's murder and Othello's suicide, there 'remains the censure of this hellish villain' (v. 2). Yet he is not the last of such villains. There follow Edmund in *King Lear* and Antonio in *The Tempest*. The former invokes 'Nature' as his goddess, and concludes in Machiavellian vein: 'All with me's meet that I can fashion fit' (i. 2). The latter spurns the thought of conscience, in his tempting of Sebastian, declaring: 'I feel not this deity in my bosom' (ii. 2).

What is common to all these villains, what is Machiavellian in them, is not just their villainy, but their lack of religious scruple in achieving their political ambition and their readiness to pretend religious scruple as a convenient means of achieving it. They put themselves and their own interests at the centre of their lives, and to this they subordinate all other considerations of humanity, justice and religion. Whether in theory they deny God or not is of secondary importance: the relevant fact is that they deny him in deeds. In Shakespeare's mind their spiritual ancestry goes back beyond Machiavelli and the medieval Vice to Judas, who betrayed his Master, to Cain, who slew his brother Abel, and to Satan, who first rebelled against God and who continues his role in time as 'slanderer'. Thus it is interesting to see how often the villains in Shakespeare's plays are paired with their victims in a blood-relationship. In *Richard III* Richard of Gloucester is contrasted from the outset with 'simple, plain Clarence' (i. 1), whom he has murdered; and the climax of his bloody path to the throne is the murder of his two little nephews, 'the most replenished sweet work of nature' (iv. 3). King John is likewise contrasted with his victim, the 'little prince' Arthur (iv. 1), and Bolingbroke with his cousin Richard II – though the latter has already indirectly been a Cain to his uncle, Thomas of Woodstock (i. 1). In *Much Ado About Nothing* we have the opposing brothers, Don Pedro and Don John; and in *As You Like It,* the two pairs of the banished Duke and his usurping brother, Duke Frederick, and the two sons of Sir Rowland de Boys, Oliver and Orlando. In *Hamlet* Claudius is brother to Hamlet's father, and consequent on his crime he feels 'the primal eldest curse' (iii. 3) – though, instead of doing penance, he goes on to contrive the son's death as well. In *Macbeth* the hero's sin in murdering Duncan is gratuitously compounded by the addition of kinship – 'as I am his kinsman' (i. 7). In *King Lear* we again have a double contrast: between Cordelia and her wicked sisters, and between Edgar and Edmund; and in each case the latter seek to do away with their fathers. Finally, in *The Tempest* the two plotters, Antonio and Sebastian, are set against their respective brothers, Prospero and Alonso. In each case, there is no doubt as to the sympathies of the dramatist. There is a clear rejection of unscrupulous self-assertion and denial of God, on the one hand; and a clear choice of meekness and patience with submission to 'the great hand of God' (*Macbeth* ii. 3), on the other hand – even if it means becoming, like Edgar, 'the lowest and most dejected thing of fortune' (*King Lear* iv. 1).

This rejection of Machiavellianism, however, may be contrasted with the evident influence on Shakespeare's plays of the sceptical mentality of Montaigne.[32] The *Essays* were first translated into English by John Florio, who had been Italian tutor to the young Earl of Southampton, and published in 1603. Even before their publication it seems that Shakespeare had read them in manuscript form, to judge from the number of verbal echoes in *Hamlet* and *Troilus and Cressida*. Montaigne himself was, of course, no atheist : he was a professed Catholic, even if his general outlook was more secular than religious. Following in the footsteps of Erasmus and other humanists, he rejected the scholasticism of the Middle Ages with its calm confidence in the power of human reason to attain absolute certainty. Rather, with Luther, he stressed the corruption in human nature, by which man had been brought even lower than the beasts; and he insisted on the need of faith to know the existence of God.[33] He did not deny 'that this vast world-frame must bear the impression of some marks therein imprinted by the hand of this great-wondrous Architect'; but he asserted that the imbecility of man is the cause 'we can nor discover nor read them'. Such practical scepticism, united though it was in Montaigne himself with a deep Christian faith, often had the effect of weakening that faith in the minds of his readers. This may well have been the case with Hamlet, if not with the creator of Hamlet; for this is the play in which Shakespeare first expresses a kind of scepticism about the after life, and in which he first shows verbal echoes of Montaigne. It is not without significance that both Hamlet and Horatio are repeatedly stated to come 'from Wittenberg' (i. 2): they might equally well come from Bordeaux.

The suggestion has been made that the book Hamlet is reading on his entry in Act III Scene 1 might have been a copy of Montaigne's *Essays*. Certainly, the soliloquy which follows is not only agnostic in thought, but also dependent for many of its verbal expressions on Montaigne as translated by Florio. Thus Hamlet's 'To die, to sleep' echoes Montaigne: 'If it [death] be a consummation of one's being, it is also an amendment and entrance into a long and quiet life. We find nothing so sweet in life, as a quiet rest and gentle sleep, and without dreams.' His 'thousand natural shocks' likewise comes from Montaigne: 'And question might be made, whether according to her [the mind's] natural condition, she might at any time be so settled; but to join constancy unto it is her last perfection; I mean, if nothing should shock her, which a thousand accidents may do.' The underlying key to Hamlet's mood may be found, not only in his previous admission to Rosencrantz and Guildenstern:

> *I have of late – but wherefore I know not – lost all my mirth, forgone all custom of exercises; and indeed it goes so heavily with my disposition that this goodly frame, the earth, seems to me a sterile promontory.* (ii. 2)

but also in the similar admission of Montaigne and his impact on Shakespeare's outlook on life: 'I wot not, whether it be without reason, I am so distasted and out of liking with the world wherein I live and frequent.' At least, in this point Montaigne would have found in Shakespeare a receptive reader – considering how many of his characters, even before Hamlet, are out of love with this world.

On the other hand, much as the dramatist may have borrowed from the essayist, he was by no means a follower or disciple of him in his scepticism. In the plays from *Hamlet* onwards, while there is scarcely one that lacks verbal echoes from the *Essays*, there is at the same time a discernible opposition to their underlying thought and outlook. Hamlet himself becomes sceptical by force not of general reflection on the human condition, but of particular experience of his own unhappy circumstances. His psychological development in the course of the play, moreover, may be seen to consist in his ability to rise above these circumstances, and the sceptical mood they engender, to a calm acceptance of life and death in view of the Christian idea of divine providence. A parallel movement, on the level of emotion rather than of intellect, may be found in *King Lear*, which is at once the masterpiece of

Shakespeare's tragic genius and the fullest extent of Montaigne's influence.[34] Both Lear and Gloucester are led along different paths of suffering to the knowledge of themselves and their human weakness; and in the depth of their downward descent they meet with the harsh echo of Montaigne's words: 'Miserable man, whom if you consider well, what is he? . . . Truly, when I consider man all naked . . . and view his defects, his natural subjection, and manifold imperfections, I find we have had much more reason to hide and cover our nakedness than any creature else.' But in this depth what they find is not only nakedness and corruption, but also new clothing and regeneration. They go on to cast aside despair and to attain the ripeness of mortal life, when joy bursts out from amid sorrow, and death gives place to immortality.

The final, and most outstanding example of Montaigne's influence on Shakespeare may be found in Gonzalo's echo of his essay 'On Cannibals' in the description of his ideal 'commonwealth' in *The Tempest* (ii. 1). But the similarity serves only to emphasize the fundamental difference between the two authors. Whereas Montaigne praises the ideal state of the 'noble savage', in contrast to the civilized society of Europe, Shakespeare implicitly ridicules the utopian commonwealth proposed by Gonzalo, not only by the mocking words of Antonio and Sebastian, but also by the confession of Gonzalo himself that this was all but 'merry fooling'. On the other hand, the reality of cannibal life is symbolized in the character of Caliban, who embodies all that is bestial in man. Yet even in him the dramatist portrays an ultimate redemption, as he leaves with the resolution to 'be wise hereafter, and seek for grace' (v. 1).

In conclusion, whatever form of atheism, agnosticism or irreligion may be distinguished among his contemporaries, we find the response of Shakespeare almost uniformly negative. Now he ridicules the folly of those who say in their heart, 'There is no God'; now he expresses loathing at the hypocrisy of those who 'with devotion's visage and pious action sugar o'er the devil himself' (*Hamlet* iii. 1); now he vents indignation against the corrupt practices of politicians which conceal 'the equivocation of the fiend' (*Macbeth* v. 5); now he struggles with the temptation to scepticism within himself, and succeeds in shaking it off. In view of all this, we may turn to the famous speeches that seem to express a pessimistic or agnostic view of life: Hamlet's 'To be or not to be' (iii. 1), Macbeth's 'Tomorrow and tomorrow and tomorrow' (v. 5), Gloucester's 'As flies to wanton boys, are we to the gods' (*King Lear* iv. 1), and Prospero's 'We are such stuff as dreams are made on' (*The Tempest* iv. 1). In the first place, they are mostly, as we have seen in an earlier chapter, a tissue of Scriptural texts, from *Job*, *Ecclesiastes*, *Isaiah* and the *Psalms*; while Prospero's speech, in particular, is also inspired by St Peter's vision of the consummation of the world (II *Pet.* iii. 7–13).[35] Further, they have to be interpreted, not merely as they sound in isolation, but as they are related to the speaker and to the total context of the play. Thus Hamlet's soliloquy expresses the temporary anguish of his mind; but this he later transcends with a renewed faith in the 'divinity that shapes our ends' and in the 'special providence' of God (v. 2). Macbeth's soliloquy expresses the last stage of despair in one who has given the 'eternal jewel' of his soul to 'the common enemy of man' (iii. 1); and it is only through his death that regeneration can come to Scotland. Gloucester's words are also an expression of despair, but in his case despair is succeeded by new hope and patience through the guidance of his faithful son, Edgar. Finally, Prospero's speech refers to the material world in which man lives, and which is destined – according to Christian expectation – to be dissolved, even as the masque of spirits has been melted, 'into thin air' (iv. 1). Such is the stuff of our present life in this world; but it is not the stuff of those spiritual values on which Prospero has just insisted so strongly with Ferdinand, and which he resolves to make the subject of his 'every third thought' on returning to Milan (v. 1).

As for Shakespeare's reversion to pagan mythology in his last plays, various reasons may be given without having to recur to a hypothetical abandonment of his Christian faith.[36] The obvious reason is the passing in 1606 of an Act to Restrain Abuses of Players, which prohibited stage-players from using the names of God, Jesus Christ, the Holy Ghost, or the Trinity, profanely or in jest.[37] The practical effect of this Act may be seen by simply comparing the text of Quartos published before 1606 with that of the Folio of 1623. Apart from *Macbeth*, the bulk of which may well have been composed before

1606, all the plays after that date have a pagan setting. A deeper reason, however, is perhaps to be found in the religious development of the dramatist – not that he was moving from Christian to pagan, but that he found it more convenient in the circumstances of his age to express his Christian vision indirectly in terms of classical mythology.[38] Already in Renaissance art there had taken place a rich fusion and vital harmony between Christian and pagan themes. It was possible for Christian thinkers, especially in the Neo-Platonic tradition, to look beyond Zeus or Jupiter to the heavenly Father, beyond Apollo and the Delphic oracle to Christ, the Word of God, and beyond the chaste Diana to the Virgin Mary. It is not without significance that these are the very deities who appear in the theophanies of *Cymbeline*, *The Winter's Tale* and *Pericles*, respectively. Although their setting is pagan and remote from Elizabethan England, their deeper content is both Christian and contemporary. The first attempt of this kind, *Pericles*, has been shown, in an earlier chapter, to have several striking points of resemblance to the medieval miracle plays of the Virgin; and it significantly culminates in a theophany of Diana.[39] The time of *Cymbeline*'s historical setting is not just Britain before Christ, but Britain at the moment of Christ's nativity – as noted by Holinshed at this place.[40] This coincidence is implied in the oracle of Jupiter, which contains no fewer than three Messianic prophecies from the Old Testament: the 'lion's whelp' from *Genesis* xlix. 9; finding 'without seeking' from *Isaiah* lxv. 1; and the branches lopped from a 'stately cedar' from *Ezekiel* xvii. 3, 6. In *The Winter's Tale* the turning-point is an oracle of Apollo, delivered to the accompaniment of a 'ceremonious, solemn and unearthly' sacrifice (iii. 1), reminiscent – as has been suggested in an earlier chapter – of a Solemn High Mass in a Catholic basilica.[41] In *The Tempest* there is, indeed, no theophany, but only a masque of spirits impersonating pagan deities, for the celebration of the betrothal between Ferdinand and Miranda. But the Christian meaning is none the less impressive: looking 'into the dark backward and abysm of time' (i. 2) to the story of Adam and Eve in Paradise, and forward to the eschatological vision of a 'brave new world' (v. 1) when the sin of man is finally forgiven.[42]

XI

Ethical Viewpoint

THE ATTRIBUTION of atheism, or at least of agnosticism, which is not infrequently made to the plays of Shakespeare, is connected with the apparent absence of a clear moral viewpoint in them. Attention is drawn in this respect to the profanity and the obscenity with which they are liberally sprinkled.[1] The dramatist is, indeed, often regarded as a kind of moral dilettante,

> *Unstaid and skittish in all motions else,*
> *Save in the constant image of the creature*
> *That is beloved. (Twelfth Night ii. 4)*

In Shakespeare's case, what is constant would presumably be the image of his beloved theatrical profession.[2] In all motions else, as Dr Johnson severely rebukes him in the *Preface to Shakespeare*, 'he sacrifices virtue to convenience, and is so much more careful to please than to instruct, that he seems to write without any moral purpose'. This criticism has been amplified in modern times by George Bernard Shaw, whose prefaces ring with denunciations of his Elizabethan predecessor. The latter is said to have 'no conscience', 'no constructive ideas', 'no conscious religion', 'no philosophy to expound', and 'no intellectually coherent drama'.[3] What is regarded by critics like Johnson and Shaw as a defect, however, is regarded by other more recent critics as a merit. For them the universal genius of Shakespeare is not to be limited by any consistent moral or religious viewpoint: his greatness rather lies in his ability to depict human nature as it really is, without judging it in the light of any moral standard.[4] Their interpretation is supported by the immense variety of characters and situations in the plays, which consequently appear to lack an underlying unity of thought. It is further encouraged by the relatively modern theory of 'art for art's sake', with the implicit desire to dissociate works of art and literature from all rules of morality.

In order to arrive at an impartial judgement in this matter, it is necessary to put aside modern preconceptions and to consider Shakespeare's plays in relation to the prevailing literary opinion of their own age. Here we find a very different approach to literature from that of today: an almost exaggerated emphasis on its essentially moral purpose. The classical exposition of this approach is, no doubt, Sir Philip Sidney's *Defence of Poesy*, where the author's principal concern is to defend poetry from the Puritan accusation of immorality, or at least of frivolity. On behalf of the poet, he makes the claim that 'his effects be so good as to teach goodness and delight the learners of it . . . Therein [in moral doctrine] he doth not only far pass the historian, but for instructing is well-nigh comparable to the philosopher, for moving leaveth him behind him.' A similar defence, on behalf of the stage, is made by Thomas Nash in *Pierce Penniless*, in a passage which includes a probable reference to Shakespeare's early history plays.[5] To prove that 'plays be no extreme, but a rare exercise of virtue', he says of their subject-matter:

For the most part, it is borrowed out of our English chronicles, wherein our forefathers' valiant acts, that have lien long buried in rusty brass and worm-eaten books, are revived, and they themselves raised from the grave of oblivion and brought to plead their aged honours in open presence, than which what can be a sharper reproof to these degenerate effeminate days of ours? How would it have joyed brave Talbot, the terror of the French, to think that after he had lien two hundred years in his tomb he should triumph again on the stage, and have his bones new-embalmed with the tears of ten thousand spectators at least, at several times, who in the tragedian that represents his person imagine they behold him fresh bleeding!

He goes on to mention various moral lessons that may also be drawn from plays:

> In plays all cozenages, all cunning drifts overgilded with outward holiness, all stratagems of war, all the cankerworms that breed on the rust of peace, are most lively anatomized. They show the ill-success of treason, the fall of hasty climbers, the wretched end of usurpers, the misery of civil dissension, and how just God is evermore in punishing of murder.

Of course, the mere fact that a theory is prevalent in an age does not mean that every author in that age necessarily follows the theory. It only warns us against interpreting the authors of that age in the light of another theory which happens to be prevalent in our own. There still remains the task of examining the plays of Shakespeare himself, to see whether and to what extent they correspond to the ideal proposed by Sidney and Nash. In undertaking this examination, it is perhaps necessary to note that for a consistent moral standard or viewpoint in the plays there is no need of an original moral philosophy in the mind of the dramatist. It is quite sufficient if there is no more than what Shaw contemptuously terms 'a mere reach-me-down', in other words, the general outlines of traditional Christian morality.[6] After all, the morality we may expect to find in poets and dramatists is less in idea than in expression, and less in expression than in the imaginative and emotional force behind the expression. Ideas are not necessarily less strong for being derived from tradition: rather, they may be all the stronger, when they are accepted with a deep faith that informs the imagination and emotions of an author.

In the plays of Shakespeare we have already noticed a prevailing tendency in favour of tradition.[7] The dramatist regularly shows his distaste for mere appearances, particularly in connection with current fashions of clothing and behaviour. He evidently sympathizes with Hotspur against the foppish lord in *Henry IV* Part I (i. 3), with Lafeu against Parolles in

All's Well That Ends Well (ii. 5), with Hamlet against Osric (v. 2), and with Kent against Oswald in *King Lear* (ii. 2). There is an interesting series of utterances put into the mouths of noble personages in many of the comedies, as though emphasizing the personal preference of Shakespeare, who is said to have himself acted in such parts. In *As You Like It* the banished Duke prefers 'old custom' to the 'painted pomp' of the 'envious court' (ii. 1). In *Twelfth Night* the Duke contrasts 'that old and antique song we heard last night' with the 'light airs and recollected terms of these most brisk and giddy-paced times' (ii. 4). In *All's Well That Ends Well* the King recalls with nostalgia his old friendship with Bertram's father, whom he contrasts with 'our young lords',

> *younger spirits, whose apprehensive senses*
> *All but new things disdain; whose judgments are*
> *Mere fathers of their garments; whose constancies*
> *Expire before their fashions.* (i. 2)

This description is subsequently applied by Lafeu to the worthless Parolles :

> *There can be no kernel in this light nut; the soul of this*
> *man is in his clothes.* (ii. 5)

In *Measure for Measure* the Duke likewise shakes his head over the 'news abroad i' the world', lamenting that

> *there is so great a fever on goodness, that the dissolution of*
> *it must cure it: novelty is only in request; and it is as*
> *dangerous to be aged in any kind of course, as it is virtuous*
> *to be constant in any undertaking: there is scarce truth*
> *enough alive to make societies secure, but security enough*
> *to make fellowships accursed.* (iii. 2)

Elsewhere Shakespeare speaks in his own person, when he complains in *Sonnet* 76, not without secret complacency, that his verse is 'barren of new pride', 'far from variation or quick change', eschewing 'new-found methods' and 'compounds strange'. If he desires newness, it is that not of mere fashion, which neglects antiquity and custom (*cf. Hamlet* iv. 5), but of tradition, which, like the sun, is daily new and old, with a newness not of time, but of eternity.

The history plays, especially when taken successively in

groups of four, or tetralogies, convey a powerful impression of unity.[8] This impression chiefly consists in a lesson of vital importance for the state : that of the need for political and moral order. In each group there emerges a central character, or protagonist – for evil, in Richard III, and for good, in Henry V. What he emerges out of is a dispute, or series of disputes, occasioned by a weak ruler, such as Henry VI and Richard II, in which the dramatist seems to suspend his judgement and to avoid taking one side or the other. Rather, in the disputes between Duke Humphrey and Cardinal Beaufort and between Somerset and York in *Henry VI*, in the quarrel between Bolingbroke and Mowbray in *Richard II*, in the successive rebellions of the Percys in the first Part and of Archbishop Scroop in the second Part of *Henry IV*, he shows a measure of right and wrong on both sides, while leaving us uncertain as to the side he favours. It seems as if he refuses to limit his view to individual causes, but directs his undivided attention to the common good of the realm.

Shakespeare is, as we have noticed in a previous chapter, by no means uncritical of the Tudor doctrine of 'divine right' of kings and 'passive obedience' of subjects.[9] He indeed upholds the monarchy, but apparently with reservations similar to those made by the author of *A Conference about the Next Succession* and by Richard Hooker in *The Laws of Ecclesiastical Policy*. He is not satisfied with the mere maintenance of outward political order, unless this is in turn based on the inner moral order, which includes the question of right. One of the main problems that recur in his plays is, in fact, the dilemma of the individual faced with a political order that is based on injustice and usurpation. This is the central problem of *Hamlet*, in which many themes of the history plays have their culmination : namely, when rulers violate the moral order in matters directly related to government, how can their subjects continue to obey without implicitly consenting to this violation? On the other hand, who is to decide when it is lawful for subjects to rise against their rulers, with the serious risk of involving the whole realm in strife and bloodshed? This is no problem for the moral dilettante, who simply chooses one side of the question, and goes on to exploit its dramatic possibilities. For Shakespeare, however, there is no such simple solution. He steadfastly faces the conflict between two apparently opposing principles, that of 'right' and that of 'order'; and thereby he succeeds in penetrating to the deep springs of human motive and action.

It has been maintained that Shakespeare's solution is one of 'individualistic, Nietzschean assertion', which spurns the claims of a petty morality designed to keep subjects in awe.[10] But it is precisely this individualism which the dramatist evidently holds in deepest abhorrence. For it is represented not in the heroes but in the villains of his plays: in Richard of Gloucester, 'I am myself alone' (*Henry VI* Part III v. 6); in Parolles, 'Simply the thing I am shall make me live' (*All's Well That Ends Well* iv. 3); in Iago, 'In following him, I follow but myself' (*Othello* i. 1); in Edmund, 'Thou, Nature, art my goddess' (*King Lear* i. 2). These are all men who unashamedly seek themselves, led by their lust, envy, anger or ambition. But their self-seeking meets with no approval within the framework of the plays, however poetically they may express themselves. Its outcome, both for themselves and for their victims, is merely chaos and confusion, the triumph of appetite, that 'universal wolf' (*Troilus and Cressida* i. 3). Adapting Berowne's words in *Love's Labour's Lost*, one might well define the moral of the tragedies as:

Self, seeking self, doth self of self beguile.

The man of ambition, by asserting himself at the expense of others, is thereby estranged both from them and from himself. Thus Macbeth confesses after his murder of Duncan: 'To know my deed, 'twere best not know myself' (ii. 2). He finds that one crime only leads to another, since 'blood will have blood'; but he feels constrained, almost in spite of himself, to continue in his path of crime, since, as he says, 'should I wade no more, returning were as tedious as go o'er' (iii. 4).

Not only does one crime lead the criminal on to another; but it also leads others to take revenge against the criminal, and so evil is multiplied till it fills the whole universe. This consequence the dramatist does not hesitate to draw with serious warning on several occasions. He draws it in More's speech to the riotous apprentices in his part of the unpublished play of *Sir Thomas More*; in the 'degree' speech of Ulysses in *Troilus*

and Cressida (i. 3); in the laments of the old king in *Henry IV*
Part II (iii. 1 and iv. 5); in the Gentleman's description of
Laertes's insurrection in *Hamlet* (iv. 5); and in Albany's
indignant rebuke of Goneril for her breach of filial piety in
King Lear (iv. 2).[11] The citation of the last-mentioned
example may serve for the rest :

> *If that the heavens do not their visible spirits*
> *Send quickly down to tame these vile offences,*
> *It will come,*
> *Humanity must perforce prey on itself,*
> *Like monsters of the deep.*

It is, however, no less disastrous – as the plays indicate – to
condone unrepented evil, leaving it unpunished, than to
oppose evil with other evil by way of revenge. Cowardice, as
Hamlet realized, is no less responsible for the rotten state of
Denmark than self-assertion. For when self-assertion passes
unchallenged, or is disguised by 'flattering unction',

> *It does but skin and film the ulcerous place,*
> *Whiles rank corruption, mining all within,*
> *Infects unseen.* (iii. 4)

In the same way, it was the too lenient administration of the
laws in Vienna which brought about the corrupt state of
affairs with which *Measure for Measure* opens –

> *When evil deeds have their permissive pass,*
> *And not the punishment...*
> *And liberty plucks justice by the nose.* (i. 3)

Justice demands the punishment of crime, as well in rulers as
in subjects. In this sense, the dramatist himself seems to
approve both the severity of Angelo and the revenge of
Hamlet. But he adds an important qualification in the choric
words of the Duke disguised as a friar :

> *He who the sword of heaven will bear*
> *Should be as holy as severe;*
> *Pattern in himself to know,*
> *Grace to stand, and virtue go;*
> *More nor less to others paying*
> *Than by self offences weighing.* (iii. 2)

Those who are charged with the restoration of moral order are often, in fact, themselves infected with the very disease they seek to relieve. The judge who condemns Claudio for the sin of fornication, the 'precise Angelo', is himself convicted of a greater sin in the same kind. He is smitten with concupiscence for the very woman who has just warned him :

> *How would you be,*
> *If he, which is the top of judgment, should*
> *But judge you as you are?* (ii. 2)

The same is true of Hamlet. From the moment he accepts the stern injunction of the ghost, he feels his inadequacy for the task :

> *The time is out of joint: O cursed spite,*
> *That ever I was born to set it right!* (i. 5)

He is a man deeply conscious not only of his own inadequacy, but also of the general inadequacy – in plain words, the sinfulness – of mankind. This is due not merely to his mood of melancholy, in which 'man delights not me' (ii. 2), but rather to his profound realization of the fact of original sin : that were one to 'use every man after his desert', none 'should 'scape whipping' (*ibid.*).

At this point Shakespeare's moral ideas appear in close connection with the moral teaching of Christ, particularly in the Sermon on the Mount. Besides the implication of the Pauline doctrine of original sin in *Romans* v, in conjunction with *Psalm* 14, 'There is none that doth good, no, not one', the words of Hamlet recall the text from the Sermon on the Mount which enters into the title of *Measure for Measure* :

> *Judge not, that you may not be judged; for with what*
> *judgment you judge, you shall be judged; and with what*
> *measure you mete, it shall be measured to you again.*

It is possibly because of his awareness of this truth that Hamlet delays his revenge; and instead he makes it his first aim to 'catch the conscience of the king' by means of his play within the play. In the event he succeeds, beyond his intention, not only in uncovering the guilt within the King's conscience, but also in moving the King close to repentance. On this occasion,

when he has a perfect opportunity for taking revenge, he hesi-
tates, not only (as he reasons to himself) because he wishes to
procure the King's eternal damnation, but also (as is theo-
logically true) because the just claims of revenge are fully
satisfied by repentance. This is, in fact, the sum of Hamlet's
aim concerning his mother, when he urges her:

> *Confess yourself to heaven;*
> *Repent what's past; avoid what is to come.*
>
> (iii. 4)

This is also the consistent aim of the Duke in *Measure for
Measure*, as he goes about in the disguise of a friar, to 'visit the
afflicted spirits in the prison' (ii. 3), after the example of
Christ in the harowing of hell (*cf.* I *Pet.* iii. 19). He instructs
Juliet 'how you shall arraign your conscience, and try your
penitence'; and he prepares Claudio to face death with
courage. He arranges the events which lead up to the final
repentance of Angelo, when the latter is finally convicted of his
sin. The play thus tends to emphasize the lesson that the way
to overcome evil is neither the laxity of mere kindness, nor the
strictness of rigid justice, but the grace of repentance. Only on
this foundation can mercy function without injury to the
claims of justice.[12] As Valentine declares at the climax of *Two
Gentlemen of Verona*,

> *Who by repentance is not satisfied*
> *Is nor of heaven, nor earth; for these are pleas'd.*
> *By penitence the Eternal's wrath's appeas'd.* (v. 4)

Repentance is the essential condition of forgiveness; and the
theme of forgiveness is close to the heart of Shakespeare's
moral viewpoint, no less than of Christ's own teaching. Such
texts as

> *I say to you: Love your enemies; do good to them that
> hate you, and pray for them that persecute and calumni-
> ate you; that you may be the children of your Father who
> is in heaven. (Matt. v. 44–5)*

and

> *Our Father, who art in heaven . . . forgive us our debts,
> as we also forgive our debtors. (Matt. vi. 9, 12)*

have their dramatic illustration in play after play. It has even been maintained, and with reason, as a general principle, that it is the acceptance or rejection of forgiveness which determines the outcome of a play – whether it is to have a happy or a sad ending, as a comedy or a tragedy.[13] In the above quotation from *Two Gentlemen of Verona*, the hero Valentine forgives his treacherous friend Proteus who has just attempted to rape his lady Silvia; and it is this rather extreme example of forgiveness, phrased in Christian terms, which abruptly transforms the play from tragedy to comedy – though at the expense of probability. There is a similar turning-point in *As You Like It*. Orlando, having been unjustly driven from home by his wicked brother Oliver, comes across an unexpected opportunity of revenge in the forest; but instead of taking the opportunity, he saves his brother's life, and is himself severely wounded in the process. Thereby Oliver is converted and adds to the happy ending of the comedy by marrying Celia, while Orlando marries Rosalind.

Yet more striking is the illustration of Christian forgiveness in *Measure for Measure*. The heroine Isabella learns that her brother Claudio has been condemned to death for fornication. When she comes to plead before the judge, Angelo, she is granted her brother's life, on condition that she commits with the judge that very sin for which he has condemned her brother. On the Duke's advice, she pretends to accept the evil proposal of Angelo, only to discover that he has none the less had her brother put to death. Finally, when Angelo is convicted of his sin and under like condemnation, she is asked by Mariana to kneel down and implore the Duke for mercy on Angelo. But the Duke first reminds her :

> *Should she kneel down in mercy of this fact,*
> *Her brother's ghost his paved bed would break,*
> *And take her hence in horror.* (v. 1)

Nevertheless, this is just what she does. She kneels down and finds reasons in her mind to extenuate Angelo's offence, seeing him to be now repentant. Thus at the end of the play, in a second judgement scene, she fulfils the ideal of mercy which in her original plea with Angelo she had derived from the example of Christ :

Why, all the souls that were were forfeit once;
And he that might the vantage best have took,
Found out the remedy. (ii. 2)

Forgiveness is not a theme peculiar to the comedies. It runs
like a golden thread through all the plays, and shines with
peculiar lustre in the tragedies. In *Hamlet* the theme of
revenge has been so emphasized in traditional criticism that
the significance of the contrary theme of repentance and forgiveness is not always noticed. As a result of his plan to 'catch
the conscience of the king', Hamlet – as we have seen – brings
Claudius to a frame of mind that is close to repentance, even
if it is short-lived.[14] He is more successful with Gertrude, who
appears to be genuinely repentant. In the outcome, he
renounces his plans of revenge and places himself as it were in
the hands of divine providence; and in this spirit, both before
and after the fatal duel, he generously exchanges forgiveness
with Laertes.[15] Similarly, the last recorded words of Ophelia
are a prayer to God for mercy 'on all Christian souls' (iv. 5).

The example of Ophelia is followed by the other tragic
heroines: by Desdemona, whose dying words are an attempt
to cover up her husband's crime, with a commendation to her
'kind lord' (*Othello* v. 2); and by Cordelia, who quite forgets
the injury done her by her father in her great pity for his
sufferings. The latter's readiness to forgive even places her in
the position of the father in Christ's parable of the Prodigal
Son, as when she exclaims:

And wast thou fain, poor father,
To hovel thee with swine and rogues forlorn,
In short and musty straw? (iv. 7)[16]

Parallel with the figure of Cordelia is that of Edgar, who likewise harbours no grudge against his father for past injuries,
but generously assists him to safety and salvation. He further
illustrates the moral ideal of patience in adversity and persecution as a living example of the last beatitude: 'Blessed are they
that suffer persecution for justice's sake (*Matthew* v. 10). He
sees himself as 'a most poor man, made tame to fortune's blows';
and he urges his despairing father to 'bear free and patient
thoughts' (iv. 6). Just as Cordelia reappears in the heroines of

the last plays, all of them models of forgiveness, so Edgar's spirit is renewed in the characters of Pericles, Belarius and Prospero. They have all been trained in the school of adversity and endurance; and they all exemplify the Christian ideals of poverty and meekness, mourning and thirst for justice, mercy and purity of heart, peace and patience under persecution. Of such, Christ says – and Shakespeare echoes him – is 'the kingdom of heaven'.

On the more positive side, the morality of Shakespeare, like that of Christ, may be aptly summarized in the one word 'love', which, as Richard of Gloucester cynically remarks, 'greybeards call divine' (*Henry VI* Part III v. 6). This word refers primarily, not to the pagan Eros, but to the Christian Agape, as described by St Paul in his famous words to the Corinthians :

> *Love suffereth long: it is bountiful: love envieth not: love doth not boast itself: it is not puffed up: it disdaineth not: it seeketh not her own things: it is not provoked to anger: it thinketh not evil: it rejoiceth not in iniquity, but rejoiceth in the truth: it suffereth all things: it believeth all things: it hopeth all things: it endureth all things.*
> (I *Cor.* xiii. 4–7)[17]

This love Shakespeare celebrates from his earliest comedies, not dissociated from, but combined with, Eros in fruitful union. It is contrasted with 'love-in-idleness' (*A Midsummer Night's Dream* ii. 1), or mere fancy that is 'engender'd in the eyes' (*The Merchant of Venice* iii. 2), and *a fortiori* with 'sweating lust' that falsely usurps the name of love (*cf. Venus and Adonis* 793–804). It has its natural culmination and its symbolic expression in the sacrament of marriage, which crowns the comedies as being the divinely appointed sign of charity. It is for this reason that plays like *The Comedy of Errors* and *The Taming of the Shrew* are strewn with echoes of St Paul's teaching on marriage in *Ephesians* v. It is also for this reason that in the climax of *Love's Labour's Lost* the happiness of marriage has to be 'merited' by the faithful performance of deeds of charity, such as visiting the 'speechless sick' and holding converse with 'groaning wretches' (v. 2).

As for the relationship between husband and wife in

marriage, it is for Shakespeare no casual contract, to be freely broken off at the will of either partner, but an 'everlasting bond of fellowship' (*A Midsummer Night's Dream* i. 1), a 'blessed bond of board and bed' (*As You Like It* v. 4), a 'contract of eternal bond of love' (*Twelfth Night* v. 1). It is a sacrament of 'faith and constant loyalty' (*Henry V* ii. 2), which is upheld with no less constancy by the dramatist through all his plays. It is a symbol of the bond which holds all creation together, and without which all things would lapse into original chaos, as Troilus recognizes in his bitter lament over Cressida's infidelity :

> *If beauty have a soul, this is not she;*
> *If souls guide vows, if vows be sanctimony,*
> *If sanctimony be the gods' delight,*
> *If there be rule in unity itself,*
> *This is not she . . .*
> *The bonds of heav'n are slipp'd, dissolv'd and loos'd.*
>
> (v. 2)

These, incidentally, are the words not of the pagan Troilus, but of a Troilus who speaks with a thousand years of Christian tradition behind him; and it is with a full awareness of this tradition that the dramatist treats of marriage even in a setting that is ostensibly pagan.[18]

The mere fact that Shakespeare occasionally introduces passages of obscenity, or lewd characters, or brothel scenes – as in the Falstaff plays, in *Measure for Measure*, and in *Pericles* – need imply no compromise with his moral ideal. What matters is not the fact that he inserts such elements into his plays, but the context and the manner in which he inserts them. Falstaff, for instance, is an immensely amusing and largely sympathetic character; nor is his claim unfounded that 'I am not only witty in myself, but the cause that wit is in other men' (*Henry IV* Part II i. 2). Yet there is another side to his character which becomes progressively apparent in the course of the two plays of *Henry IV* – that ugly side which is described by the Prince as 'that reverend Vice, that grey Iniquity, that Father Ruffian, that Vanity in years' (ii. 4). It is this moral ugliness which has to be rejected, not only by the Prince on attaining the maturity of his kingship, but also by the audience and the literary critics, who are commonly swayed by sentiment.[19]

In this context, there occur two important passages which serve to explain, not only the Prince's attitude to his dissolute companions, but also the deeper reasons of Shakespeare for introducing obscene words and situations into his plays. The first passage in the Prince's soliloquy on his companions at the very beginning of *Henry IV* Part I :

> *I know you all, and will a while uphold*
> *The unyok'd humour of your idleness;*
> *Yet herein will I imitate the sun,*
> *Who doth permit the base contagious clouds*
> *To smother up his beauty from the world,*
> *That when he please again to be himself,*
> *Being wanted, he may be more wonder'd at,*
> *By breaking through the foul and ugly mists*
> *Of vapours that did seem to strangle him.* (i. 2)

The second passage, from Part II, is the Earl of Warwick's defence of the Prince's behaviour before the King his father – with a more explicit reference to language :

> *The prince but studies his companions*
> *Like a strange tongue, wherein, to gain the language,*
> *'Tis needful that the most immodest word*
> *Be look'd upon, and learn'd; which once attain'd,*
> *Your highness knows, comes to no further use*
> *But to be known and hated.* (iv. 4)

As for the brothel scenes in *Measure for. Measure* (ii. 1 and iii. 2) and *Pericles* (iv. 2 and 6), the way of life they depict is shown, not as a pleasurable alternative to the strict morality of Christian marriage, but as a sordid contrast to the bright chastity of the heroines, Isabella and Marina. In *Measure for Measure*, in particular, no attempt is made to extenuate the guilt even of Claudio and Juliet, though their fault is small enough in comparison with Angelo's proposed seduction of Isabella and with the general background of organized prostitution. It was, indeed, 'upon a true contract' that Claudio got possession of Juliet's bed, and all he lacked was 'the denunciation of outward order' (i. 2). Yet he admits his 'too much liberty' to Lucio (*ibid.*); and Juliet freely confesses her sin to the Duke in disguise, repenting of it, not merely as it is the cause of her present shame, but 'as it is an evil' (ii. 3). In the case of Isabella, moreover, there is no real implication that she should have consented to Angelo's wicked proposal to save her brother's life. Claudio's plea on this occasion, 'Sweet sister, let me live' (iii. 1), is shown by the context to proceed not from reason, but from selfish fear. In fact, Isabella's resolute adherence to moral principle, even if expressed with undue indignation, serves ultimately to expose the injustice of Angelo and to restore true order. Had she yielded to mere sentiment, like her critics, she would only have helped, like Hamlet's mother, to 'skin and film the ulcerous place', and so to prevent the remedy. In any case, even when she seems to give her consent and deceives the unjust judge, her brother remains without the promised reprieve – as though to emphasize the emptiness of any compact with iniquity.[20]

This firm grasp of Christian morality, retaining the clear ideal, while making allowances for human frailty, continues to characterize Shakespeare's attitude to sex (sometimes mistakenly interpreted as a Puritan attitude) in the last plays. Particular attention has been paid to two passages in *The Winter's Tale* (iv. 3) and *The Tempest* (iv. 1), where premarital intercourse is frowned upon, even between promised spouses.[21] This is, however, no puritanical restriction, but a wise reminder of the true nature of human marriage, rooted in Christian tradition. This is not just a pleasurable association of two private individuals, but a contract of love between two responsible human persons, ratified by the society in which they live and to which they are expected to make their rightful contribution.

Such is the ideal of human love and marriage which we find in Shakespeare's plays, and which accords with the teaching of Christ, while paying due regard to the respective claims of mercy and justice. Here, too, as in affairs of state, the dramatist stresses the need of maintaining justice and lawful order for the health of society; otherwise, men will only 'make a scarecrow of the law' (*Measure for Measure* ii. 1). He is not swayed by sentimental exaggeration of individual cases, so as to overlook the common good which has to be preferred before that of individuals. He recognizes, like Hamlet, that often one has to 'be cruel only to be kind' (iii. 4). Yet while upholding justice, he remembers the frailty of human nature; and this restrains him from requiring, like Angelo, more than fallen nature can bear, or from insisting, like Shylock, on strict right at the expense of mercy and charity. In this respect, his ideal is that of the medieval Morality plays, the *Ludus Coventriae* and the *Castle of Perseverance*, in which the four Daughters of God, Truth and Mercy, Justice and Peace, discuss the fate of fallen mankind and agree on a plan that satisfies their several claims – the incarnation of the Son of God.[22] Interestingly enough, this plan is traditionally represented in the symbolism of marriage, both in *Psalm* 85 :

> *Mercy and Truth have met each other, Justice and Peace have kissed each other.*

and in its elaboration by the Fathers, who explain the Incarnation as a marriage between the Son of God and human nature in the bridal chamber of the Virgin's womb. This tradition is echoed by Shakespeare in the happy endings of his comedies, especially in Hymen's Song (with its echo of *Luke* xv. 7, 10) at the end of *As You Like It* :

> *Then is there mirth in heaven,*
> *When earthly things made even*
> *Atone together.* (v. 4)

In contrast to this ideal of the comedies, the common theme of the tragedies is the grievous rent made in the moral being of man by the rejection of love. One might even say that Shakespeare identifies this moral being with love, so that, when love once given is withdrawn, nothing is left but 'chaos is come again' (*Othello* iii. 3). In *Hamlet* Polonius is not wide of the mark when he attributes the 'head and source' of the Prince's distemper to the 'neglected love' of Ophelia; only, he overlooks the deeper reason for it, namely, the previous separation of Hamlet from his father by death and from his mother by her 'o'erhasty marriage' (ii. 2). Particularly in the marriage of his mother with his uncle, following so soon on his father's death, Hamlet senses the 'most wicked speed' of matrimonial infidelity, both to her first husband and to her son by that husband (i. 2). In his present situation he feels, like Troilus, as if 'the bonds of heav'n are slipp'd, dissolv'd and loos'd' (*Troilus and Cressida* v. 2), and he consequently wishes his own being at an end :

> *O, that this too, too solid flesh would melt,*
> *Thaw and resolve itself into a dew.* (i. 2)

His feelings of disgust with the world, with women, with all mankind, with himself, his doubts, delays and hesitations, all proceed from the same emotional cause : his realization of the frailty of his mother, which he finds reflected in Ophelia's compliancy to her father's will. He finds himself alone, not through his own selfish choice, like the Machiavellian villains of other tragedies, but by the force of unchosen circumstances. It is only the friendship of Horatio that enables him to survive, and to achieve a measure of reconciliation, by way of death, with his mother and with Ophelia.

Still more grievous is the rent made in the moral being of Othello by the apparent infidelity of his wife Desdemona, and by his consequent abjuration of love for her. The manner of his abjuration is deeply impressive. Once he has been persuaded of her infidelity by Iago, he declares in a fit of passion :

> *All my fond love thus do I blow to heaven:*
> *'Tis gone.*
> *Arise, black vengeance, from the hollow hell!*
> *Yield up, O love, thy crown and hearted throne*
> *To tyrannous hate.* (iii. 3)

But the outcome of his hate proves to be a return to chaos and a moral vacuum – as he realizes, when it is too late, the moment after he has murdered his wife :

> *My wife! my wife! what wife? I have no wife.*
> *O insupportable, O heavy hour!*
> *Methinks it should be now a huge eclipse*
> *Of sun and moon, and that the affrighted globe*
> *Should yawn at alteration.* (v. 2)

This is also the case with Macbeth, whose moral chaos after the murder of Duncan is likewise presented in religious and eschatological terms. Only, he has gone further than Othello.

He has given his full consent to the temptation of evil, knowing
it to be evil. He has cut himself off from his kinsman and
sovereign, and from the company of good men, preferring to
remain with his wife, who has already given herself over to
those 'spirits that tend on mortal thoughts' (i. 5), and whose
personality thereafter disintegrates into madness. From the
moment of his sacrilegious murder, it is borne in upon him
that henceforth

> *There's nothing serious in mortality,*
> *All is but toys; renown and grace is dead,*
> *The wine of life is drawn, and the mere lees*
> *Is left this vault to brag of.* (ii. 3)

He finds that he has merely given the 'eternal jewel' of his soul
to 'the common enemy of man' (iii. 1), and that it is 'the
equivocation of the fiend' to demand all and to give nothing
substantial in return (v. 5). For him, but not for Shakespeare,
life is now no more than 'a tale told by an idiot, full of sound
and fury, signifying nothing' (*ibid.*).

The moral consequence of love's rejection is further developed, in cosmic terms, in *King Lear* and *Timon of Athens*. In
the former play, the old king, after rejecting the love of his
youngest daughter, is himself rejected by his elder daughters,
to whom he has given his all. In his excess of indignation he
summons the frame of things to disjoint, in witness to 'the
bond cracked' between father and daughters. Out in the
tempest he calls on the wild elements:

> *Blow, winds, and crack your cheeks! rage, blow,*
> *You cataracts and hurricanoes! spout*
> *Till you have drench'd our steeples, drown'd our cocks!*
> *You sulphurous and thought-executing fires,*
> *Vaunt-couriers to oak-cleaving thunderbolts,*
> *Singe my white head! and thou, all-shaking thunder,*
> *Smite flat the thick rotundity o' the world!*
> *Crack nature's moulds, all germens spill at once*
> *That make ingrateful man!* (iii. 2)

His curses are echoed by Timon, who has been rejected and
abandoned by his former friends and fellow-citizens of Athens,

and who now wishes to involve the whole of mankind in chaos.
Thus he prays to the earth :

> *Common mother, thou,*
> *Whose womb unmeasurable and infinite breast*
> *Teems and feeds all . . .*
> *Ensear thy fertile and conceptious womb,*
> *Let it no more bring out ingrateful man!* (iv. 3)

In the case of Lear, unlike that of Timon, the storm both without and within blows over, and moral order is restored through
the forgiving love of Cordelia. The scene of reconciliation
between father and daughter is, indeed, one of the most
moving scenes in human drama; and it re-echoes through the
last plays, which seem to be devoted to this one theme. In their
reunion the old king turns to his daughter with the words :

> *When thou dost ask me blessing, I'll kneel down*
> *And ask of thee forgiveness.* (v. 3)[23]

Thus the wheel of the tragedies comes full circle; and human
love is restored in a divine blessing.

In the last plays Shakespeare deals with the morality of the
relationship, not between husband and wife, nor between
sovereign and subject, but between parent and child – or,
more precisely, between father and daughter, as in *King Lear.*
He makes the daughter an ideal heroine, illustrating the virtues of constancy, fidelity, filial piety, and gratitude; and he
renews the character of Cordelia in Marina, Imogen, Perdita
and Miranda, in uninterrupted succession. In a variety of
situations he presents us with human love, first separated from
its object, whether physically (as in *Pericles*) or morally (as in
The Winter's Tale), but finally reunited in such a way that
the sorrow of separation is outweighed by the joy of reunion.
This reunion is, moreover, represented as the outcome not of
mere natural power, but of divine grace working both in and
above nature.[24] This is a theme already developed in *Macbeth,*
where the supernatural evil centred on Macbeth is dissipated
by 'the grace of Grace' (v. 7). In *King Lear* this grace is
embodied in the person of Cordelia, who is implicitly compared to Christ himself, in that she 'redeems nature from the
general curse' (iv. 6). The heroines of the subsequent

romances continue her function of embodying divine grace; and the happy ending they help to bring about is also shown as a miraculous intervention of divine providence.

Thus in the climax of *Pericles* the aged hero, looking on Marina whom he has not yet recognized as his long-lost daughter, exclaims:

> *Falseness cannot come from thee, for thou look'st*
> *Modest as justice, and thou seem'st a palace*
> *For the crown'd truth to dwell in.* (v. 1)

Then, when he at last recognizes her, he feels as if a 'great sea of joys' were overbearing 'the shores of my mortality', and he hears as it were the 'music of the spheres' (*ibid.*). Finally, through a heavenly vision of the goddess Diana, he is reunited with his lost wife Thaissa, whom he had believed dead; and joy is crowned by joy. Similarly, in the final scene of *Cymbeline*, knot after knot is untied in bewildering succession, culminating in the reconciliation of the aged king with his daughter Imogen, who has helped to bring this about by her chastity and her patience.[25] Cymbeline, like Pericles, feels as though struck 'to death with mortal joy'; for it is indeed, as the Soothsayer declares, 'the fingers of the powers above' which have tuned 'the harmony of this peace' (v. 5).

In *The Winter's Tale* there is a further elaboration of this theme, with the quality of divine grace embodied equally in 'the gracious queen', Hermione, and in her daughter Perdita, who is described as 'grown in grace equal with wondering' (Chorus to Act IV).[26] Here, too, the intervention of divine providence is evident: first, in the proclamation of Apollo's oracle and Leontes's miraculous punishment for his disobedience; and secondly, in the scarcely less miraculous restoration of Hermione to Leontes after his sixteen years of penitence. Again, there is mention of a joy that 'wades in tears', as though at the news 'of a world ransomed, or one destroyed' (v. 2). Finally, in *The Tempest* there is Miranda, who is seen from the beginning through the eyes of Ferdinand as a goddess filling his spirit with wonder (i. 2). Through their union the 'heavens rain grace', not only 'on that which breeds between them' (iii. 1), but on all the characters of the play. Here is no miraculous intervention of a deity, as in the pre-

vious plays; but all is guided to its happy outcome by Prospero's magic power. Yet here, more than in any of the previous
plays, all is attributed to the kindly guidance of 'immortal
providence', operating through the pair of lovers; and this is
emphasized by Gonzalo in his concluding prayer to the gods,
who 'have chalked forth the way which brought us hither'
(v. 1).

Among the later plays of Shakespeare, however, there is one
which has raised serious doubts concerning his adherence to
the moral ideal of Christianity. This is the Roman play of
Antony and Cleopatra, which has been hailed by Coleridge as
'of all perhaps of Shakespeare's plays the most wonderful'. The
hero is a married man seeking the embraces of another woman,
who dallies with him like a 'strumpet' (i. 1). Yet the movement of the play tends to glorify this illicit love-affair; and the
imagery of the wide world is exploited to magnify 'such a
mutual pair and such a twain' (*ibid.*), as if they were another
phoenix and turtle.[27] The culmination is reached in the
successive suicides of hero and heroine, as if they were another
Romeo and Juliet; and even more than in the early tragedy
there seems to be glory in such an end. It is not surprising,
therefore, that critics have found the poetic values of the play
dependent on the immoral acts, and have seen in the sympathy
with which these acts are portrayed a blow to traditional
morality.[28] Precisely because Antony indulges his passion for
Cleopatra with regard neither for public duty nor for private
shame he seems to vindicate a new morality – that of the
Nietzschean Superman, as adumbrated in the 'Herculean
hero' of Renaissance drama.[29] His love, repudiated though it
is by Christian ethics, is seen as somehow heavenly, involving
the noble values of loyalty and abnegation.

In order to understand the moral standard implied in
Antony and Cleopatra, it is necessary to bear in mind the total
context of Shakespearian drama. In this context we find certain plays grouping themselves in recognizable patterns. One
such pattern constitutes a prolonged study, in dramatic terms,
of the romantic conceptions of love and honour, which were
integral to the medieval ideal of chivalry and courtly love. The
conception of love is examined in *Romeo and Juliet*, where it
is shown sympathetically in the persons of the two young

lovers, but at the same time critically through the eyes of the wise old friar. His warning to them, which is repeated with variations in other plays of the same period, seems to echo the dramatist's own conviction:[30]

> These violent delights have violent ends,
> And in their triumph die, like fire and powder,
> Which, as they kiss, consume; the sweetest honey
> Is loathsome in his own deliciousness
> And in the taste confounds the appetite;
> Therefore love moderately; long love doth so;
> Too swift arrives as tardy as too slow. (ii. 6)

The parallel conception of honour is examined soon after in *Henry IV* Part I, and is implicitly criticized through the contrasting attitudes of Henry Hotspur and Prince Hal. The former is passionate in his youthful idealism, unrestrained by motives of prudence, and rushes headlong into lawless insurrection. The latter, though tempted for a time by 'riot and dishonour' (i. 1), 'in the likeness of a fat old man' (ii. 4), redeems both his time and his honour by defending the right of the king his father; and by defeating Hotspur at Shrewsbury, he crops 'the budding honours' on his crest 'to make a garland' for his own head (v. 4).[31]

The two conceptions are examined together, in a more critical vein, in *Troilus and Cressida*, where they are represented in excess without the guidance of right reason.[32] The ideal of honour is connected with the background of war, as providing the motive governing the policy of the Trojans; but it is an honour that is dishonourably rooted in adultery and injustice. Its main exponent is Troilus, who silences the opposition of Hector by his reasoning against reason:

> Nay, if we talk of reason,
> Let's shut our gates and sleep; manhood and honour
> Should have hare-hearts, would they but fat their thoughts
> With this cramm'd reason; reason and respect
> Make livers pale, and lustihood deject. (ii. 2)

It is interesting to compare his attitude with that, not only of Hotspur in *Henry IV* Part I, but also of Richard III and

Hamlet in their talk of conscience and cowardice. In the fore-ground of the dramatic action, the ideal of love is also cham-pioned by Troilus, and in the same spirit, with passion taking the place of reason. In eager anticipation of Cressida's love, he declares:

> *Even such a passion doth embrace my bosom;*
> *My heart beats thicker than a fev'rous pulse;*
> *And all my powers do their bestowing lose,*
> *Like vassalage at unawares encountering*
> *The eye of majesty.* (iii. 2)

The outcome of his attitude is, however, merely 'the expense of spirit in a waste of shame', which is defined in *Sonnet* 129 as the fruit of lust in action. It is a descent from the eternity of true love to the 'formless ruin of oblivion' which is graphically presented in the latter part of the play – in anticipation of Macbeth's hopeless 'Tomorrow and tomorrow and tomorrow' (v. 5).

These twin conceptions of love and honour are further examined in the two Roman plays to which Shakespeare turned after his great tragedies.[33] In *Coriolanus* he deals once more with the conception of honour, as embodied in a great military leader. The hero is renowned for nobility and valour, but no less for pride and fierce anger. He is magnificent as a warrior, in the conduct of war, but incapable as a statesman, in the management of peace. He is compared, not only to a god, 'made by some other deity than Nature' (iv. 6), but also to 'a lonely dragon' (iv. 1). In his triumph over Corioli, whence he derives his name, he is described – in reminiscence of Macbeth – as 'a thing of blood' whose every motion is 'timed with dying cries' (ii. 2; *cf. Macbeth* i. 2). This study of honour in *Coriolanus* is paralleled by the further study of love in *Antony and Cleopatra*. Both conceptions are here shown on a grand scale, grand in nobility and individual self-assertion, and grand in disregard of the general community of mankind. On the one hand, Antony is described as 'the demi-Atlas of this earth, the arm and burgonet of men' (i. 5) and as 'ne'er lust-wearied' (ii. 1). His grandeur is summed up by Cleopatra in a kind of panegyric:

His legs bestrid the ocean; his rear'd arm
Crested the world; his voice was propertied
As all the tuned spheres, and that to friends;
But when he meant to quail and shake the orb,
He was as rattling thunder. For his bounty,
There was no winter in't, an autumn 'twas
That grew the more by reaping; his delights
Were dolphin-like, they show'd his back above
The element they liv'd in; in his livery
Walk'd crowns and crownets, realms and islands were
As plates dropp'd from his pocket. (v. 2)

All this, however, he abandons out of lust for her, as he
wittingly makes 'his will lord of his reason' (iii. 11). Ignorant
of himself, he seeks his own harm, which, as Menecrates points
out, the wise powers would have denied him for his good (ii.
1). Only when it is too late, and he has become hardened in
vicious habit, he realizes his true situation.

But when we in our viciousness grow hard, –
O misery on't! – the wise gods seel our eyes;
In our own filth drop our clear judgments; make us
Adore our errors; laugh at's while we strut
To our confusion. (iii. 11)

Nevertheless, Antony never loses his natural nobility; but he
appears, like Milton's Satan, 'Archangel ruin'd, and th' excess
of glory obscur'd' (*Paradise Lost* I, 593–4). For this reason
the prevailing imagery of the play is splendid in its vastness,
reflecting the prodigality of his lust; but it is merely the
glittering splendour and empty vastness of the material universe. There is nothing of the metaphysical universality of
King Lear or the power of stirring the heart of man to its
depths. Even its concluding scenes are moving less in a tragic
than in a symbolic sense. They convey an impression, not so
much of tragedy, as of a drama played out in the rich
imaginations of Antony and Cleopatra. Critics may identify
themselves with these imaginations, as they have identified
themselves with the imaginations of Richard III, of Falstaff, of
Macbeth, and of Edmund.[34] But this does not mean that the
dramatist identified himself with them, thus deliberately limit-

ing the universality of his imagination. Rather, within the framework of a Roman play he is developing the conception of romantic love to its utmost limits, so as to lay bare its intrinsic contradiction between 'the nobleness of life' and the self-assertion of the lovers. Thus, while we can sympathize with the hero and heroine, we are prevented, both by the play itself and by its wider dramatic context, from giving them our undivided sympathy.

As for the problem of suicide, which is raised in the same play, it also has to be considered in view of its total dramatic context. Other plays of Shakespeare have a similar climax in suicide; and together they form another dramatic pattern. *Antony and Cleopatra* may be compared to a mighty river fed by tributaries, the previous Roman play, *Julius Caesar*, on the one hand, and the previous romantic tragedies, *Romeo and Juliet* and *Othello*, on the other. In all of these plays suicide seems to appear in a sympathetic light, as a justifiable means of 'taking arms against a sea of troubles' (*Hamlet* iii. 1). But once again we have to beware of deception by 'false seeming' and examine the cases of suicide in the context of each play and of all the plays together. In *Romeo and Juliet*, not only is the conception of romantic love implicitly criticized from the viewpoint of the friar, but Romeo's proposal to commit suicide out of despair is roundly condemned by him :

> *Hold thy desperate hand!*
> *Art thou a man? Thy form cries out thou art;*
> *Thy tears are womanish; thy wild acts denote*
> *The unreasonable fury of a beast;*
> *Unseemly woman in a seeming man,*
> *Or ill-beseeming beast in seeming both!* (iii. 3)

When Romeo finally does commit suicide beside the lifeless form of Juliet, it is presented as the fruit of misunderstanding and as a 'lamentable chance' (v. 3). When Juliet adds her self-immolation to his, she does but bring a 'glooming peace' to the morning (*ibid.*). In their tragic end is no rejoicing but only woe, even if good is drawn out of the evil by the subsequent reconciliation of Montague and Capulet.

In *Julius Caesar*, as being a Roman play and therefore pre-Christian in setting, there is a larger measure of sympathy for

the suicides of Cassius and Brutus. But even here the two
tragedies are prefaced with expressions of disapproval. Before
his death, Brutus himself avows :

> *I do find it cowardly and vile,*
> *For fear of what might fall, so to prevent*
> *The time of life; arming myself with patience,*
> *To stay the providence of some high powers*
> *That govern us below.* (v. 1)

Later, Messala attributes the too hasty death of Cassius to
mere error :

> *O hateful error, melancholy's child!*
> *Why dost thou show to the apt thoughts of men*
> *The things that are not? O error, soon conceiv'd,*
> *Thou never com'st unto a happy birth,*
> *But kill'st the mother that engender'd thee.* (v. 3)

It is indeed error, guided by the avenging ghost of Caesar,
which turns the swords of Cassius and Brutus into their
'proper entrails' (v. 3), and causes them to be their own
executioners for the crime of Caesar's murder.

Similarly in *Othello* it is error, guided by the spirit of
revenge incarnated in Iago, which turns the hero's sword
against himself, once he has recognized his injustice in murdering Desdemona. He is noble in death, and 'great of heart' even
in the act of suicide; but he is 'perplex'd in the extreme' (v .2).
Subjectively, he is convinced of his own damnation, as he
exclaims in a fit of remorse :

> *O cursed, cursed slave! Whip me, ye devils,*
> *From the possession of this heavenly sight!*
> *Blow me about in winds! Roast me in sulphur!*
> *Wash me in steep-down gulfs of liquid fire!* (v. 2)

In the same spirit, he implicitly compares himself to Judas, the
'base Judean', who also kissed his Master before killing him,
and who also committed suicide in remorse.[35]

In other tragedies suicide is contemplated, but not consum-
mated. These have also to be taken into account in determining
the dramatist's attitude. From the beginning of *Hamlet*, we
find the hero considering the possibility, even the desirability

of suicide. He only refrains in view of the canon fixed by the Everlasting ' 'gainst self-slaughter' (i. 2). In his later soliloquy, 'To be or not to be', he is still preoccupied with the same possibility; but he still shrinks from taking 'arms against a sea of troubles', not so much because of a canon to the contrary, but because of his 'dread of something after death' – the nightmare that may come to trouble his eternal sleep (iii. 1). He reproaches himself with cowardice in following his conscience, instead of prosecuting his revenge (like Laertes) or yielding to his despair (like Ophelia). But he does, in effect, follow his conscience, and so he comes to perceive a truth he had hitherto overlooked, namely that

> *There's a divinity that shapes our ends,*
> *Rough-hew them how we will.* (v. 2)

Consequently, when he finds his friend Horatio about to share his fate by way of suicide, he angrily restrains him in words that recall those of the friar to Romeo :

> *As thou'rt a man,*
> *Give me the cup; let go; I'll have't.* (v. 2)

Stronger still is the disapproval of suicide in *King Lear*. Both Lear and Gloucester are tempted by the extremity of their sufferings to take their own lives. The first concern of Cordelia on arriving in Britain is to find out her mad father,

> *Lest his ungovern'd rage dissolve the life*
> *That wants the means to lead it.* (iv. 4)

Similarly, but more graphically, when the afflicted Gloucester is driven by desperation to throw himself down a cliff, he is – as it seems to him, miraculously – preserved from death by his faithful son, Edgar. Thenceforth he resolves to 'bear affliction till it do cry itself, Enough, enough'; and in his resolution he is warmly seconded by Edgar : 'Bear free and patient thoughts' (iv. 6). Soon afterwards, on finding his father again 'in ill thoughts', Edgar renews his exhortation in words that may be said to sum up the moral lesson of the play :

> *Men must endure*
> *Their going hence, even as their coming hither;*
> *Ripeness is all.* (v. 2)

In the final scene it has been maintained that Kent, like Horatio, is thinking of suicide when he speaks of a journey 'shortly to go' in the footsteps of his royal master.[36] But from the previous speech of Edgar we know that he is in any case on the point of death, and his 'strings of life' are already beginning to crack for grief (v. 3).

As for *Macbeth*, suicide is mentioned only with contempt, by Macbeth himself in his hour of despair, in words that may have reference either to Brutus and Cassius or to Antony:

> *Why should I play the Roman fool, and die*
> *On mine own sword?* (v. 7)

In conclusion, it may be said that the prevailing tendency in the plays of Shakespeare, from first to last, is an insistence on the search for reality beneath outward appearances and for truth behind the deceptiveness of ornament. This is his aim in every question – whether of political order, as in the histories and tragedies, or of romantic love and honour, as in the comedies and Roman plays. This aim is more and more clearly defined in terms of a true knowledge of man, which means a true knowledge of oneself – a definition which, as we have seen, owes as much to the *Homilies* and the homiletic tradition of the Middle Ages as to Montaigne and the secular tradition of the Classics. For Shakespeare, as for the homilist, to know oneself means primarily 'to remember what we be of ourselves', namely, that we are 'but ground, earth and ashes, and that to earth and ashes we shall return', and this is 'the most commendable virtue of humility' ('Of the Misery of All Mankind'). Such is indeed the main emphasis of the great tragedies, from *Hamlet* to *King Lear*, with their penetrating analysis of the psychology of sinful man. What they propose is no mere speculative Narcissism, but a self-knowledge that leads, in a practical way, to repentance and forgiveness, in view of St Paul's teaching that 'all have sinned and do need the glory of God' (*Rom.* iii. 23).[37] It is in so far as man learns, with Lear, to recognize his sinfulness, as reflected in the wretched condition of the mad beggar, that he enters on the way of salvation.[38] In this recognition he is reconciled to his better self (Cordelia) and weaned away from his baser self (Goneril and Regan); and at the same time he perceives his relationship with all men, particularly with the 'poor naked wretches' who are unprotected by the pomp and commodity of this world (iii. 4). Finally, in his reconciliation with his better self, he perceives his relationship, not only with his fellow-men, but also with Christ (as he is figured in Cordelia), and he receives the spirit of repentance, which is the condition of his forgiveness.

Thus it is that in play after play – from *Two Gentlemen of Verona*, where the principle is first stated by Valentine (v. 4), to *The Tempest*, where the repentance solemnly urged by Ariel (iii. 3) is crowned by Prospero's final words of forgiveness (v. 1) – Shakespeare rings the changes on the themes, not only of recognition and acceptance, but also of repentance and forgiveness. And in repentance what he evidently prizes most of all is the first beatitude of the Sermon on the Mount, which he rephrases as 'the blessedness of being little' (*Henry VIII* iv. 2).

XII

Theology

IMPLICIT IN Shakespeare's moral viewpoint are certain theological presuppositions, inasmuch as his philosophy is not confined to the earthly life of man, but

> *Like to the lark at break of day arising*
> *From sullen earth, sings hymns at heaven's gate.*
>
> (*Sonnet* 29)

Deep in his poems and his plays is a divine impatience with the limitations of 'this vile world' (*Sonnet* 71; *Henry VI* Part II v. 2), 'sad mortality' (*Sonnet* 65), and 'devouring Time' (*Sonnet* 19; *Love's Labour's Lost* i. 1). Conversely, there is an undying fascination in what lies beyond the temporal arena of this world, counterbalancing that 'dread of something after death' which is the burden of Hamlet's melancholy reflections (iii. 1). It is precisely this movement of his thought which imparts to Shakespeare's work its peculiar tone of profundity and resonance, distinguishing it from that of his contemporaries. Yet it has been interpreted by his critics in a strange variety of senses. The fascination itself is undeniable; but doubt is often expressed concerning its utterances – whether they are consistent with the orthodox Christian tradition, or even consistent among themselves. Some critics fail to find any consistency in these utterances, and regard the poet as merely utilitarian in his approach to theology, making use of theological concepts merely for their poetic or dramatic value.[1]

Others find a consistent theology, whether Scholastic or Neo-
Platonic, within particular plays, but not in all the plays
together.[2] Others find in the plays a consistent refusal to
dramatize theological concepts, but justify this refusal with
reference to contemporary theological opinion.[3] Others again
detect a deeper consistency in Shakespeare's theological utterances, but maintain that it is fundamentally at variance with
orthodox Christianity.[4]

A contemporary proof of Shakespeare's 'heterodoxy' (in the
Catholic meaning of that word) has been found in the
thorough censorship of the Second Folio of the plays by a
Jesuit priest, William Sankey, acting on behalf of the Spanish
Inquisition in the mid-seventeenth century.[5] In addition to
various deletions made in the name of sexual morality, after
the fashion of Thomas Bowdler in the nineteenth century,
Sankey was particularly severe with the passages in *King John*
and *Henry VIII* which contain anti-Roman sentiments, such
as John's defiance of the Pope (iii. 1) and Cranmer's prophetic praise of Queen Elizabeth (v. 5). Above all, he cut out
Measure for Measure altogether, though it has since been
recognized as the most Christian of Shakespeare's plays. This
has been attributed to the fact that the Duke in the play
assumes the habit and the prerogatives of a priest – a presum-
able outrage to orthodox Catholic feeling. On the other hand,
none of the deletions have any direct bearing on theological
questions; and it might be argued that their purpose is wholly
practical – not to condemn the dramatist, but to avoid the
danger of scandal to Catholic schoolboys, that is to say, to the
boys at the English College, Valladolid, where Sankey 'was in
charge and signed the books'. From the nature of his deletions
it seems that he paid attention rather to the individual meaning of phrases and speeches than to the general meaning of the
context. His rejection of *Measure for Measure* probably has
less to do with the Duke's disguise, which in a play is hardly
objectionable even for Catholics, than with the pervading
reference to sexual immorality, whose piecemeal deletion
would have left the play unintelligible as a whole.

Returning to the plays themselves, it is important for their
proper understanding to put aside the modern prejudices
against 'orthodoxy' and 'dogma', which have little relevance

to the sixteenth century. When we calmly consider the way Shakespeare refers to various points of theology, we find that he refers to them far more extensively than is commonly realized. We also find that he observes an inner consistency both within his plays as a whole and with the theological tradition of Christianity – parallel to that which we have noticed in his moral viewpoint. This consistency is not necessarily the outcome of original thought or profound speculation. Rather, it may be seen as the expression of a deep personal faith, enriched by the theological inheritance of the Middle Ages, and stimulated by the continuing concern of medieval theologians and Renaissance thinkers for a synthesis between reason and revelation, between the Book of Nature and the Book of Scripture.[6]

If the moral philosophy of Shakespeare may be said to consist, like that of Socrates, in the task of preparing for a good death – as in Hamlet's 'The readiness is all' (v. 2) and Edgar's 'Ripeness is all' (*King Lear,* v. 2); his theology may be seen as having its point of departure in the consideration of death itself and of what lies beyond. In this respect, he follows the popular (as distinct from the scholastic) tradition of theology, which may be called a theology of 'the four last things' – death, judgement, hell, and heaven.[7]

In the first place, Shakespeare's view of death is by no means limited to the famous passages on the fear of death in *Hamlet* and *Measure for Measure*. When Hamlet speaks of his 'dread of something after death' (iii. 1), he utters a natural sentiment without necessarily retracting his Christian conviction of the existence of heaven and hell, which he subsequently takes for granted in the prayer-scene with Claudius. Similarly, when Claudio betrays his human fear of death – 'Ay, but to die and go we know not where' (iii. 1) – he is not necessarily calling in question his previously expressed faith in 'the words of heaven' (i. 2). Besides these passages there are others, no less significant, though less famous, which reiterate the Christian view of death as a separation of soul and body, each returning to its native abode, the body to its mother, the earth, and the soul to its heavenly Father. Thus in *Romeo and Juliet* the friar comforts the parents of Juliet as they mourn for her apparent death :

> *Heaven and yourself*
> *Had part in this fair maid: now heaven hath all,*
> *And all the better is it for the maid;*
> *Your part in her you could not keep from death,*
> *But heaven keeps his part in eternal life.* (iv. 5)

In similar terms Balthasar, a layman, brings Romeo the news of Juliet's death:

> *Her body sleeps in Capel's monument,*
> *And her immortal part with angels lives.* (v. 1)

This antithesis of body and soul, earth and heaven, is repeated again and again in the history plays. In *Richard III* the dying King Edward declares to those around his bed:

> *And more in peace my soul shall part to heaven,*
> *Since I have made my friends at peace on earth.*
>
> (ii. 1)

Later, the condemned Duke of Buckingham punningly contrasts the day of his execution, 'All-Souls' Day', with the event that is to take place, 'my body's doomsday' (v. 1). In *King John* the dying words of Prince Arthur are: 'Heaven take my soul, and England keep my bones!' The subsequent death of the King is also represented as a separation between the 'clod' or 'clay' of his body, which remains on earth, and his soul, which takes its flight to 'lasting rest' in heaven (v. 7). In *Richard II* there is an even greater abundance of such expressions. Bolingbroke declares before Mowbray that for what he speaks

> *My body shall make good upon this earth,*
> *Or my divine soul answer it in heaven.* (i. 1)

After the suspension of their combat at Coventry, he further declares:

> *By this time, had the king permitted us,*
> *One of our souls had wander'd in the air,*
> *Banish'd the frail sepulchre of our flesh.* (i. 3)

Later, on his return to England, he arrests Bushy and Green for their evil counsel to Richard, and tells them that 'presently your souls must part your bodies' (iii. 1). Richard himself, in the following scene, speaks of 'this flesh which walls about our life' (iii. 2); and in the moment of death he exclaims:

> *Mount, mount, my soul! thy seat is up on high,*
> *Whilst my gross flesh sinks downward, here to die.*
>
> (v. 5)

The fate of Mowbray after his banishment is described by the Bishop of Carlisle, culminating in his death at Venice, where he gave

> *His body to that pleasant country's earth,*
> *And his pure soul unto his captain Christ.* (iv. 1)[8]

Naturally, these expressions mainly occur in a Christian context, that of Renaissance Italy and medieval England; but the frequency with which they recur is impressive. They are also echoed by the poet speaking in his own person, in the most religious of his *Sonnets*, which is based on this very contrast between his 'poor soul' and his 'sinful earth'. The latter is but a 'fading mansion', to which Death comes at the end of 'hours of dross'; whereas the former looks to 'terms divine' that follow and transcend Death (146). The same idea is finally ratified, in more openly Christian terms, in the formula of his will, to which Shakespeare attached his signature: 'I commend my soul into the hands of God my Creator, hoping and assuredly believing through the only merits of Jesus Christ my Saviour to be made partaker of life everlasting, and my body to the earth whereof it is made.'

Human life itself is occasionally described as a 'way to heaven' through the performance of good deeds, by Corin in *As You Like It* (ii. 4) and by Ophelia in *Hamlet* (i. 3). The issue of salvation or damnation is evidently regarded by Shakespeare as an intensely serious matter, providing him with the mainspring of tragedy in such plays as *Othello* and *Macbeth*. Yet he can also treat it light-heartedly – as he treats the grim facts of contemporary tortures and executions – in the amusing malapropisms of Dogberry in *Much Ado About Nothing*: 'Thou wilt be condemned into everlasting redemption for this' (iv. 2), and of the grave-digger in *Hamlet*: 'Is she to be buried in Christian burial that wilfully seeks her own salvation?' (v. 1). Similarly, he finds in it matter for the comic repartee between the Clown and Olivia in *Twelfth Night* :

C.   *Good madonna, why mournest thou?*
O.   *Good fool, for my brother's death.*
C.   *I think his soul is in hell, madonna.*
O.   *I know his soul is in heaven, fool.*
C.   *The more fool, madonna, to mourn for your*
     brother's soul being in heaven. (i. 5)

Such passages further imply the traditional belief in the immortality of the soul and in the after life, including reward in heaven and punishment in hell. This belief furnishes a climax to *Hamlet* in Horatio's farewell to the dying prince :

> *Good night, sweet prince,*
> *And flights of angels sing thee to thy rest!* (v. 2)

In *Measure for Measure* the theme of preparation for death, which is underlined by the Duke in his activities as a friar, culminates in the contrast drawn in the last scene between the 'stubborn soul' of Barnardine, who 'apprehends no further than this world', and Isabella's expectation of 'another comfort than this world'. This comfort is precisely identified by the Duke as that 'better life, past fearing death', in heaven (v. 1). In *Othello* the immortality of the soul is implied by Cassio, when filled with remorse for his drunkenness he exclaims: 'I have lost the immortal part of myself, and what remains is bestial' (ii. 3). Similarly, in *Macbeth* the hero realizes after he has murdered Duncan that he has given his 'eternal jewel' to 'the common enemy of man' (iii. 1). Moreover, the theological foundation of immortality, that man is created to the image and likeness of God (*cf. Gen.* i. 27), is alluded to several times in the plays : in *Measure for Measure*, 'heaven's image' (ii. 4); in *Henry VIII*, 'the image of his Maker' (iii. 2); and in *Richard III*, 'the precious image of our dear Redeemer' (ii. 1), with reference to the new creation of mankind through Christ's redemption.

As for the life after death, the traditional distinction between a particular judgement soon after death and the general judgement at the Last Day is implied in the different references, on the one hand, to death as the day of doom for each individual and, on the other hand, to the general Doom, or Doomsday. Examples of the former occur in two early plays: in *Titus Andronicus*: 'This is the day of doom for Bassianus' (ii. 3); and – as noted above – in *Richard III*: 'Then All-Souls' Day is my body's doomsday' (v. 1). References to the general judgement are, however, more widely extended through all the plays and have an important role in the imagery of the tragedies. In *Romeo and Juliet* the heroine, on hearing the news of Romeo's duel with Tybalt, fears the worst and exclaims: 'Then, dreadful trumpet, sound the general doom!' (iii. 2). The same thought occurs to the hero, as he awaits the prince's judgement in the friar's cell: 'What less than dooms-day is the prince's doom?' (iii. 3). Even in the Roman plays there is mention of 'doomsday': in *Julius Caesar*, where immediately after Caesar's murder Trebonius describes how

> *Men, wives and children stare, cry out and run*
> *As it were doomsday.* (iii. 1)

And in *Antony and Cleopatra*, where Cleopatra prepares for her death, assuring Charmian:

> *And when thou hast done this chare, I'll give thee leave*
> *To play till doomsday.* (v. 2)

In *Hamlet* the former mention is recalled by Horatio on the occasion of the ghost's appearance, though he refers rather to the portents in Rome 'a little ere the mightiest Julius fell', when the moon 'was sick almost to doomsday with eclipse' (i. 1). In *Othello* the imagery of the culminating scene seems to move between an allusion to the 'huge eclipse of sun and moon' that took place at the death of Christ (*Luke* xxiii. 45) and a pre-monition of the great 'compt' when the hero fears a look from his wife 'will hurl my soul from heaven, and fiends will snatch at it' (v. 2). In *Macbeth*, above all, we have a dramatic representation of 'the great doom's image', when Duncan's murder is followed by the ominous knocking at the gate. Macduff cries out, 'Awake! awake!' and more significantly, 'As from your graves rise up, and walk like sprites', like an Angel of Judgement.[9] He calls for 'the alarum-bell'; but Lady Macbeth hears it as 'a hideous trumpet', as it were the Angel's trumpet sounding the general doom (ii. 3).

The issue of the judgement, in terms of eternal salvation or damnation, is also an underlying feature in the imagery particularly of the tragedies. One might even say that the doctrine of heaven and hell is no less essential to the imagery of these plays than to the teaching of Christ himself. It recurs in them again and again, and fills them with their deep and universal resonance.[10] In *Romeo and Juliet* the imagery of hell is used in the parallel scenes which represent the similar reactions of Juliet and Romeo to the news of the latter's banishment. In Juliet's case, she is indignant with her Nurse for the ominous uncertainty in which she veils the fate of Romeo:

> *What devil art thou that dost torment me thus?*
> *This torture should be roar'd in dismal hell.* (iii. 2)

As for Romeo, on hearing of his banishment from the friar, he exclaims in protest:

> *There is no world without Verona's walls,*
> *But purgatory, torture, hell itself.*
> *... Banished!*
> *O friar! the damned use that word in hell.*
>
> (iii. 3)[11]

On the other hand, heaven is presented by the friar as the agent both of the marriage:

> *So smile the heavens upon this holy act.* (ii. 6)

and of its tragic outcome:

> *Bear this work of heaven with patience.* (v. 3)

Among the history plays, this contrast between heaven and hell is particularly marked in *Richard II*. On the one hand, heaven is seen as the place of comfort – by York: 'Comfort's in heaven; and we are on the earth' (ii. 2), and by Green: 'My comfort is, that heaven will take our souls' (iii. 1). On the other hand, Green in the same passage calls down 'the pains of hell' on his enemies; and Richard in his final scene first strikes a servant, exclaiming: 'Go thou and fill another room in hell', and then on being himself struck down by Exton continues:

> *That hand shall burn in never-quenching fire*
> *That staggers thus my person.* (v. 5)

Heaven is also mentioned by York as the supreme arbiter in earthly disputes, in words that echo those of the friar in *Romeo and Juliet* :

> *But heaven hath a hand in these events,*
> *To whose high will we bound our calm contents.*
>
> (v. 2)

In *Hamlet* the contrast enters into the deep framework of the play, largely owing to the presence of the ghost, who serves to raise 'thoughts beyond the reaches of our souls' (i. 4). The eternal dimension which he introduces is expressed in the words of Hamlet, both at the first encounter :

> *Angels and ministers of grace, defend us!*
> *Be thou a spirit of health, or goblin damn'd,*
> *Bring with thee airs of heaven, or blasts from hell.*
>
> (i. 4)

and at his disappearance :

> *O all you host of heaven! O earth! what else?*
> *And shall I couple hell?* (i. 5)

This dimension is again apparent in the climax of the play, when Hamlet senses hell itself breathing out 'contagion to the world' (iii. 2), and when he only refrains from killing Claudius at prayer on reflecting that 'so he goes to heaven', whereas it is his avowed intention to

> *Trip him, that his heels may kick at heaven,*
> *And that his soul may be as damn'd and black*
> *As hell, whereto it goes.* (iii. 3)

The moment passes; and in his subsequent interview with his mother, when he persuades her to repentance, the emphasis is no longer on hell, but on heaven, which is mentioned no less than five times. Even the second appearance of the ghost evokes no thought of hell, but only an appeal for the protection of 'heavenly guards' (iii. 4).

It is above all in *Othello* and *Macbeth* that a central place is given to the imagery of heaven and hell. In the former play, 'hell and night' (i. 3) are indicated as the spiritual habitat of Iago who, as a 'demi-devil' (v. 2), engineers both the death of Desdemona and the 'damnation' of Othello. Whereas Desdemona is welcomed to Cyprus by Cassio with 'the grace of heaven' (ii. 1), Othello shows how far he has yielded to Iago's temptation when he displaces the thought of heaven for that of hell:

> *All my fond love thus do I blow to heaven:*
> *'Tis gone.*
> *Arise, black vengeance, from the hollow hell!*
>
> (iii. 3)

In the tragic outcome, whereas Desdemona dies with a prayer for the mercy of heaven on her lips, Othello is filled with remorse at the sight of her corpse and anticipates his damnation:

> *O cursed, cursed slave! Whip me, ye devils,*
> *From the possession of this heavenly sight!*
> *Blow me about in winds! roast me in sulphur!*
> *Wash me in steep-down gulfs of liquid fire!* (v. 2)

As for *Macbeth*, the atmosphere of hell pervades the play from the beginning, with the appearance of the witches as 'instruments of darkness' (i. 3), and the opening invocation by Lady Macbeth:

> *Come, thick night,*
> *And pall thee in the dunnest smoke of hell,*
> *That my keen knife see not the wound it makes,*
> *Nor heaven peep through the blanket of the dark,*
> *To cry, Hold, hold!* (i. 5)

The subsequent murder of Duncan is announced beforehand – in Macbeth's imagination – by the 'bell' that is a 'knell' summoning him 'to heaven or to hell' (ii. 1). Its immediate consequence is as it were to transform the castle, for all its 'delicate air' outside (i. 6), into a replica of hell, guarded by the 'porter of hell-gate' (ii. 3). From this moment, Macbeth proceeds along a path of crime that turns him into a 'hellhound' (v. 7), till Macduff can exclaim of him:

> *Not in the legions*
> *Of horrid hell can come a devil more damn'd*
> *In evils to top Macbeth.* (iv. 3)

In contrast, the two legitimate kings, Duncan of Scotland and
Edward of England, are attended by the sanctity of heaven.
The murder of Duncan is 'most sacrilegious' (ii. 3), not only
because he is invested with the sacred office of kingship, but
also because in his personal life he

> *Hath borne his faculties so meek, hath been*
> *So clear in his great office, that his virtues*
> *Will plead like angels trumpet-tongu'd against*
> *The deep damnation of his taking off.* (i. 7)

Macduff openly calls him 'a most sainted king' and adds concerning his queen – apparently confusing her with St Margaret of Scotland, who was historically Malcolm's queen –
that she was 'oft'ner upon her knees than on her feet' and
'died every day she liv'd' (iv. 3). As for Edward, the 'sanctity'
of his touch, the efficacy of his 'holy prayers', and his 'heavenly
gift of prophecy' are emphasized in such a way as to suggest
that the restoration of peace and justice to Scotland is the work
of heaven. And at the end the new king Malcolm proposes to
set about his task 'by the grace of Grace' (v. 7).

In addition to the fundamental contrast between heaven
and hell, there are occasional references in the plays to the
Catholic beliefs in limbo, or *limbus patrum*, and purgatory.
Limbo is mentioned four times : by Dromio of Syracuse in *The
Comedy of Errors*: 'He's in Tartar limbo, worse than hell' (iv.
2); by Titus in *Titus Andronicus*: 'As far from help as limbo
is from bliss' (iii. 1); by Parolles in *All's Well That Ends Well*:
'Of Satan, and of limbo, and of Furies' (v. 3); and by the
Porter in *Henry VIII* : 'I have some of 'em in Limbo Patrum'
(v. 4). Purgatory is mentioned by name only twice : in *Romeo
and Juliet*, where the hero exclaims: 'There is no world without Verona's walls, but purgatory . . .' (iii. 3); and in *Othello*,
where Emilia says she 'should venture purgatory' for the whole
world (iv. 3). The latter belief, however, has a deeper influence on Shakespeare's imagination than is often realized. In
Hamlet there is a clear implication of purgatory in the ghost's

description of 'the secrets of my prison-house', which are all the more impressive for his refusal to divulge them. The purgatorial nature of his pains is deduced from the temporal limit of his punishment,

> *Till the foul crimes done in my days of nature*
> *Are burnt and purg'd away.* (i. 5)[12]

The implication of purgatory is later confirmed by the oddness of Hamlet's oath, 'by Saint Patrick' – with reference to the legendary St Patrick's Purgatory, of which mention has been made in an earlier chapter.[13]

Various apocryphal ideas of purgatory that were current in the Middle Ages, without belonging to the official teaching of the Church, are echoed in several plays. In *Measure for Measure* Claudio imagines the fate of his spirit after death :

> *To bathe in fiery floods, or to reside*
> *In thrilling region of thick-ribbed ice;*
> *To be imprison'd in the viewless winds,*
> *And blown with restless violence round about*
> *The pendant world.* (iii. 1)[14]

Likewise, in *Othello* the hero draws on his imagination of the after life in calling down punishment on himself for his crime :

> *Blow me about in winds! roast me in sulphur!*
> *Wash me in steep-down gulfs of liquid fire!* (v. 2)

Parallel ideas to these have been noted in *The Golden Legend*, which was very popular in England up to the time of the Reformation, and before that in Chaucer's *Parliament of Fowls* :

> *But brekers of the lawe, soth to seyne,*
> *And likerous folk, after that they ben dede,*
> *Shul whirle aboute th'erthe alwey in peyne,*
> *Tyl many a world be passed, out of drede.* (78–81)

Persons, too, in his *Christian Directory*, speaks of the punishments that await sinners after death, where the fire, whether of purgatory or of hell, is said to have 'contrary extreme effects, both of heat and cold'.

Above all, the pains of purgatory may be found dramatized

in an earthly setting in *King Lear*; for what the old king goes through is a purgatory on earth. For his fault in banishing Cordelia and listening to his wicked daughters, he is punished by exposure to 'the fretful elements' (iii. 1). Accepting his punishment, he calls on the 'sulphurous and thought-executing fires' to singe his 'white head' (iii. 2). Subsequently, in his delirious imagination he feels himself 'bound upon a wheel of fire, that mine own tears do scald like molten lead' (iv. 7) – with reference not merely to classical legend, but also to the apocryphal tradition of the Middle Ages.[15] His sufferings are not only comparable to medieval representations of purgatory, but – what is more important – they have a purgatorial effect in cleansing his soul of pride, and in teaching him the humility appropriate to 'unaccommodated man' (iii. 4). They serve to prepare him for the culminating moment of his reunion with Cordelia, when he looks on her as though she were 'a soul in bliss' (iv. 7).

This reunion of Lear with Cordelia is the turning-point not only of *King Lear*, but of Shakespeare's whole dramatic career. It expresses in dramatic form his deeply experienced solution to the problem of evil, which he has explored so painfully in *Othello* and *Macbeth*. It thus forms a bridge of his imagination from the 'inferno' of the tragedies to the 'paradiso' of the last plays.[16] In these last plays, it seems as if the dramatist is aiming time and time again to recapture the bliss of that reunion between Lear and Cordelia. As he is to her, so Pericles is to Marina, Cymbeline is to Imogen, and Leontes is to Perdita. In each case, the loss or separation of father from daughter is comparable to purgatory; and the subsequent recovery and reunion of father with daughter is comparable to paradise, where the previous experience of sorrow only serves to augment the supervening joy. In *Pericles* the change from sorrow to joy is so sudden that the father fears lest 'this great sea of joys' may overbear the shores of his mortality; and he hears that 'music of the spheres' which is granted only to immortal souls (v. 1; *cf. The Merchant of Venice* v. 1). In *Cymbeline*, too, the father feels in his reunion with his daughter that 'the gods do mean to strike me to death with mortal joy'; and in his further reunion with his long-lost sons he declares they are 'worthy to inlay heaven with stars' (v. 5). In

The Winter's Tale the father experiences a similar mixture of 'joy and sorrow' in the return home of his lost daughter; and in his eventual reunion with his wife his joy is presented in terms of resurrection and new life (v. 3). Finally, in *The Tempest* all leads up to the concluding scene of reconciliation between the two fathers, cemented in the union of their son and daughter – looking towards a 'brave new world' and rejoicing 'beyond a common joy' which is hardly that of earth, but of heaven (v. 1).

Concerning this word 'heaven', we may further note that it is used by Shakespeare not only as a place of future reward, among the 'four last things', but also as a present influence on human life. In this sense it becomes a synonym for God himself, according to the common idiom of the New Testament. From this point, therefore, we may go on to examine the various names attributed to God in the plays and the extent to which they indicate the underlying thought of the dramatist. No doubt, many of the utterances concerning God may be described as 'virtual clichés, ranging from conventional piety to conventional expletive'; but it is interesting to see how, taken together, they grow 'to something of great constancy' (*A Midsummer Night's Dream* v. 1).[17]

In the early plays 'heaven' is often mentioned as God's dwelling-place, as in the opening words of the Lord's Prayer. Thus in *Richard III* Richard of Gloucester refers to 'the King of heaven' (i. 2); and in *Richard II* Northumberland speaks of God in the same manner (iii. 3). In *Henry VI* Part II the pious king uses the plural form in his invocation, 'O thou eternal Mover of the heavens!' (iii. 3). In *Romeo and Juliet* invocation is made by the Nurse to 'God in heaven' (ii. 4); and in other plays of the period the simpler form 'above' is often used.

The attribute of justice is noticeable in the early history plays, where the general theme of retribution is strongly emphasized. Thus in *Henry VI* Part II the King makes his prayer:

> *O thou that judgest all things, stay my thoughts . . .*
> *For judgment only doth belong to thee.* (iii. 2)

In *Richard III* Queen Margaret, as the mouthpiece of divine retribution in the play, makes her appeal to the 'upright, just and true-disposing God' (iv. 4). In *King John* the dispute between the two kings over the possession of Angiers is deepened by the appeal of either king to divine justice. Whereas John claims to be 'God's wrathful agent', Philip appeals on behalf of Arthur to 'that supernal Judge, that stirs good thoughts' (ii. 1). The best known of all Shakespeare's references to God's justice, however, occurs in Claudius's soliloquy in *Hamlet*, where the King recognizes the contrast between this world below, with all its bribery and corruption, and heaven 'above':

> *There is no shuffling, there the action lies*
> *In his true nature, and we ourselves compell'd*
> *Even to the teeth and forehead of our faults*
> *To give in evidence.* (iii. 3)

On the other hand, the complementary attribute of mercy also has its roots in the early plays, especially in the opening scene of *Titus Andronicus*, where Tamura pleads with Titus for the life of her son:

> *Wilt thou draw near the nature of the gods?*
> *Draw near them then in being merciful.* (i. 1)

The sentiment has its well-known development in Portia's appeal to Shylock in the trial-scene of *The Merchant of Venice*:

> *The quality of mercy is not strain'd . . .*
> *But mercy is above this sceptred sway,*
> *It is enthroned in the hearts of kings,*
> *It is an attribute to God himself.* (iv. 1)

And this is in turn elaborated by Isabella in her corresponding appeal to Angelo in *Measure for Measure*:

> *No ceremony that to great ones 'longs,*
> *Not the king's crown, nor the deputed sword,*
> *The marshal's truncheon, nor the judge's robe,*
> *Become them with one half so good a grace*
> *As mercy does.* (ii. 2)

Other significant references occur in the plays of the early period to the power of God in controlling human events. In *Romeo and Juliet* the friar comments on the tragic end of the lovers:

> *A greater power than we can contradict*
> *Hath thwarted our intents.* (v. 3)

In *King John* the citizens of Angiers reject the claim of the English king, saying, in similar words:

> *A greater power than we denies all this.* (ii. 1)

In *Richard II* the divine power is associated with the 'divine right' of the king, both in Carlisle's exhortation:

> *Fear not, my lord; that power that made you king*
> *Hath power to keep you king in spite of all.* (iii. 2)

and in Richard's own defiance of Northumberland:

> *Yet know, my master, God omnipotent*
> *Is mustering in his clouds on our behalf*
> *Armies of pestilence.* (iii. 3)

In the same scene Richard also uses the Scriptural metaphor of 'the hand of God'; and this is further used on several occasions in *Henry V*. In the latter play, the King, whose piety is hardly inferior to that of his son, the pious King Henry VI, from the beginning entrusts his 'puissance into the hand of God' (ii. 2). Then, in the hour of crisis he assures his brother, 'We are in God's hand' (iii. 6). Finally, on hearing of his victory at Agincourt, he ascribes it to the divine power:

> *O God, thy arm was here;*
> *And not to us, but to thy arm alone,*
> *Ascribe we all.* (iv. 8)

Echoes of this may be heard in Banquo's assurance, spoken as much for himself as for those around: 'In the great hand of God I stand' (*Macbeth* ii. 3).

The related attribute of majesty is also present in the history plays, in view of the theme of kingship treated in them. Thus in *Richard III* God is mentioned, not only by Gloucester as 'king of heaven' (i. 2), but also by his two brothers, Clarence, as 'the great King of kings' (i. 4), and the dying Edward, as 'the supreme King of kings' (ii. 1). Conversely, in *Richard II* the earthly king is represented by the Bishop of Carlisle as 'the figure of God's majesty' (iv. 1).

Out of these references to God's justice, power and majesty, there emerges in the mature plays of Shakespeare an important emphasis on divine providence, conceived as governing the exercise of justice and power. In *As You Like It* this theme is expressed in the pious words of Adam, combining echoes from the Old Testament (*Ps.* cxlvi) and the New Testament (*Luke* xii 6, 24):

> *Take that; and he that doth the ravens feed,*
> *Yea, providently cater for the sparrow,*
> *Be comfort to my age!* (ii. 3)

In *Hamlet* the theme is again taken up in the dramatic outcome, where the hero shows his new spirit of resolution in the face of death :[18]

> *Not a whit, we defy augury: there's a special providence*
> *in the fall of a sparrow. If it be now, 'tis not to come; if it*
> *be not to come, it will be now; if it be not now, yet it will*
> *come: the readiness is all.* (v. 2)

The Christian spirit implicit in these words seems to accord with Hamlet's previous recognition that

> *There's a divinity that shapes our ends,*
> *Rough-hew them how we will.* (*ibid.*)

and with his belief that even in the sealing of the alternative document, which was to send Rosencrantz and Guildenstern to their fate, 'was heaven ordinant' (v. 1).

There is a marked contrast between Shakespeare's frequent use of the name of God in his early plays and his later preference for the indirect form of Heaven. This is most evident in the two 'problem' comedies, *All's Well That Ends Well* and *Measure for Measure*. In the former play, the name of Heaven is particularly associated with the theme of divine power operating through a human instrument. Thus the Countess charges Helena, 'as heaven shall work in me for thine avail', to confess 'the mystery of your loneliness' (i. 3). Shortly

afterwards, Helena herself adopts the same language in persuading the old king to accept her remedy, attributing its
efficacy not to her art, but to the grace of heaven :

> *But most it is presumption in us when*
> *The help of heaven we count the act of men.*
> *Dear sir, to my endeavours give consent;*
> *Of heaven, not me, make an experiment.* (ii. 1)

In his answer, the king likewise looks beyond her earthly words
to the heavenly power that inspires her :

> *Methinks in thee some blessed spirit doth speak*
> *His powerful sound within an organ weak.* (*ibid.*)

The miraculous effect of her remedy is admired by Lafeu as
the 'showing of a heavenly effect in an earthly actor', the 'very
hand of heaven', and 'in a most weak and debile minister, great
power, great transcendence' (ii. 3). In the same scene, Helena
herself makes the announcement that 'heaven hath through
me restor'd the king to health'. From a merely naturalistic
point of view, all this must seem awkward and unreal. But its
very awkwardness serves to emphasize an allegorical and theological meaning implicit in the action of the play and in the
character of the heroine.[19]

A similar meaning is apparent in *Measure for Measure*,
which almost defies a naturalistic interpretation. From the beginning the theme of divine power operating through a human
instrument is touched upon by the Duke as he outlines his plans:

> *Heaven doth with us as we with torches do,*
> *Not light them for themselves; for if our virtues*
> *Did not go forth of us, 'twere all alike*
> *As if we had them not.* (i. 1)

To this Angelo responds with the pious wish : 'The heavens
give safety to your purposes !' It is not only in the Duke, but
also in Isabella, that the operation of heaven becomes apparent, especially in the 'moving graces' that inspire her plea with
Angelo on behalf of her brother (ii. 2). In the course of her
plea, it is noticeable that she mentions 'heaven' no less than
eight times – with not so much as one mention of 'God'. She
makes her appeal, above all, to 'merciful heaven'; and in the

subsequent development of the play this attribute of mercy is skilfully interwoven with that of providence. If the former attribute is represented by Isabella, the latter is represented by the Duke, who in his disguise as a friar takes advantage of every accident 'that heaven provides', teaches Isabella to make 'heavenly comforts of despair', and exhorts her to 'give your cause to heaven' (iv. 3). Thus, in the eventual union of the Duke with Isabella, there is more than the natural significance of a happy ending: there is also the theological symbolism of a union between mercy and providence.

In the later plays there is a noticeable increase of subjects with a pagan setting; and in keeping with this setting it is natural that 'God' should be declined in the plural. To judge from the epithets ascribed to the gods in these plays, it seems that the dramatist wishes to lay special emphasis on the attributes of immortality, wisdom and justice. In *Troilus and Cressida* he speaks of 'the gods above' (iii. 2), the 'immortal gods' (iv. 2), the 'blessed gods' (iv. 4), and the 'everlasting gods' (v. 3). The constancy and wisdom of the gods above are, in particular, contrasted with the fickleness and folly of men below. Thus Cressida declares, with ironical reference to the love of Troilus:

> To be wise, and love,
> Exceeds man's might; that dwells with gods above.
>
> (iii. 3)

It is the absence of this wisdom from his love, where reason is violently displaced by feverish passion, that deprives Troilus's vows of sanctimony, 'the gods' delight' (v. 2). He is warned by his sister Cassandra, but fails to heed her warning:

> The gods are deaf to hot and peevish vows;
> They are polluted offerings, more abhorr'd
> Than spotted livers in the sacrifice. (v. 3)

Such references provide a divine basis for judging the confused events of love and war that take place on earth.

The theme of divine wisdom is taken up, and conjoined with that of divine justice, in *King Lear* and *Antony and Cleopatra*. The former tragedy, as it moves towards its climax, increasingly points beyond the apparent injustice of things to a supreme, if mysterious, justice. Amid the storm on the heath what troubles Lear is the injustice not of the heavens, but of men, who have left himself and other 'poor naked wretches' to wander abroad in the 'pitiless storm'. Even in their unkindness the heavens give a salutary 'physic' to 'pomp', and thereby vindicate their justice (iii. 4). Their function in punishing crime is underlined not only in general terms by Lear:

> *Let the great gods,*
> *That keep this dreadful pother o'er our heads,*
> *Find out their enemies now.* (iii. 2)

but also on two particular occasions by Albany, who almost seems a mouthpiece for the moral of the play. As though in response to his appeal to the heavens to send down 'their visible spirits . . . to tame these vile offences', news is brought that Cornwall has been struck down in the very act of putting out Gloucester's eyes. Thereat Albany exclaims:

> *This shows you are above,*
> *You justicers, that these our nether crimes*
> *So speedily can venge!* (iv. 2)

Similarly, in the final scene news is brought of the deaths of the two sisters, Regan by Goneril's poison, and Goneril by her own knife; and Albany recognizes in it the 'judgment of the heavens, that makes us tremble' (v. 3). In contrast, the heavens are charged with ethical irresponsibility by Gloucester in words which have made a deeper impression on readers and critics than the above-quoted comments of Albany:

> *As flies to wanton boys, are we to the gods;*
> *They kill us for their sport.* (iv. 1)

But these words of his are hardly spoken in a calm frame of mind. Subsequently he learns better thoughts under the encouragement of Edgar, who is as though sent from heaven to preserve his father's life:

> *Think that the clearest gods, who make them honours*
> *Of men's impossibilities, have preserv'd thee.* (iv. 6)

In Gloucester's case, the mercy of the heavens is shown in his miraculous preservation; but their justice has been vindicated in his sufferings – as Edgar comments at the end:

> *The gods are just, and of our pleasant vices*
> *Make instruments to plague us.* (v. 3)

In *Antony and Cleopatra* the wisdom of the gods, together with their justice and providence, is contrasted with the wilful life of Antony. The general moral is pointed out by Mene-crates:

> *We, ignorant of ourselves,*
> *Beg often our own harms, which the wise powers*
> *Deny us for our good; so find we profit*
> *By losing of our prayers.* (ii. 1)

The converse truth is only recognized by Antony when it is too late – as it seems to him – to mend:

> *When we in our, viciousness grow hard, –*
> *O misery on't! – the wise gods seel our eyes;*
> *In our own filth drop our clear judgments; make us*
> *Adore our errors; laugh at's while we strut*
> *To our confusion.* (iii. 11)

The outcome of Shakespeare's meditations on the divine nature, as we have followed them, would seem to be his noticeable emphasis on the attribute of providence in the last plays. The action of each play in turn leads up to a theophany in which the merciful providence of the gods is presented as drawing good out of evil and joy out of sorrow – beyond all expectation. Pericles is overwhelmed by the 'present kindness' of the gods, which 'makes my past miseries sport' (v. 3) – where 'sport' is interestingly used in a sense precisely counter to that of Gloucester quoted above. Cymbeline also feels as if 'the gods do mean to strike me to death with mortal joy' (v. 5). In both plays the 'best wills' of the gods are seen as directing human troubles and mishaps to a divine harmony and peace. So, too, behind the events of *The Winter's Tale* we are made aware of 'powers divine' who behold 'our human actions' (iii. 2). Their influence strikingly appears in the scene of Her-mione's trial, when her innocence is vindicated by Apollo's oracle and Leontes is punished for his contempt of the god. In his punishment, however, Leontes recognizes his own guilt and the justice of the gods:

> *Apollo's angry; and the heavens themselves*
> *Do strike at my injustice.* (iii. 2)

The just anger of the gods is further emphasized in the tempest-scene, when the mariner exclaims:

> *In my conscience,*
> *The heavens with that we have in hand are angry,*
> *And frown upon's.* (iii. 3)

To this Antigonus replies: 'Their sacred wills be done!' But as their wills are done, their anger is replaced by forgiveness in view of Leontes's repentance, as Cleomenes reassures his royal master at the beginning of the final act. From their 'sacred vials' graces are now poured in profusion, both on Perdita who has been found, and on Leontes who has found himself in her and in his queen.

Finally, it is in *The Tempest* that we find the culminating expression of this theme of 'providence divine' (i. 1). It operates, for the most part, through the agency of Prospero, who, like the Duke in *Measure for Measure*, takes the advantage of his 'zenith' (i. 2) to bring about the happy reconciliation of the ending. He operates, in turn, through the agency of Ariel, who presents himself as the minister, not only of Prospero, but also of 'fate' and the higher 'powers' (iii. 3). From first to last everything seems to be securely under the control of Prospero and Ariel; but in the outcome all is attributed to the blessing of the gods, who answer Prospero's prayer and 'rain grace' on his daughter's happy union with Prince Ferdinand (iii. 1; v. 1). At the same time, while it was by Prospero's contrivance that he first met Miranda, Ferdinand recognizes that 'by immortal providence she's mine'. His father Alonso is filled with like wonder, and looks beyond the mortal instruments to the immortal agent:

> *There is in this business more than nature*
> *Was ever conduct of.* (v. 1)

All these references to God, or to the gods, taken separately, may seem conventional enough; but taken together, they fall

into the order outlined above, which implies a comprehensive
– if traditional – view of theology. This view is, moreover,
discernible not only in the more obvious references to God and
religious worship, but also in the various human relationships
which constitute the essence of drama. On the ordinary level
of human life these relationships belong to the world of
'nature'; but they rarely remain on this level, being either
attracted upwards by the drawing of 'grace' or pulled down-
wards by the tempting of 'sin'. Here we have a triangular
distinction between 'nature' and 'grace' and 'sin', which
increasingly enters into the meaning of Shakespeare's plays and
imparts a deep structure to his dramatic presentation of man's
condition in this world.

A preliminary statement of this distinction may be found in
the opening speech of Friar Laurence in *Romeo and Juliet* :

> *O mickle is the powerful grace that lies*
> *In herbs, plants, stones, and their true qualities;*
> *For nought so vile that on the earth doth live*
> *But to the earth some special good doth give,*
> *Nor aught so good, but strain'd from that fair use*
> *Revolts from true birth, stumbling on abuse . . .*
> *Two such opposed foes encamp them still*
> *In man as well as herbs, grace and rude will.* (ii. 3)

His words are later recalled by the aged Belarius in *Cymbeline*,
with reference to the two young princes :

> *Nature hath meal and bran, contempt and grace.*
> (i.2)

In both these statements 'nature' seems inclusive of both good
and evil, 'grace' and 'sin'; but in their dramatized expression
– as in the medieval Morality plays – the latter appear as conflicting influences from without, swaying the will of man now
one way, now another. As a result of this spiritual conflict,
within and yet beyond the will of man, 'nature' itself becomes
divided between better and baser, as it is acted upon by 'two
spirits' – 'the better angel' and 'the worser spirit' (*Sonnet*
44).[20]

Since it is out of the background of 'sin' that 'grace' comes
to appear in 'nature', we may begin by noting various signifi-

cant allusions in the plays to the Christian doctrine of original sin. First, in the history plays, the many evils of the Wars of the Roses are duly traced to the unlawful deposition and murder of Richard II by Bolingbroke; but Shakespeare goes beyond the Tudor historiographers by conceiving the crime in universal terms as a type of original sin. In the garden-scene of *Richard II*, the Queen sees the crime as 'a second fall of cursed man' (iii. 4); and in the deposition-scene itself Carlisle warns the assembly:

> *O, if you rear this house against this house,*
> *It will the woefullest division prove*
> *That ever fell upon this cursed earth.* (iv. 1)

In the final play of the sequence, *Henry V*, the crime of the father is to some extent redeemed by the son, when he succeeds to his father's throne; for, in the words of the Archbishop of Canterbury,

> *Consideration, like an angel, came*
> *And whipp'd the offending Adam out of him,*
> *Leaving his body as a paradise,*
> *To envelop and contain celestial spirits.* (i. 1)

But he realizes that 'all that I can do is nothing worth' (iv. 1); and, in fact, he does not so much redeem as postpone the payment of the terrible debt of blood.

In turning from the histories to the tragedies, we turn not only from the general to the individual, but also from the individual to the universal. In *Hamlet* significant emphasis is laid on the theme of original sin in the heated declarations of the Prince, first to Polonius: 'Use every man after his desert, and who should 'scape whipping?' (ii. 2), and subsequently to Ophelia in the nunnery-scene: 'We are arrant knaves all, believe none of us!' (iii. 1).[21] It is as though his knowledge of the combined guilt of his uncle and his mother has induced in Hamlet an awareness of the universal sinfulness of mankind, including himself; and in this knowledge he finds it difficult, if not impossible, to take any redemptive action. His words to Ophelia are further echoed in Malcolm's puzzling speech of self-depreciation to Macduff, acknowledging in himself 'all the particulars of vice' and enlarging on his 'confineless harms'

(*Macbeth* iv. 3). Malcolm is, of course, testing the faith of Macduff by means of this his 'first false speaking'; but implicit in his untruth is the deeper truth, that this is precisely what he would be but for the grace of God. In each of these plays, which somehow come together at this point, there is an interesting contrast between the sinfulness in the foreground and a suggestion of the symbolical background of Eden. In *Hamlet* the two grave-diggers claim to 'hold up Adam's profession', with the implication that gardening has since turned to grave-digging (v. 1). In *Macbeth* the 'pleasant seat' and delicate air of Macbeth's castle (i. 6) is the ironical setting for the foul crime of husband and wife, who are themselves deceived by 'the equivocation of the fiend' (v. 5).

Other allusions to the doctrine occur in *Measure for Measure*, where Isabella reminds Angelo that 'all the souls that were were forfeit once', and goes on to appeal to his conscience :

> *Go to your bosom;*
> *Knock there, and ask your heart what it doth know*
> *That's like my brother's fault.* (ii. 2)

The immediate reference of her words is, no doubt, to a particular form of personal sin; but they also imply the general fact that Angelo is, like other men, a sinner. They may also be connected with the words of her brother Claudio, who, in acknowledging his sin, brings out its natural and universal character :

> *Our natures do pursue –*
> *Like rats that ravin down their proper bane –*
> *A thirsty evil, and when we drink we die.* (i. 2)

In *King Lear* the universal misery of mankind, represented in the person of the old king, is implicitly presented as 'the penalty of Adam' (*As You Like It* ii. 1). There is an interesting contrast between Lear's readiness to cry grace of 'these dreadful summoners' in the onset of the storm, recognizing his sinfulness, albeit 'more sinn'd against than sinning', and his later readiness in the mock-trial to dispense general absolution – almost in defiance of the universality of sin : 'None does offend, none, I say none.' This contrast leads up to the declaration of the Gentleman, which puts the preceding scenes into a theological context :

> *Thou hast one daughter,*
> *Who redeems nature from the general curse*
> *Which twain have brought her to.* (iv. 6)

What has gone before, in Lear's experience, is 'the general curse' – not only on himself as an individual, but also on all mankind of whom he is the representative. What is to come after is the redemption of nature by 'one daughter'.

The theological context is perhaps most fully developed in *The Winter's Tale*, where Lear is continued in Leontes, and Cordelia in both Hermione and Perdita.[22] From the beginning there is significant reference to 'the doctrine of ill-doing' and 'the imposition . . . hereditary ours' (i. 2). So long as Leontes is united with Hermione, his 'gracious queen' (i. 2), he remains his noble self; but when he rejects her from his grace, it is he himself who loses his grace – and this loss is symbolized in his loss of his daughter, Perdita. The same truth is expressed in Angelo's words of remorse in *Measure for Measure* :

> *Alack, when once our grace we have forgot,*
> *Nothing goes right; we would, and we would not.*
>
> (iv. 4)

So too, Claudius laments at the end of his fruitless soliloquy :

> *My words fly up, my thoughts remain below:*
> *Words without thoughts never to heaven go.* (iii. 3)

The truth is also exemplified in Prince Hal, when he sees himself 'violently carried away from grace' by a devil 'in the likeness of a fat old man' (*Henry IV* Part I ii. 4); and in Lord Pandarus, when he counters the naive remark of a servant, that he is 'in the state of grace', with the punning response: 'Grace! not so, friend; honour and lordship are my titles' (*Troilus and Cressida* iii. 1). Conversely, the state of sin is so widely depicted in the plays – in Bertram and Angelo, in Othello and Macbeth and Lear – that it hardly requires elaboration.

One might even say that, while the state of sin seems to receive much attention in the tragedies, what is chiefly important for the dramatist is the initial loss and the final recovery of grace. It is in this latter direction that everything may be said to move – through the suffering that is born of sin, the self-knowledge that is born of suffering, and the repentance that is born of self-knowledge. In dramatic terms the final recovery of grace is represented in terms of the union or reunion between hero and heroine, according to the principle stated in *A Midsummer Night's Dream* that graces dwell in love (i. 1). The ideal of grace, as we have already seen in a previous chapter, is regularly associated in Shakespeare's plays with the person of the heroine. She is invariably described as 'full of grace'; and she further communicates her grace to others, or at least intercedes for grace on behalf of others.[23] Her influence is of cardinal importance in *Measure for Measure* (as intercessor), and in *All's Well That Ends Well* (as mediator). In tragedies like *Othello* and *King Lear* it is the rejection of her influence which brings about their sad ending, and which in the meanwhile lends poignancy to the state of sin. In the latter play, however, the recovery of grace is represented – though the word is not used – in the reconciliation-scene between Lear and Cordelia; and it is this scene which provides the fundamental pattern of the last plays, turning as they do on the theme of 'a world ransomed' (*The Winter's Tale* v. 2).

It is in *Macbeth* that the full theological force of 'grace' is felt most vividly, by contrast to the sacrilegious sin that has put an end to 'renown and grace' (ii. 3).[24] Images of grace cluster particularly round the throne of 'gracious England' (iv. 3), from which the forces are sent to restore order in Scotland. Consequently, Malcolm looks forward to disposing all things in his new reign 'by the grace of Grace' (v. 7). Here, however, there is no heroine to embody the ideal of grace : only two successive sovereigns, Duncan and Malcolm, of Scotland, and Edward of England. This lack is supplied in *The Winter's Tale* by two heroines, mother and daughter, who may be said to represent the two stages of grace for Leontes – before and after its loss by sin. Hermione, his Queen, is from the first characterized in terms of grace. Not only is she regularly described – like Edward in *Macbeth* – as 'our gracious lady' (ii. 2), 'the gracious queen' and 'our most gracious mistress' (i. 2); but in her opening conversation with Polixenes she implies that women are, through the grace of marriage, the providential means of counteracting the 'hereditary imposition' of original sin in men (i. 2). After her marriage with Leontes, therefore, she was not only 'in his grace', but also 'merited to be so' (iii. 2). Through his rejection of her, however, Leontes loses his grace and is doubly punished, by the sudden news of his son's death and the apparent death of Hermione. His slow return to grace, through his 'saint-like sorrow' of sixteen years, is symbolized by the growth of his lost daughter Perdita in distant Bohemia – 'in grace equal with wondering' (iv. chorus). It is materialized on her return to Sicily with Prince Florizel, in whom the marital relation between Leontes and Hermione appears renewed. Then, in the joyful reunion of father and daughter, it seems as if 'every wink of an eye some new grace will be born' (v. 2). The subsequent reunion of husband and wife, and of mother and daughter, is attended by a further outpouring of graces at the prayer of Hermione; and this prayer, which she makes for Perdita, applies no less to Leontes, of whom she is the better self. In her all that he has lost by sin he now finds again by grace. The same theme of losing and finding is repeated in *Pericles*, with respect to a wife and a daughter, in *Cymbeline*, with respect to a daughter and two sons, and in *The Tempest*, with respect – as Gonzalo points out – to everyone. In the last-mentioned play, even Caliban may be said to find himself at the end, when he departs with the words: 'I'll be wise hereafter, and seek for grace' (v. 1).

In general, the effect of grace, as shown in the last plays, is to transform the nature of man by bringing good out of evil and 'redeeming the time' – the aim which Prince Hal sets for himself in *Henry IV* Part I (i. 2), but which it is not within man's power to realize by himself. Through the influence of divine mercy man is 'new made' (*Measure for Measure* ii. 2), and under the continued guidance of divine providence the way is chalked for a 'brave new world' (*The Tempest* v. 1). In this vision, which is the eschatological vision of Christianity, Prospero foresees that 'the cloud-capp'd towers, the gorgeous palaces, the solemn temples' which form the 'insubstantial pageant' of this material world will all disappear. But beyond 'this our little life' there remains the unchanging Word of God,

and the word of man, too, in so far as it is – like the promise
made in marriage – ratified and sanctified by the Word of
God. Here is the deep meaning, not only of *The Tempest*, but
of the whole dramatic development of Shakespeare – from the
self-confident declaration of *Sonnet* 18 :

> *So long as men can breathe, or eyes can see,*
> *So long lives this, and this gives life to thee.*

to the humbler conclusion of *Sonnet* 146 :

> *So shalt thou feed on Death, that feeds on men,*
> *And Death once dead, there's no more dying then.*

Conclusion

The Heart of Shakespearian Drama and of Christian Tradition

BY WAY of conclusion, I would like to recall and restate the aim of this book : to examine the extent to which Shakespeare was influenced in his plays by the various religious currents of his age, and the manner in which he responded to those currents. Most of his readers are vaguely aware of a religious element in the plays; but few of them realize how deeply pervasive is that element, or how varied are its ramifications. Even many ideas that seem secular to us today would have been intended by the dramatist and understood by his audience in a religious sense.

While concentrating on the religious element, it has not, of course, been my intention to minimize the other elements that enter into the rich variety of Shakespearian drama. Every element has its proper place in the harmony of the whole. But for a deeper appreciation of the whole, it is often beneficial to limit one's attention now to one part, now to another – the nautical, the culinary, the biological, the botanical, the economical, the legal, the heraldic, the proverbial, the literary, the classical, the medieval, the theatrical, the metaphysical, and so on. Not least among these elements is the religious, though it is all too often neglected by scholars and critics for reasons I have touched on in the Introduction.

In this book I have endeavoured to give as detailed and as comprehensive a survey as possible of this religious element,

and so to provide, not only a convenient handbook to the many
religious allusions in the plays, but also a clue to their underlying inspiration. In my concern for completeness I may have
accumulated items of evidence in such numbers as to leave this
clue in some obscurity. So it is perhaps necessary for me at this
point to retrace the main lines of thought implied in my presentation of the evidence.

First of all, it seems to me that the deepest inspiration in
Shakespeare's plays is both religious and Christian. In view of
the religious background of his age, and the circumstances of
his dramatic composition, one may interpret the plays as
Shakespeare's personal response to the major problem of his
age, which was fundamentally a religious problem. Further, it
seems to me that, as a deeply religious man, Shakespeare was
grieved by the 'breach in nature' brought about, both in the
English nation and in himself as an Englishman, by the
Reformation. Not that he approved of every aspect of Catholic
life in the Middle Ages. Nor that he disapproved of every
proposal urged by the Protestant reformers. But beneath all
his plays may be heard the 'still, sad music of humanity',
lamenting the plight of his 'poor country' since the day Henry
VIII decided to break with Rome.

His lament is 'cries countless', sent up in a rising crescendo
from all his plays taken together – from the theme of mistaken
identity in the comedies, through that of usurpation and civil
strife in the histories, to that of sin and suffering in the
tragedies. The culmination may be heard in the pitiful prayer
of Cordelia to the 'kind gods' in the crucial scene of *King Lear*,
followed by the *rallentando* of the last plays with their hope of
ultimate reunion.

Inevitably he expresses his thoughts in a secular form, in
keeping with the drama of his age and the expectations of his
audience. But, as I have tried to show, this secular form is itself
allegorical, or rather, analogical, of the religious situation of
his time. A search for this kind of meaning, or a recognition of
its presence, in the plays is not necessarily an attempt – as is
often asserted – to force them into preconceived patterns of
thought, or a departure from 'the plain road of common
sense'. Analogy of one kind or another is natural to human
thought, particularly in the endeavour to apprehend and

express religious meaning. What is deepest in human nature can, in fact, be expressed only by means of analogy or allegory. At first, the expression may seem fragmentary; but with time and reflection the fragments come together in a unity of thought and experience such as we find in the plays from *Hamlet* onwards.

The inspiration of Shakespeare may indeed be explained in part by his patriotic concern for national unity, an aim which may seem secular enough. But in the setting of the sixteenth century, even this aim is not entirely secular. Rather, it comes directly from the religious ideal of the Middle Ages, when England was no self-enclosed entity, but an integral part of Christendom. During that time the political aspiration of Europe was parallel to the religious aspiration of Christendom : even as the memory of a united Roman Empire was parallel to the desire of perfect spiritual unity among Christians. But in the sixteenth century this aspiration had been seriously undermined by the growth of a nationalistic spirit and the emergence of religious sectarianism in different countries of Europe, and not least in England.

In Shakespeare's plays this aspiration may be seen moving beneath the surface with gathering momentum. The history plays reveal, by the side of his English patriotism, an unwillingness to attach himself to any partisan spirit which might impair the unity of England – whether for or against Richard II, whether for or against Henry IV. Thereafter his attention moves from Henry V to Julius Caesar, from the narrow confines of England to the vast extent of the Roman Empire, and from the limits of the Elizabethan Age to the universality of Christian Rome. The culmination of this movement may be found in the vision at the end of *Cymbeline*, in which 'a Roman and a British ensign wave friendly together' (v. 5).

At a deeper level, this vision is concerned not only with the unity of a group, but also with the more intimate unity in man himself. For it is primarily in the heart of man that the unity of Christendom has been broken, by a defect of charity on both sides : by the rigid legalism of ecclesiastical organization, on the one side, and by the fanaticism of individualistic opposition, on the other. It may have been with this in mind that Shakespeare dealt in his comedies with the strange situations that

arise out of mutual understanding – 'O devilish-holy fray!' –
and in his tragedies with the sad alienation of men from one
another and from their own true selves that arises out of an
original alienation from God. As I have pointed out, what is
fundamental to Shakespeare's conception of tragedy is a rend-
ing of the moral being of man which depends on love. In
Othello's prophetic words, 'When I love thee not, chaos is
come again!' Conversely, what is fundamental to his conception of romance in his last plays is a restoration of moral harmony to man, effected by forgiveness and love.

Here is the highest Christian ideal, both secular and religious, both human and divine. The more it is realized, first in
individuals, then in small groups, the more it spreads out, until
it fills 'the wide vessel of the universe'. It is to this ideal of unity
that Shakespeare directs his ultimate attention, just as from it
he receives his original inspiration – not merely as a Platonic
idea above the world of shadows, but as a Christian ideal to be
realized in and through this world 'by doing deeds of hospitality'. This is what constitutes, in its deepest being, that
Christian tradition which, while ever developing in time, has
continued unchanged through the varying phases of human
culture, from Roman to Renaissance, from medieval to
modern. And this is also what constitutes, in its deepest meaning, the Christian drama of Shakespeare, which looks at once
backward through the Renaissance and the Middle Ages to
the classical era of Greece and Rome, forward into the
unknown future of mankind, our own age and beyond, outward to the most distant lands, 'states unborn and accents yet
unknown', inward to the deepest recess of the human heart,
and upward to the very 'crown and hearted throne' of divine
love.

Notes

I Family Background

1 Cited by P. Hughes, *The Reformation in England,* Vol. III, p. 127, with similar statements of many other bishops.

2 The whole survey is reported by W. R. Trimble, *The Catholic Laity in Elizabethan England,* p. 26. The Bishop of Worcester reported forty-six of the gentry unfavourable to the changes, thirty-six favourable, and thirty neutral (i.e. not favourable). The Bishop of Coventry and Lichfield reported twenty unfavourable, forty favourable, and six neutral.

3 Cf. E. I. Fripp, *Shakespeare, Man and Artist,* Vol. I, p. 41.

4 The poem is quoted, and its occasion described, by Bede Camm, *Forgotten Shrines,* p. 185.

5 The Puritanism of John Shakespeare is maintained by T. Carter, *Shakespeare Puritan and Recusant;* and by E. I. Fripp, *Shakespeare Studies,* pp. 81–97, and *Shakespeare, Man and Artist,* Vol. I, pp. 196–203, 305–8.

6 The arguments for John Shakespeare's Catholicism are set forth by J. H. de Groot, *The Shakespeares and the Old Faith,* and by J. S. Smart, *Shakespeare, Truth and Tradition,* pp. 69–71.

7 The evidence was first presented by H. Thurston, 'A controverted Shakespeare Document', *The Dublin Review,* October–December 1923.

8 Letter of 7 November 1583.

9 Doubt is expressed by Sir S. Lee, *A Life of Shakespeare,* pp. 284–5; but J. S. Smart, *op. cit.* pp. 61–4, defends the connection with the Ardens of Parkhall.

10 Cf. Sir E. Chambers, *William Shakespeare,* Vol. II, pp. 257, 265.

11 Cf. G. R. French, *Shakespeareana Genealogica,* pp. 354–5.

12 The suggestion is made by the Countess de Chambrun, *Shakespeare, A Portrait Restored,* p. 374; but it is criticized by J. H. de Groot, *op. cit.* pp. 103–4.

II Religious Formation

1 Mentioned by J. Gillow, *Bibliographical Dictionary of English Catholics* Vol. V, p. 498 (under 'Shakespeare').

2 Cf. H. S. Bowden, *The Religion of Shakespeare,* pp. 12, 262, and J. Crehan, 'Shakespeare and the Sarum Ritual', *The Month,* July–August 1964, pp. 47–50.

3 Cf. J. M. Nosworthy, New Arden edition of *Cymbeline,* p. 18, and R. G. Hunter, *Shakespeare and the Comedy of Forgiveness,* p. 148. But neither author

notices the allusion to the Angelus, which had become a widespread custom by the end of the Middle Ages.

4 Cf. H. S. Bowden, *op. cit.* pp. 270, 312, and C. Devlin, *Hamlet's Divinity*, p. 31.

5 Cf. Baldwin Peter, 'Hamlet and In Paradisum', *Shakespeare Quarterly,* July 1952, pp. 279–80, and M. J. Quinlan, 'Shakespeare and the Catholic Burial Services', *ibid.* Summer 1954, pp. 303–6. Other parallels are given by R. M. Frye, *Shakespeare and Christian Doctrine*, pp. 135–6.

6 J. M. Nosworthy, *op. cit.* p. 51, ascribes this prayer to the Collect for Aid against Perils in *Evening Prayer:* 'Lighten our darkness, we beseech thee, O Lord, and by thy great mercy, defend us from all perils and dangers of this night.'

7 Cf. H. S. Bowden, *The Religion of Shakespeare*, p. 271, and H. Mutschmann and K. Wentersdorf, *Shakespeare and Catholicism,* pp. 215–16.

8 C. Devlin, *Hamlet's Divinity*, pp. 26, 40, sees in the apparition of Hamlet's father 'the ghost of the old religion', and considers it would 'in the minds of many of Shakespeare's audience inevitably recall the old religion, with its doctrinal, psychological, *and* political implications'.

9 In describing Saint Patrick's Purgatory on Lough Derg, Campion professes to discharge himself 'of my readers' expectation'. The saint in question was not the Apostle of Ireland, as often thought, but a later abbot of the same name.

10 The question of the 'maimed rites' is discussed by J. D. Wilson, *What Happens in Hamlet*, pp. 68–70, 295–300, and by R. Noble, *Shakespeare's Biblical Knowledge*, pp. 84–6.

11 Cf. E. I. Fripp, *Shakespeare, Man and Artist*, Vol. I, pp. 52–9.

12 On Hell-Mouth, cf. M. D. Anderson, *Drama and Imagery in English Churches*, pp. 126–9; and with special reference to *Othello*, cf. John Vyvyan, *The Shakespearean Ethic*, pp. 145–6.

13 Cf. M. D. Anderson, *op. cit.* p. 145.

14 Cf. R. Noble, *Shakespeare's Biblical Knowledge*, pp. 103–4.

15 This connection is pointed out by H. Matthews, *Character and Symbol in Shakespeare's Plays*, p. 82, and by R. G. Hunter, *op. cit.* p. 206.

16 W. M. Merchant, 'Shakespeare's Theology', *REL* October 1964, p. 73, speaks of 'elements which relate Shakespeare to the Wakefield Master'.

17 Cf. J. D. Wilson, *The Fortunes of Falstaff*, p. 18, and Sir A. Quiller-Couch, *Shakespeare's Workmanship*, pp. 108–11.

18 Cf. F. D. Hoeniger, New Arden edition of *Pericles*, pp. lxxxviii–xci, and R. G. Hunter, *op. cit.* pp. 139–40, 177–83, 114.

19 Cf. M. D. Anderson, *op. cit.* pp. 188–92, 202.

20 Cf. *ibid.* pp. 202–3. The motif of the pound of flesh occurs in the legend of St Helen's expedition in search of the True Cross.

21 The survey is included in *The Second Part of a Register*, intended for publication by the Puritans about 1593 (edited by A. Peel in 1915).

22 The marriage licence was issued on 27 November 1582, for William Shaxpere and Anne Whateley of Temple Grafton; and on the next day a bond was signed by Fulke Sandells and John Richardson, guaranteeing there were no legal impediments between William Shagspere and Anne Hathwey of Stratford. Cf. H. Mutschmann and K. Wentersdorf, *op. cit.* pp. 85–95.

23 Cf. T. W. Baldwin, *William Shakspere's Petty School*, pp. 174–86.

24 The affirmative is maintained by T. W. Baldwin, *William Shakspere's Small Latine & Lesse Greeke*, p. 685; but the negative is defended by R. Noble, *op. cit.* p. 46.

25 Cf. J. H. Pollen, 'A Shakespeare Discovery: His Schoolmaster afterwards a Jesuit', *The Month*, October 1917, pp. 317–23, and November 1917, pp. 401–8.

26 Cf. H. A. Shield, 'A Stratford Schoolmaster', *The Month*, August 1961, pp. 109–11.

27 Cf. E. I. Fripp, *op. cit.* p. 92; and H. Mutschmann and K. Wentersdorf, *op. cit.* pp. 79, 327.

28 Cf. Sir E. Chambers, *William Shakespeare*, Vol. II, p. 254.

29 The main proponents of this theory are: O. Baker, *In Shakespeare's Warwickshire and the Unknown Years*, Ch. XIV; Sir E. Chambers, *Shakespearean Gleanings*, pp. 52–6; L. Hotson, *Shakespeare's Sonnets Dated*, pp. 127–32; A. Keen and R. Lubbock, *The Annotator;* and R. Stevenson, *Shakespeare's Religious Frontier*, pp. 67–83.

30 Accounts of John Shakespeare and John Taylor, 1564–5; at the Shakespeare Birthplace Library.

31 Stratford records for February 1580 and January 1581; cf. H. A. Shield, *op. cit.* p. 111.

32 The tradition is mentioned by A. Keen, *op. cit.* p. 50; and the connection with Savage is also explored by L. Hotson, *op. cit.* pp. 126–32.

33 Cf. Sir E. Chambers, *William Shakespeare*, Vol. II, pp. 551–4, and A. Keen, *op. cit.* p. 202. Doubt is expressed in *The Reader's Encyclopedia of Shakespeare*, p. 821, without sufficient reason given for the doubt.

III   English Jesuits

1 Cf. Notes 25 and 26 to Ch. II.

2 Cf. C. Devlin, *Life of Robert Southwell*, p. 263.

3 Cf. Bede Camm, *Forgotten Shrines*, p. 184.

4 Cf. H. Ross Williamson, *The Day Shakespeare Died*, p. 14 and note.

5 The main source for the life of Robert Persons (which has yet to be written) is *The Letters and Memorials of Fr. R. Persons, S.J.*, Vol. I: to 1588, ed. L. Hicks, Catholic Record Society, No. 39. There is a popular account of his life by D. Meadows, *Elizabethan Quintet*. His writings are discussed by A. Southern, *Elizabethan Recusant Prose, 1559–82*, by J. Crehan, 'The Prose of Robert Persons', *The Month*, May 1940, pp. 366–75, and by T. Clancy, *Papist Pamphleteers*. (The spelling 'Persons' is his own preferred spelling of his name).

6 Cf. H. Thurston, 'Father Parsons' *Christian Directory*', *The Month*, December 1894, pp. 457–76; R. McNulty, 'The Protestant Version of Persons' *Christian Exercise*', *Huntington Library Quarterly*, 1959, pp. 271–300; and C. Devlin, *Hamlet's Divinity*, pp. 36–41.

7 In addition, Baxter declares in his *Autobiography* (published posthumously in 1696) that while reading *The Resolution* 'it pleased God to awaken my soul'. Dean Swift also commends the prose style of Persons, with that of Hooker, in his essay 'On Corruptions of Style', *The Tatler* No. 230.

8 Cf. J. Crehan, 'Father Persons, S.J.', in *English Spiritual Writers* (ed. C. Davis), p. 86.

9 K. Muir, New Arden edition of *King Lear*, p. 122, cites parallel passages in Florio's Montaigne.

10 The authorship is uncritically assigned to Persons by L. Campbell, *Shakespeare's Histories*, pp. 176–88, and by E. W. Talbert, *The Problem of Order*, pp. 66–7. A more critical study is undertaken by L. Hicks, 'Father

Robert Persons and the Book of Succession', *Recusant History*, 1957, pp. 104–37.

11 Abednego Seller, *A History of Passive Obedience since the Reformation* (1689), charges Milton with deriving his reasons 'from Doleman, i.e. Parsons the Jesuit'. Sir George Mackenzie, *Jus Regium* (1684), professes to maintain 'the just and solid foundations of monarchy' against Dolman, Milton and others. T. Clancy, *op. cit.* p. 212, notes the frequent accusation 'that the Whigs, and even Milton, were really Jesuits in disguise'!

12 The simplified exposition of Shakespeare's political theory in E. M. W. Tillyard, *Shakespeare's History Plays*, is criticized by L. C. Knights, *Shakespeare: the Histories*, p. 8: 'We shall be very careful not to assume that Shakespeare, in any play, is simply reflecting "Tudor ideas", or that he is accepting them uncritically as a premise for dramatic action.'

13 Cf. Sir E. Chambers, *William Shakespeare*, Vol. II, p. 213.

14 The patron of Shakespeare's company was Lord Hunsdon – first the father, then the son. The father died in 1596, and his son succeeded to the title and the patronage, but not to the office of Lord Chamberlain. The office first went to Lord Cobham, who, however, died soon afterwards in 1597; and so it reverted to Lord Hunsdon (son).

15 A similar complaint is made by Thomas Fuller in his *Church History* (1655) and in his *Worthies of England* (1662); cf. Sir E. Chambers, *op. cit.* pp. 217, 244.

16 Cf. J. Phelps, 'Father Parsons in Shakespeare', *Archiv für das Studium der neueren Sprachen und Literaturen*, 1915, pp. 66–86.

17 The contemporary setting of the play is thoroughly examined by F. Yates, *A Study of Love's Labour's Lost*.

18 The exorcisms are described from opposite viewpoints in two contemporary documents: Weston's own *Autobiography* (1611), edited by P. Caraman in 1955; and S. Harsnet's hostile *Declaration of Egregious Popish Impostures* (1604).

19 Cf. T. W. Baldwin, *On the Compositional Genetics of the Comedy of Errors*, Ch. III.

20 'Darrel's tricks', as Ben Jonson called them in *The Devil is an Ass* (1616), were exposed by S. Harsnet in his *Discovery of the Fraudulent Practices of John Darrel* (1599), to which Darrel replied with his *True Narration* (1600).

21 K. Muir examines Harsnet's influence on Shakespeare, in *Shakespeare's Sources*, p. 70, in 'Samuel Harsnett and *King Lear*', *RES*, January 1951, pp. 11–21, and in the New Arden edition of *King Lear*, pp. 253–6. F. W. Brownlow has an exhaustive study of Harsnet's *Declaration* in a lengthy doctorate thesis for the University of Birmingham (Shakespeare Institute), 1963.

22 For Southwell's published works, cf. R. A. Morton, *An Appreciation of Robert Southwell*, pp. 97–9, C. Devlin, *Life of Robert Southwell*, App. D, and J. H. McDonald, *The Poems and Prose Writings of Robert Southwell, S.J.: A Bibliographical Study*. A bibliographical account of the poems is also included in the latter's *Poems of Robert Southwell, S.J.*, pp. xxxv–civ.

23 Cf. L. Martz, *The Poetry of Meditation*, pp. 199–203, and C. Devlin, 'Robert Southwell and Contemporary Poets', *The Month*, 1950, pp. 169–80, 309–19.

24 Cf. Genealogy given by C. Devlin, *Life of Robert Southwell*, p. 15.

25 R. Barnfield, *Poems in Divers Humours* (1598), F. Meres, *Palladis Tamia* (1598), the anonymous play *The Return from Parnassus* (1599–1601); quoted by Sir E. Chambers, *op. cit.* pp. 194–5, 200–1.

26 Cf. C. Devlin, *op. cit.* Ch. 18: 'Master W.S.'; and G. R. French, *Shakespeareana Genealogica*, p. 489.

27 The parallel is developed by C. Devlin in his *Life,* pp. 268–73, and in his article for *The Month,* pp. 176–80, following the suggestion of Prof. Hales in his Preface to Ward's *English Poets: 'Saint Peter's Complaint* reminds one curiously of the almost exactly contemporary poem, Shakespeare's *Lucrece.'*

28 L. Hotson, *Shakespeare's Sonnets Dated,* p. 31, refers to 'the short-laid Jesuit plots to cut down Elizabeth', such as the Babington Plot of 1586 – though, in fact, the Jesuits had no hand in this, or in any other plot against Elizabeth's life. A. L. Rowse, *William Shakespeare, A Biography,* p. 187, suggests the names of Cornelius, Southwell, and Walpole in this context. J. B. Leishman, *Themes and Variations in Shakespeare's Sonnets,* p. 15, puts his finger on 'the Jesuit conspiracies at the beginning of James I's reign'.

29 The other commentators are, respectively, G. Steevens, as quoted in Malone's Variorum edition of *Shakespeare's Plays;* T. Tyler, *Shakespeare's Sonnets,* p. 283; and J. A. Fort, *A Time Scheme for Shakespeare's Sonnets,* p. 140. An interesting parallel is noted by G. Wilson Knight, *The Mutual Flame,* in the death of the Thane of Cawdor (*Macbeth* i. 4).

30 The account is cited by P. Caraman in his edition of Weston's *Auto-biography,* p. 67, n3 – annotating Weston's variant account, pp. 61–2.

31 Cf. C. Devlin, *op. cit.* pp. 333–5; also P. Caraman, *John Gerard, the Autobiography of an Elizabethan,* p. 154 and App. E, pp. 299–300.

32 Cf. J. D. Wilson, New Cambridge edition of *Hamlet,* p. 236.

33 Cf. P. Caraman, *Henry Garnet and the Gunpowder Plot,* pp. 406–19 and 447–8.

34 Cf. H. L. Rogers, '*Double Profit' in Macbeth.*

35 Cf. L. Hotson, *I, William Shakespeare,* p. 197, and the genealogical table in H. Mutschmann and K. Wentersdorf, *Shakespeare and Catholicism,* p. 422.

36 Cf. T. Clancy, *Papist Pamphleteers,* pp. 82–106, P. Caraman, *op. cit.* pp. 284–301, H. Mutschmann and K. Wentersdorf, *op. cit.* pp. 22–6.

37 The campaign goes back to W. Charke's official answer to Campion's 'Brag', *An Answer to a Seditious Pamphlet lately cast abroad by a Jesuit, with a discovery of that blasphemous sect* (1580), and to Sir William Cecil's *The Execution of Justice in England* (1583). Cf. J. H. Pollen, 'The Politics of English Catholics during the Reign of Queen Elizabeth', *The Month,* 1902, pp. 43–60, 131–48, 290–305, 394–411, 600–18; 71–87, 176–88.

IV Catholic Clergy

1 Cf. E. I. Fripp, *Shakespeare, Man and Artist,* Vol. I, pp. 408–11.

2 Cf. T. W. Baldwin, *Shakespeare Adapts a Hanging,* and *On the Compositional Genetics of the Comedy of Errors,* pp. 352–53.

3 Cf. Sir E. Chambers, *William Shakespeare,* Vol. II, p. 252.

4 Robert Persons, for example, was variously addressed in letters from England as 'Mark Mercante, Florence', and 'Mr Luke, merchant, at Venice'; cf. H. Foley, *Records of the English Province, S.J.* Series IX–XI, pp. 588–89, Vol. V, p. 853.

5 Cf. C. Devlin, *Hamlet's Divinity,* pp. 20–2. There may be other echoes of the locality in *Two Gentlemen of Verona,* 'by the abbey wall' (v. 1), and in *Romeo and Juliet,* 'behind the abbey wall' (ii. 4).

6 Comments on journalism in *The Sanity of Art* (1908).

7 For an account of the rack and other tortures used on priests, cf. P. Caraman, *John Gerard,* pp. 132–43, and *The Other Face,* pp. 233–44, also A. Meyer, *England and the Catholic Church under Elizabeth,* pp. 179–88.

8 Quoted by J. Morris, *The Troubles of Our Catholic Forefathers,* Vol. III, p. 20.

9 Thomas Fitzherbert 'entered into bonds to give £5,000 unto Topcliffe, if he would persecute his father and his uncle unto death' (letter of Garnet to Persons, 1594; Foley, *Records* Vol. IX, p. 49); cf. C. Devlin, *op. cit.* pp. 65–6.

10 These words of Cecil may also be echoed in Lucio's description of the Duke in *Measure for Measure* (iv. 3) as 'the old fantastical duke of dark corners', who goes around in the disguise of a friar.

11 G. Wilson Knight, *The Wheel of Life*, p. 207, compares Prospero with each of the friars, as all figures of providence.

12 R. M. Frye, *Shakespeare and Christian Doctrine*, p. 136, says of his advice: 'I see no possibility of finding in it even a single attitude which is distinctively Christian.'

13 Cf. *ibid.* pp. 291–2.

14 Cf. my article, 'What's in a Name? – A study of Shakespearian Nomenclature', *English Literature and Language* (Tokyo), 1969, pp. 1–11.

15 The image of a jewel is frequently used by Shakespeare to signify chastity, good name, and the immortal soul; cf. T. W. Baldwin, *On the Compositional Genetics*, p. 179.

16 Cf. discussion on pp. 37–38.

17 This sonnet, if addressed to the young Earl of Southampton, may well have particular reference to the ruins of Beaulieu Abbey, which formed a major part of the Southampton estate.

18 The authenticity of *Henry VI*, especially Part I, has been cast in doubt since Edmund Malone published his *Dissertation on the Three Parts of Henry VI* (1790). His doubts have been upheld by J. D. Wilson, *The Essential Shakespeare*, pp. 44–8, 'Malone and the Upstart Crow', *Shakespeare Survey* No. 4, pp. 56–68, and the New Cambridge edition of *Henry VI* Part I, pp. xxi–xxxi. Few scholars today, however, agree with him.

19 There is a tendency among scholars today to date *King John* before *The Troublesome Reign*. The evidence is given by E. A. J. Honigmann, New Arden edition of *King John*, pp. xi–xxxiii.

20 Article 37 reads: 'The king's majesty hath the chief power in this realm of England, and other his dominions, unto whom the chief government of all estates of this realm, whether they be ecclesiastical or civil, in all causes doth appertain, and is not nor ought to be, subject to any foreign jurisdiction . . The Bishop of Rome hath no jurisdiction in this realm of England.'

21 Cf. R. M. Frye, *op. cit.* pp. 275–93.

22 The authenticity of *Henry VIII* in part has been cast in doubt since the appearance of James Spedding's article, 'Who Wrote Shakespeare's *Henry VIII*?' in *The Gentleman's Magazine* (1850). His conclusions are supported by M. Mincoff, '*Henry VIII* and Fletcher', *The Shakespeare Quarterly*, Summer 1961, pp. 239–60. The authenticity is, however, defended by G. Wilson Knight, *The Crown of Life*, pp. 256–336, and *Shakespeare and Religion*, pp. 75–82, and by R. Foakes, New Arden edition of *Henry VIII*, pp. xvii–xxvi. Cf. fuller discussion of the play on pp. 165–6.

23 Cf. L. Campbell, *Shakespeare's Histories*, pp. 230–7, where a particular parallel is drawn between Scroop and John Leslie, Bishop of Ross.

24 Detailed comparisons between *King John* and *The Troublesome Reign* appear in J. H. de Groot, *The Shakespeares and the Old Faith*, and in H. Mutschmann and K. Wentersdorf, *Shakespeare and Catholicism*, pp. 309–19. L. Campbell, *op. cit.* Ch. XII, presents the play in relation to its Elizabethan background.

V The Bible

1 R. Noble gives a complete summary account of 'Tudor Printed Versions of Scripture' in *Shakespeare's Biblical Knowledge*, pp. 1–17; but he mistakenly attributes the Rheims version to the Jesuits. The professors at Rheims were all members of the secular clergy; but the seminary priests were often mentioned in contemporary writings in the same breath as Jesuits.

2 Cf. R. Noble, *op. cit.* Ch. IV, 'Which Version did Shakespeare use?'; also C. Wordsworth, *Shakespeare's Knowledge and Use of the Bible*, and T. Carter, *Shakespeare and Holy Scripture*.

3 Cf. R. Noble, *op. cit.* p. 88, and C. de Chambrun, *Shakespeare, A Portrait Restored*, p. 23.

4 R. M. Frye, *Shakespeare and Christian Doctrine*, p. 43, maintains that 'Shakespeare's works are pervasively secular'; but from a deeper viewpoint they may equally be described as pervasively religious.

5 The criticism of Sir A. Quiller-Couch, *Shakespeare's Workmanship*, pp. 60–1, may be set beside the appreciation of J. Vyvyan, *Shakespeare and the Rose of Love*, pp. 130–5.

6 Cf. reference on p. 58. There is a possible allusion here to the controversy over the rendering of *Rom.* xiii. 10: whereas other versions had 'love', the Bishops' Bible had 'charity'; cf. R. Noble, *op. cit.* pp. 70–1.

7 The allusions are to the story of Adam in *Genesis*, the parable of the Prodigal Son in *Luke* xv, and St Paul's warning in II *Corinthians* xi against Satan who transforms himself into an angel of light.

8 Cf. my article on 'Shakespeare and the Prodigal Son', *The Bible Today*, December 1970, pp. 172–9. Shakespeare evidently thought of the Parable in pictorial as well as printed terms: cf. *Henry IV* Part II ii. 1, and *The Merry Wives of Windsor* iv. 5.

9 Cf. W. J. Birch, *An Inquiry into the Philosphy and Religion of Shakspere*, p. 12: 'The clowns, and Falstaff, *et hoc genus omne,* are exponents of the altered state of theatrical theology.'

10 Cf. J. Palmer, *Comic Characters of Shakespeare*, who remarks, p. 25, that Shakespeare tends to 'identify himself with the object of his mirth'.

11 Cf. discussion on Persons and Falstaff, pp. 51–2, and Falstaff as Puritan, pp. 165–6. J. D. Wilson, *The Fortunes of Falstaff*, p. 16, remarks: 'Traces of Lollardry may still be detected in Falstaff's frequent resort to Scriptural phraseology and in his affectation of an uneasy conscience.'

12 Cf. N. Coghill, 'The Basis of Shakespearian Comedy', *Essays and Studies* 1950, pp. 18–23.

13 Cf. p. 23; also R. G. Hunter, *Shakespeare and the Comedy of Forgiveness*, pp. 129–30.

14 Cf. J. Vyvyan, *Shakespeare and Platonic Beauty;* also my *Christian Themes in English Literature*, pp. 174–6.

15 Cf. *Matt.* xix. 14 and 24, or *Luke* xviii. 16 and 25. It is significant that both words of Christ occur in the same chapter of the Gospel.

16 Cf. John Vyvyan, *The Shakespearean Ethic,* pp. 102, 149.

17 Cf. R. Noble, *Shakespeare's Biblical Knowledge*, pp. 90–3, Roy Battenhouse, 'Shakespearean Tragedy, a Christian Approach', in *Approaches to Shakespeare*, p. 209; also my article, 'The Base Judean', *Shakespeare Studies* 1962, pp. 6–14.

18 Cf. F. E. Halliday, *Shakespeare in his Age*, p. 290, R. Noble, *Shakespeare's Biblical Knowledge*, p. 82, and V. Whitaker, *Shakespeare's Use of Learning*, p. 18.

19 The character of Lear is interpreted generally as Everyman by J. Danby, *Shakespeare's Doctrine of Nature*, pp. 170–1, and M. Mack, *King Lear in Our Time*, p. 57; specifically as Adam by Roy Battenhouse, 'Shakespearean Tragedy, a Christian Approach', p. 206, and P. Siegel, *Shakespearean Tragedy and the Elizabethan Compromise*, p. 186. Cf. also my article, 'Shakespeare and the Prodigal Son', *The Bible Today*, 1970, pp. 172–9.

20 K. Muir, Arden edition of *King Lear*, identifies the 'twain' as Goneril and Regan; but the theological overtones of the words, 'redeems', 'nature', 'general curse', as well as 'twain', point to a deliberate ambiguity.

21 M. Mack, *King Lear in Our Time*, p. 86, makes but a passing mention of the *pieta* in this connection. Otherwise this significant analogy is passed over in silence by the majority of commentators. Cf. my article, 'The Religious Dimension of *King Lear*', *Shakespeare Studies*, 1969–70, pp. 48–74.

22 Jan Kott, *Shakespeare Our Contemporary*, p. 118, develops an unashamedly existentialist and Beckettian interpretation. W. R. Elton, *King Lear and the Gods*, is a more scholarly exponent of the same theory.

23 The influence of the *Book of Job* on *King Lear* is emphasized in my article, *op. cit.* pp. 67–8. It is entirely overlooked by R. Noble in *Shakespeare's Biblical Knowledge*.

24 This 'kneeling-resurrection' pattern is noted by P. Siegel, *Shakespearean Tragedy*, pp. 181, 185, 230–1, and *Shakespeare in His Time and Ours*, pp. 108–21.

25 John Vyvyan writes to me, in a letter dated 17 August 1965: 'Since talking to you about the final plays an idea struck me that I will just mention but I have no idea how it would work out in detail. I think I told you my opinion that the theme of "man new made" of the earlier plays develops into "the brave new world" or the world new-made in the end plays. At the end of the love tragedies, the actual world still does not measure up to love's standard. But at the end of "The Tempest" it does. That is surely the development of a line of intense thought. Now the theme of man new made obviously comes from the Gospels; and then it struck me for the first time that the idea of the world new made might very well come from St Paul. In fact it could be Shakespeare's version of the Christian hope as St Paul puts it – "the hope being that creation as well as man would one day be delivered from its thraldom, etc." Suppose one were to press very hard on what *exactly* St Paul means in that passage, "The showing forth of the sons of God" is the condition that comes first. Could Shakespeare be presenting that as "man new made" and the "brave new world" as its consequence? Could Prospero's "magic" fit in there? the "rough magic" that was discarded and replaced by something more spiritual? And Ariel first bound and then set free in two stages, could that be symbolic of the nature that now "sighs and throbs with pain" *waiting* for the manifestation of the divine in man through which it will be set free?'

26 G. Wilson Knight, *The Crown of Life*, pp. 76–128, interprets Paulina as the personified Conscience of Leontes and connects her words (following the suggestion of her name) with those of St Paul.

27 Cf. p. 29.

28 Cf. R. M. Frye, *op. cit.* p. 43.

29 R. Noble, *op. cit.* p. 43, and T. W. Baldwin, *William Shakspere's Small Latine & Lesse Greeke*, p. 687, draw attention to the dramatist's familiarity with the 'wisdom' literature of the Old Testament.

VI Anglican Liturgy

1 Heminges and Condell, Shakespeare's fellow-actors and editors of the First Folio, were active in the parish affairs of St Mary's, Aldermanbury: Condell was sidesman in 1606, and Heminges churchwarden in 1609. The name of Augustine Phillips also appears in connection with St Savior's, Southwark. The opinion that Shakespeare, too, was a conforming member of the Church of England is upheld, among others, by E. I. Fripp, *Shakespeare, Man and Artist*, Vol. II, p. 919; by Ivor Brown, *Shakespeare*, p. 331; by T. W. Baldwin, *William Shakspere's Petty School*, p. 221; by A. L. Rowse, *William Shakespeare*, p. 43; and by R. M. Frye, *Shakespeare and Christian Doctrine*, p. 89, who says very confidently: 'We do know that he was a conforming member of the Church of England.'

2 Cf. R. Noble, *Shakespeare's Biblical Knowledge*, pp. 76–82.

3 Cf. *ibid*. p. 168.

4 Cf. *ibid*. p. 86.

5 In these words Shakespeare significantly departs from his source to emphasize that Othello is a baptized Christian.

6 Cf. Noble, *op. cit.* pp. 29–30. The fact that Beatrice is unmarried leaves her without the shelter promised by the *Psalm*.

7 This indebtedness is emphasized by G. R. Owst, *Literature and Pulpit in Medieval England*, pp. 9, 591, 593; and by J. W. Blench, *Preaching in England in the Late 15th and 16th Centuries*, Ch. VI.

8 Cf. the pioneering work of A. Hart, *Shakespeare and the Homilies*, Ch. I, followed by E. M. W. Tillyard, *Shakespeare's History Plays*, and by M. M. Reese, *The Cease of Majesty*.

9 A wider use of the *Homilies* is made by T. W. Baldwin, *On the Compositional Genetics of the Comedy of Errors*; cf. also my article, 'The Homiletic Tradition in Shakespeare's Plays', *Shakespeare Studies* (Tokyo) 1966–7, pp. 72–87.

10 A. Hart, *op. cit.* p. 26, points out how Shakespeare, in common with the dramatists of his age, ascribes to Richard II 'an anachronistic belief in the divine right of kings'.

11 Parallel passages have been noted in Sir Thomas Elyot's *Book of the Governor* (1531) and in Hooker's *Laws of Ecclesiastical Polity* Book I (1594); cf. E. M. W. Tillyard, *The Elizabethan World Picture*, pp. 18–28, and V. K. Whitaker, *Shakespeare's Use of Learning*, pp. 197–9.

12 T. W. Baldwin, *On the Compositional Genetics*, p. 182, requires a careful reading of 'all three parts of the sermon on adultery' before any more ink is spilt on *Measure for Measure*.

13 Cf. L. Campbell, *Shakespeare's Histories*, p. 304.

14 Cf. G. R. Owst, *op. cit.* p. 392, and J. W. Blench, *op. cit.* pp. 342–4.

VII Smith and Hooker

1 Cf. M. Maclure, *The Paul's Cross Sermons*, 1534–1642, pp. 81–6.

2 The life of Henry Smith was written by Thomas Fuller and published in the 1657 edition of his *Sermons*; cf. J. F. Lievsay, 'Silver-tongued Smith, Paragon of Elizabethan Preachers', *Huntington Library Quarterly*, 1947, pp. 13–36.

3 Veiled allusions to *Pierce* in *Love's Labour's Lost* are indicated by F. Yates, *A Study of Love's Labour's Lost*, p. 4. In *Pierce* are to be found a famous defence of stage-plays, with a probable reference to Shakespeare's *Henry VI Part I*, and several interesting parallels with *Hamlet*.

4   Field printed *Venus and Adonis* in 1593, *The Rape of Lucrece* in 1594, and *The Phoenix and the Turtle* in 1601 (as part of *Love's Martyr*).
5   Cf. W. Haller, *The Rise of Puritanism*, pp. 32–4.
6   Cf. my article, 'The Homiletic Tradition in Shakespeare's Plays', *Shakespeare Studies* (Tokyo) 1966–7, pp. 72–87.
7   Cf. V. K. Whitaker, *op. cit.* p. 208: 'Hooker was also of great value to Shakespeare in another way. He organized into a coherent system both the religious doctrines that Shakespeare had learned at school and church and the psychology of which increasing fragments appear in the earlier plays'; also his 'Philosophy and Romance in Shakespeare's "Problem Comedies"', *The Seventeenth Century*, pp. 339–54.
8   Cf. P. Hughes, *The Reformation in England*, Vol. III, p. 227, and L. B. Wright, *Middle-Class Culture in Elizabethan England*, p. 294.
9   Cf. Sir E. Chambers, *William Shakespeare*, Vol II, p. 193. Covell's reply to *A Christian Letter* was entitled *A Just and Temperate Defence of the five books of Ecclesiastical Polity, written by Mr Richard Hooker* (1603).
10   The agnosticism of Shakespeare has been maintained by J. M. Robertson, *Montaigne and Shakespeare*, p. 191; G. Seibel, *The Religion of Shakespeare*, p. 72; I. Brown, *Shakespeare*, p. 331; and E. I. Fripp, *Shakespeare, Man and Artist*, Vol. II, p. 919, who speaks of 'his Reverent Liberalism'. Cf. the discussion on pp. 212–13.
11   Cf. V. Whitaker, *op. cit.* pp. 197–9.
12   Cf. R. W. Chambers, 'Shakespeare and the Play of *More*', *Man's Unconquerable Mind*, pp. 204–49, and 'The Expression of Ideas', *Shakespeare's Hand in The Play of Sir Thomas More*, pp. 142–88.
13   V. Whitaker, *op. cit.* p. 294, draws particular attention to the coincidence between Hooker's ideas in this section and the psychology of *Macbeth*.

VIII   Parsons and Puritans

1   Cf. Sir E. Chambers, *William Shakespeare*, Vol. II, p. 253.
2   Don Armado has been variously identified as Sir Walter Raleigh, Antonio Perez, Gervase Markham and John Florio; Holofernes as Gabriel Harvey, John Florio, George Chapman, Richard Lloyd and Alexander Aspinall; cf. R. Gittings, *Shakespeare's Rival*, F. Yates, *A Study of Love's Labour's Lost*, and R. David, New Arden edition of *Love's Labour's Lost*. Of course, there is no reason why several persons may not be reflected in the same stage character.
3   Cf. G. K. Chesterton, 'On *A Midsummer Night's Dream*', *The Common Man*, pp. 10–21, and 'On Stage Costume', *The Uses of Diversity*, pp. 132–7.
4   Cf. pp. 37–38.
5   Cf. L. Hotson, *The First Night of Twelfth Night*, pp. 99–118, where Malvolio is convincingly identified as Sir William Knollys, Comptroller of the Queen's Household. However, C. de Chambrun, *Shakespeare, A Portrait Restored*, p. 175, relates him to John Florio; and A. L. Rowse, *William Shakespeare*, p. 335, to Sir Thomas Hoby.
6   The anonymous author of the first *Admonition* (1572), in appealing 'to the Christian Reader', takes his stand on 'the testimony of a good conscience'. Subsequently, Cartwright in his *Reply* to Whitgift (1573) professes to 'stay ourselves with the testimony of our own consciences'. The phrase itself is from II *Corinthians* i. 12.
7   *A Dialogue, wherein is plainly laid open the tyrannical dealing of L. Bishops*

against God's children (1590), probably by Job Throckmorton.

8 In his *Reply* Cartwright speaks of 'what time there was more than Egyptiacal and palpable darkness over the face of the whole earth'; and in his English translation of Travers's *Full and Plain Declaration* (1574) he likewise speaks of 'that Egyptiacal darkness of Popery'. This Biblical image is used, with like reference to the age of Popery, in Jewel's *Apology*.

9 Cf. K. Muir, *Shakespeare's Sources*, p. 70, and H. S. Bowden, *The Religion of Shakespeare*, p. 281. The *True Narration* was written in reply to S. Harsnet's *Discovery of the Fraudulent Practices of John Darrell* (1599); cf. p. 54.

10 Cf. W. P. Kennedy, *Parish Life under Queen Elizabeth*, Ch. III, P. Hughes, *The Reformation in England*, Vol. III, pp. 133–46, and R. Bayne, 'Religion', *Shakespeare's England*, Vol. I, pp. 59–61. The general scene in the seventies is described by Bishop Frere, *A History of the English Church in the Reigns of Elizabeth and James I*, p. 208: 'The sacraments had dropped almost out of sight, the churches were profaned and closed, piety was decayed, and a gloom of spiritual apathy had settled over the land.'

11 In his *Reply* to Whitgift.

12 In his *Answer* to the *Admonition* (1572), where he also pleads: 'If tag and rag be admitted [to the ministry] . . it is the fault of some, not of all, nor of the law.'

13 K. Muir, New Arden edition of *King Lear*, p. 111, points out that these verses are a parody of some pseudo-Chaucerian verses to be found in Puttenham's *Art of English Poesy* (1589): 'When faith faileth in priest's saws . . then shall the land of Albion be brought to great confusion.' The anonymous author of *A Declaration of the True Causes* (probably R. Verstegan) introduces his book as 'a commentary upon Chaucer's prophecy'.

14 In his *Admonition to the People of England* (1589).

15 Cf. E. I. Fripp, *Shakespeare, Man and Artist*, Vol. I, pp. 203–5, H. S. Bowden, *op. cit.* p. 113. The identification with Job Throckmorton goes back to Matthew Sutcliffe, *An Answer unto a certain calumnious letter published by Mr Job Throckmorton* (1595).

16 Cf. F. Yates, *A Study of Love's Labour's Lost*.

17 The former interpretation of this passage is given by J. H. Pafford, New Arden edition of *The Winter's Tale*, p. 84; the latter by R. Noble, *Shakespeare's Biblical Knowledge*, p. 183. It may be further illustrated by the account of the dying Martin Marprelate in the anonymous *Martin's Month's Mind* (1589): 'He would have a hornpipe at any hand, because he loved that instrument above measure.'

18 Cf. Josias Nichols, *The Plea of the Innocent* (1602): 'Whoso feareth an oath, or is an ordinary resorter to sermons, earnest against excess, riot, popery, or any disorder, they are called in the university precisians, and in other places puritans.'

19 Cf. B. Johansson, *Religion and Superstition in the Plays of Ben Jonson and Thomas Middleton*.

20 Thus in Middleton's play, *A Trick to Catch the Old One* (1608) a creditor says: 'Do you call us devils? You shall find us Puritans.'

21 The *Second Admonition*, which is sometimes attributed to Cartwright, speaks of 'the time-servers, and such as dally with the shame of nakedness in this time', and elsewhere of 'all other time-servers' and 'men-pleasers'. In his *Reply* to Whitgift's *Answer*, Cartwright accuses his adversary: 'You do *servire scaenae*, that is, you are a time-server.'

22 L. Hotson, *The First Night of Twelfth Night*, pp. 93–118, points out that

Banbury, the seat of Knollys, was a hot-bed of Puritanism, as well as being famous for its cakes and ale.

23 Cf. M. M. Knappen, *Tudor Puritanism*. This tenet of the Puritans was generally held as orthodox teaching in the Church of England, as expressed in the *Lambeth Articles* in 1595; but other views were coming to the fore about this time, particularly at Cambridge, where the Calvinist theologians found themselves confronted by a growing tendency to Arminianism.

24 Cf. discussions on Falstaff, pp. 51, 94.

25 Cf. the Genevan note to II *Thess*. iii. 10: 'Then by the word of God none ought to live idly, but ought to give himself to some vocation.'

26 The anonymous author of *A Defence of the Ecclesiastical Regiment* (1574) speaks of 'our precise apostles', 'our precisians', 'such precise correctors', 'that so precisely stand on trifles of very small account'. In two later Puritan dialogues, a usurer calls the Puritans 'these precise and hot preachers' (Udall's *Diotrephes*), and a papist remarks, 'I care for none of these precise fellows' (*A Dialogue, wherein is plainly laid open*. . .).

27 From his *Modest and Reasonable Examination* (1604), written in answer to Nichols's *Plea of the Innocent* (1602).

28 Cf. D. McGinn, 'The Precise Angelo', *Joseph Quincy Adams Memorial Studies*, p. 132.

29 In his *Second Reply* (1575) to Whitgift's *Second Answer*.

30 Cf. P. N. Siegel, 'Shylock and the Puritan Usurers', *Studies in Shakespeare*, pp. 129–38; also my article, 'The Religious Implications of *The Merchant of Venice*', *English Literature and Language* (Tokyo) 1969, pp. 62–80.

31 Cf. G. Wilson Knight, *The Crown of Life*, pp. 253–55, and C. Leech, *Shakespeare's Tragedies*, pp. 137–58.

32 Cf. G. Wilson Knight, *op. cit.* pp. 244, 253.

33 Cf. E. I. Fripp, *op. cit.* Vol. II, pp. 838–45.

34 Cf. H. A. Hanley, 'Shakespeare's Family in Stratford Records', *TLS*, 21 May 1964.

35 Cf. E. I. Fripp, *op. cit.* Vol. II, pp. 881–2, and H. Mutschmann and K. Wentersdorf, *Shakespeare and Catholicism*, pp. 181–4.

IX   Henry VII and Elizabeth

1 This may be hinted at in the words of Ulysses, *Troilus and Cressida* iii. 3: 'There is a mystery – with whom relation durst never meddle – in the soul of state.' There is a supreme irony in them.

2 Cf. Note 3 to Ch. VIII, p. 286.

3 Cf. Note 22 to Ch. IV, p. 282.

4 Cf. *Johnson on Shakespeare*, ed. Sir Walter Raleigh, p. 152: 'The genius of Shakespeare comes in and goes out with Catherine.'

5 *Shakespeare Commentaries*, (1852) translated by F. Bunnett (1863), p. 823.

6 Cf. St Augustine, *Confessions* X. 27: 'Too late have I loved you, Beauty so ancient and so new, too late have I loved you!' – also echoed in *Romeo and Juliet* i. 5: 'My only love. . . too early seen unknown, and known too late!'

7 In essay on 'Dante', *Selected Essays*, p. 245.

8 This parallel was first noted by R. Simpson, and incorporated in H. S. Bowden, *The Religion of Shakespeare*, pp. 289–90. Cf. also p. 26.

9 Cf. interpretation proposed on pp. 83–4.

10 Cf. Isaac's blessing of Esau in *Gen*. xxvii. 39: 'Thy dwelling shall be the fatness of the earth, and of the dew of heaven from above.'

11 Imogen is likewise called 'goddess-like' (iii. 2) and 'angel-like' (iv. 2).

12 Cf. interpretation proposed on p. 83.

13 'Paragon' is a word used also of Desdemona in *Othello* ii. 1, and of the ideal man in *Hamlet* ii. 2.

14 J. M. Nosworthy, New Arden edition of *Cymbeline*, p. 185, is at a loss to explain the words 'upon a rock'; but the mention of 'holy water' a few lines later suggests an ecclesiastical reference, to *Matt.* xvi. 18: 'Upon this rock I will build my church.' Cf. *King Lear* iv. 3, where Cordelia's tears are similarly described as 'the holy water from her heavenly eyes'.

15 *The Blanket of the Dark* (1931).

16 Quoted in *The Life of Sir Thomas More*, by his great-grandson Thomas More (Cresacre More) (1726), p. 289.

17 *The Life of Sir Thomas More* (from the Latin work, *Tres Thomae*, 1588), translated and edited by E. Reynolds, p. 191.

18 Cf. J. D. Wilson, *What Happens in Hamlet*, pp. 28–9, and New Cambridge edition of *Hamlet*, p. 149.

19 I.e. her references to 'cockle hat and staff', emblems of the medieval pilgrims, and her prayer, 'God ha' mercy on his soul, and of all Christian souls! I pray God.' (iv. 5).

20 Cf. arguments to the contrary, that *The Troublesome Reign* was composed after *King John*, in E. A. J. Honigmann, New Arden edition of *King John*, pp. xi–xxxiii.

21 Cf. discussion on p. 78.

22 Cf. L. Hotson, *The First Night of Twelfth Night*, pp. 121ff.

23 W. H. Matchett, *The Phoenix and the Turtle*, leads up to the conclusion, p. 202: 'Shakespeare in 1601, in the poem(s) we have come to know as "The Phoenix and the Turtle", paid tribute to Essex and Elizabeth, but qualified the tribute by introducing an ultimately negative rational evaluation.'

24 Cf. Sir E. Chambers, *William Shakespeare*, Vol. II, p. 266.

25 Cf. *ibid.* p. 189.

26 Cf. L. B. Campbell, *op. cit.* pp. 126–67.

27 In his *Defence of the Right High, Mighty and Noble Princess Mary Queen of Scotland* (1569), quoted by L. B. Campbell, *op. cit.* pp. 143–4.

28 Cf. R. Simpson, 'The Political Use of the Stage in Shakespeare's Time', *New Shakespeare Society's Transactions*, 1874, and E. Albright, 'Shakespeare's Richard II and the Essex Conspiracy', *PMLA*, 1927, p. 686.

29 Cf. L. B. Campbell, *op. cit.* p. 161, and A. Fraser, *Mary Queen of Scots*, pp. 634–5.

30 Cf. L. B. Campbell, *op. cit.* pp. 232–5; also the discussion of Scroop above, pp. 85–6.

31 Cf. V. McNabb, 'Is *Macbeth* a Study of Queen Elizabeth?', *Dublin Review*, July 1902, pp. 97–110.

32 This account was first published in Persons's *Judgment of a Catholic Englishman* in 1608. Cf. P. Caraman, *The Other Face*, pp. 285–7, and T. H. Clancy, *Papist Pamphleteers*, pp. 190–1, 229.

33 Cf. L. B. Campbell, *op. cit.* pp. 306–34.

34 Camden notes in his *Annales* (1615) that 'openly he was accounted in the number of commendable men, but privily he was ill spoken of by the most sort'. A contemporary epitaph on the Earl is given in P. Caraman, *op. cit.* pp. 282–3, concluding with the lines: 'Here lies the Earl of Leicester/Whom earth and heaven hates.'

35 Cf. note 32.

36 Cf. Sir E. Chambers, *op. cit.* p. 326.

37 Cf. J. D. Wilson, *What Happens in Hamlet*, pp. 28–30, and New Cambridge edition of *Hamlet*, pp. 148–9; also G. Wilson Knight, *Byron and Shakespeare*, p. 5.

38 The advice given by Euphues to Philautus in Lyly's *Euphues his England* (1580).

39 Campion's last words were a prayer 'for Elizabeth your Queen and my Queen, unto whom I wish a long quiet reign with all prosperity'. Cf. the anonymous *True report of the death and martyrdom of Mr Campion Jesuit and priest*, attributed to Thomas Alfield (1582).

40 Cf. P. Hughes, *The Reformation in England*, Vol. III, pp. 379–83, and J. B. Code, *Queen Elizabeth and the English Catholic Historians*, pp. 40–3.

41 A. L. Rowse, *William Shakespeare*, p. 392, notes the parallel between the characters of Antony and Essex. That between Cleopatra and Elizabeth is implied poetically by T. S. Eliot in *The Waste Land*.

42 Cf. Sir E. Chambers, *op. cit.* p. 255.

X   Elizabethan Atheism

1 Cf. John Carpenter, *A Preparative to Contentation* (1597): 'In this world, Diagoras the Atheist . . and the Cyclopical Epicures do take their pleasure to jest at the providence of God' – quoted by W. R. Elton, *King Lear and the Gods*, pp. 22–3.

2 A similar complaint was made by Augustine Baker, who was converted from Anglicanism in 1607: he observes how thousands of Catholic youths, 'in tract of time and sensim, and indeed as it were unawares to themselves, become neutrals in religion.' A case in point is that of the young John Donne. Cf. P. Hughes, *The Reformation in England*, Vol. III, p. 60.

3 Cf. references on Shakespeare's 'agnosticism', note 10 to Ch. VII.

4 Cf. W. J. Birch, *An Inquiry into the Philosophy and Religion of Shakespeare*, p. 10. He there cites the authority of Gifford and Johnson, who both 'expressed themselves most decidedly in reference to the irreligion of Shakespeare.'

5 Cf. H. Thurston, 'Catholic Writers and Elizabethan Readers: I', *The Month*, December 1894, p. 475.

6 Cf. H. Thurston, 'The Spiritual Testament of John Shakespeare', *The Month*, November 1911, p. 488. A similar opinion is voiced by Newman in a letter dated 7 June 1874, 'that he was probably a Catholic in his general sentiments', but that like so many of his fellow-countrymen he had lapsed into a practical irreligion. Cf. his lecture on 'Catholic Literature in the English Tongue', in *The Idea of a University*, and Macaulay's essay on 'Lord Burleigh and his Times'.

7 Cf. G. T. Buckley, *Atheism in the English Renaissance*, pp. 18–19: 'Stoicism made for rationalism because it laicized morals, removed them from the church and placed them in the sphere of reason . . . it drew men's minds to other religious systems and suggested a comparison not always unfavourable to the non-Christian creeds.'

8 Cf. W. K. Wimsatt, 'Poetry and Morals', *Thought*, June 1948, p. 286.

9 Cf. G. Wilson Knight, *The Crown of Life*, pp. 96–7, 128, and *Shakespeare and Religion*, p. 299.

10 N. Coghill, 'The Basis of Shakespearian Comedy', *Essays and Studies*, 1950, pp. 1–28, develops the thesis that Shakespeare's comedies follow 'a tradition that evolved during the Middle Ages', a tradition not of satire, but of romance. Cf. also G. K. Chesterton, 'The Humour of King Herod', *The Uses*

of Adversity, pp. 96–100, and J. Vyvyan, Shakespeare and the Rose of Love.

11 Compare the opposing views on Falstaff of A. C. Bradley, 'The Rejection of Falstaff', Oxford Lectures on Poetry (1909), and J. D. Wilson, The Fortunes of Falstaff (1943).

12 Cf. W. R. Elton, op. cit. p. 334.

13 Cf. J. Vyvyan, Shakespeare and Platonic Beauty, and R. Simpson, An Introduction to the Philosophy of Shakespeare's Sonnets; also in general, L. Einstein, The Italian Renaissance in England.

14 On Bruno's visit to England, cf. F. A. Yates, Giordano Bruno and the Hermetic Tradition, pp. 205–56; J. M. Stone, 'Giordano Bruno in England', Studies from Court and Cloister, and 'Atheism under Elizabeth and James I', The Month, June 1894, pp. 174–87; and R. McNulty, 'Bruno at Oxford', Renaissance News, 1960, pp. 300–5. An interesting contemporary account is given by G. Abbot, The Reasons which Doctor Hill hath brought. . . (1604): 'That Italian Kidnapper. . . undertook among very many other matters to set on foot the opinion of Copernicus, that the earth did go round and the heavens did stand still; whereas in truth it was his own head which rather did run round, and his brains did not stand still.'

15 Cf. F. A. Yates, op. cit. pp. 356–47, and A Study of Love's Labour's Lost, pp. 89–136. On Bruno's possible influence on Hamlet, cf. G. Brandes, William Shakespeare, a Critical Study, and J. M. Robertson, Montaigne and Shakespeare.

16 The theory of the 'school of night' is developed by A. Acheson, Shakespeare and the Rival Poet, M. C. Bradbrook, The School of Night, and F. A. Yates, A Study of Love's Labour's Lost; cf. also W. Oakeshott, The Queen and the Poet, pp. 100–27.

17 G. T. Buckley, op. cit. p. 137, dismisses Persons's information with contempt as that of 'a notorious plotter who had barely escaped from England with his life on account of his complicity in the famous Babington plot'. But besides the facts that Persons had nothing to do with this plot and had left England some five years earlier, he was remarkably well informed about events in England, as superior of the Jesuits there.

18 Cf. C. Tucker Brooke, The Life of Marlowe, pp. 56–64, 97–107, and appendices on Greene's admonition, Baines' deposition, and Kyd's statements; P. Kocher, 'Marlowe's Atheist Lecture', Marlowe (Twentieth Century Views), pp. 159–66; G. T. Buckley, 'The Atheism of Christopher Marlowe', op. cit. pp. 121–36; and Roy Battenhouse, Marlowe's Tamburlaine.

19 Cf. G. B. Harrison, edition of Willobie his Avisa, pp. 255–71; G. T. Buckley, op. cit. pp. 137–52; Roy Battenhouse, op. cit. pp. 50–68.

20 Cf. F. A. Yates, op. cit. pp. 74–88, and G. B. Harrison, introduction to Willobie his Avisa. Harvey refers scornfully to 'the multiplying spirit . . of the villanist, that knocketh the nail on the head, and spurreth out farther in day than the quickest artist in a week'.

21 Cf. V. K. Whitaker, Shakespeare's Use of Learning, p. 100–1, where he suggests that 'his befuddlement by Chapman perhaps resulted in brilliant comedy'.

22 Cf. Roy Battenhouse, op. cit. pp. 69–85.

23 Among recent exponents of the theory that Marlowe is the rival poet are A. L. Rowse, William Shakespeare, and L. Hotson, Mr W.H.

24 Cf. T. H. Clancy, Papist Pamphleteers, pp. 159–91, where he deals with 'political atheism', especially as attacked by T. Fitzherbert, Treatise Concerning Policy and Religion (1606, 1610).

25 Cf. G. T. Buckley, op. cit. pp. 35–6; L. Einstein, op. cit. pp. 291–4; also F. Raab, The English Face of Machiavelli.

26 The Machiavellianism of Raleigh is discussed by F. Raab, *op. cit.* pp. 70–6.
27 The letter to Cecil is quoted by L. Hicks, 'Sir Robert Cecil, Father Persons and the Succession', *Archivum Historicum* 1955, pp. 103–4.
28 For the influence of Machiavelli on Marlowe's plays, cf. L. Einstein, *op. cit.* pp. 368–9; Roy Battenhouse, *op. cit.* pp. 206–16.
29 The literary and dramatic ancestry of the stage Machiavel is traced by B. Spivack, *Shakespeare and the Allegory of Evil*, pp. 28–59, by D. Cole, *Suffering and Evil in the Plays of Christopher Marlowe*, pp. 23–38, and by M. M. Reese, *The Cease of Majesty*, pp. 92–104.
30 E. M. W. Tillyard, *Shakespeare's History Plays*, p. 208, remarks that in these plays 'Respublica or England is the hero, invisible yet present'; cf. also my article, 'Shakespeare's Medieval Inheritance', *Shakespeare Studies* (Tokyo) 1963, pp. 49–62.
31 Cf. S. L. Bethell, 'Shakespeare's Imagery: the Diabolic Images in *Othello*', *Shakespeare Survey* 5, p. 70: 'The beliefs already ascribed to Iago are made with sufficient point for him to be recognized by an Elizabethan audience as an "atheist" . . We could accept Iago as a "practical atheist", one who lives by an atheistic code without making any deliberate intellectual rejection of religion.'
32 Cf. J. M. Robertson, *Montaigne and Shakespeare*; G. C. Taylor, *Shakespeare's Debt to Montaigne*; and T. Spencer, *Shakespeare and the Nature of Man*, pp. 32–40. D. G. James, *The Dream of Learning*, pp. 57–58, also draws attention to the influence of Montaigne on *Hamlet* and *Troilus and Cressida*.
33 Montaigne did not agree with 'the new fangles of Luther'; but in his 'Apology of Raymond Sebond' he criticizes the critic of Luther for his excessive trust in the 'discourse of reason'.
34 Cf. K. Muir, New Arden edition of *King Lear*, pp. 249–53: App. 6. Florio and *King Lear*; also W. R. Elton, *op. cit. passim*. The latter draws attention to Montaigne's quotation of Plautus, à propos of Gloucester's cry of despair 'The gods play at hand-ball with us, and toss us up and down on all hands', and notes the further echo in *Pericles* ii. 1.
35 Cf. discussion on p. 106, with note 29 to Ch. V.
36 This is often implied in the interpretation of the last plays as seasonal myths; cf. C. Still, *Shakespeare's Mystery Play: a Study of the Tempest*, and G. Wilson Knight, *The Crown of Life*. This approach is criticized by P. Edwards, 'Shakespeare's Romances: 1900–1957', *Shakespeare Survey* 11, pp. 6–12.
37 Cf. discussion on p. 100, with note 18 to Ch. V.
38 Cf. R. Speaight, *Christian Theatre*, p. 78: 'New myths must be found to clothe the old truths, and they were ready to hand in the rediscovered classics.'
39 Cf. discussion on p. 36, with note 18 to Ch. II.
40 Cf. R. Moffet, '*Cymbeline* and the Nativity', *Shakespeare Quarterly*, spring 1962, pp. 207–18.
41 Cf. discussion on p. 29.
42 Cf. N. Coghill, 'The Basis of Shakespearian Comedy', *Essays and Studies*, 1950, p. 25: 'What story, familiar to Shakespeare and to his audience, does this *Tempest* story of a man and a woman exiled from their natural inheritance for the acquisition of a forbidden knowledge resemble? An answer leaps readily to the mind; it resembles the story of Adam and Eve, type-story of our troubles'; also M. D. Parker, *The Slave of Life*, pp. 188–9.

XI Ethical Viewpoint

1 Cf. W. J. Birch, *An Inquiry into the Philosophy and Religion of Shakespeare*, p. 3.
2 This is the repeated assertion of I. Brown: *Shakespeare*, pp. 20, 331–2, and *How Shakespeare Spent the Day*, p. 10.
3 From Shaw's Prefaces to *Man and Superman*, *Back to Methuselah*, and *Plays Unpleasant*; cf. E. Wilson, *Shaw on Shakespeare*.
4 G. Wilson Knight, *Principles of Shakespearian Production*, p. 17, rejects as meaningless the notion of any religious philosophy in the plays: 'His massed statement includes many philosophies, but is subject to none.'
   In 1592 Henslowe records in his Diary the success of a new play, 'Harey the vi', which is commonly identified as Shakespeare's *Henry VI* Part I (cf. p. 38); and *Pierce Penniless* belongs to the same year.
6 In his Preface to *The Irrational Knot*.
7 Cf. discussion on p. 81.
8 Cf. John Barton, *The Wars of the Roses* – being the revised text of the first tetralogy of history plays, as produced at Stratford in the centenary year, 1964, with introduction.
9 Cf. L. C. Knights, *Shakespeare: The Histories*, p. 8; cf. discussion on pp. 142–3.
10 Cf. G. Wilson Knight, 'Shakespeare and Theology', *Essays in Criticism*, January 1965, p. 101 (later republished in *Shakespeare and Religion*, 'Christian Doctrine', pp. 293–303); with my criticism of his article in the *Critical Forum*, January 1966, pp. 118–22. Cf. also my article, 'Shakespeare and Wilson Knight', *Shakespeare Studies* (Tokyo) 1967–8, pp. 75–93.
11 Cf. R. W. Chambers, 'Shakespeare and the Play of *More*', *Man's Unconquerable Mind*, pp. 204–49.
12 M. D. Parker's *The Slave of Life* is sub-titled 'A Study of Shakespeare and the Idea of Justice' – with the complementary idea of Mercy; cf. also H. Matthews, *Character and Symbol in Shakespeare's Plays*, pp. 108–16.
13 Cf. J. Vyvyan, *The Shakespearean Ethic*, p. 38: 'It is a principle with Shakespeare that if the hero's actions are right, the tragic ending does not take place'; and *Shakespeare and Platonic Beauty*, p. 104: 'It is the law with Shakespeare that the measure his characters mete is meted to them again'; cf. also my *Christian Themes in English Literature*, pp. 55–6.
14 Cf. discussion on pp. 222–3.
15 On the regeneration of Hamlet, cf. I. Ribner, *Patterns in Shakespearian Tragedy*, p. 80 (where a full bibliography of this point is given); also C. S. Lewis, 'Hamlet: the Prince or the Poem?', *Studies in Shakespeare*, p. 212: 'The world of Hamlet is a world where one has lost his way. The Prince also has no doubt lost his, and we can tell the precise moment at which he finds it again.' The opposite opinion is expressed by J. Vyvyan, *The Shakespearean Ethic*, p. 59: 'There is no regeneration in the last act'; also by Roy Battenhouse, *Shakespearean Tragedy*, p. 250.
16 Cf. Roy Battenhouse, 'Shakespearean Tragedy: a Christian Approach', *Approaches to Shakespeare*, p. 207: 'Another way to viewing the logic of Lear would be to say that its hero is analogous to the prodigal son'; and D. G. James, *The Dream of Prospero*, p. 24: 'Shakespeare seems here to develop lines in the old play of *King Lear* as to invoke the thought of the Prodigal'; also the discussion on p. 93, and note 8 to Ch. V.
17 G. Wilson Knight, 'Jesus and Shakespeare', *Shakespeare and Religion*, p. 71, draws a contrast between the love of Christ and 'the Shakespearian Eros'; but J. Vyvyan, *Shakespeare and the Rose of Love*, p. 59, notes that while

remaining 'close to the spirit of the Gospels', Shakespeare 'preserves the essence of the Rose'.

18 Cf. H. Charlton, *Shakespearian Comedy*, p. 48, in speaking of *The Comedy of Errors*.

19 J. D. Wilson, *The Fortunes of Falstaff*, p. 11, remarks that 'it is the critics, and not Shakespeare, who have been swept off their feet by Falstaff'.

20 Isabella is defended against her critics by R. W. Chambers, *'Measure for Measure', Man's Unconquerable Mind*, pp. 277–310, and by C. J. Sisson, 'The Mythical Sorrows of Shakespeare', *Studies in Shakespeare*, pp. 21–2.

21 Cf. G. Wilson Knight, *The Crown of Life*, pp. 253–55, and C. Leech, *Shakespeare's Tragedies*, Ch. VII; also discussion on p. 172.

22 For the impact of this traditional theme on Shakespeare's plays, cf. Roy Battenhouse, '*Measure for Measure* and the Christian Doctrine of the Atonement', *PMLA*, December 1946, pp. 1029–59; N. Coghill, 'The Basis of Shakespearian Comedy', *Essays and Studies* 1950, pp. 50–1; H. Matthews, *Character and Symbol in Shakespeare's Plays*, pp. 71–82; R. G Hunter, *Shakespeare and the Comedy of Forgiveness*, pp. 17–20; and discussion on pp. 33–4.

23 P. Siegel, *Shakespearian Tragedy and the Elizabethan Compromise*, pp. 174–81, and *Shakespeare in His Time and Ours*, pp. 108–21, notes the significance of the 'kneeling-resurrection pattern' in *King Lear*.

24 Cf. D. Traversi, *Shakespeare, The Last Phase*, p. 119: '"Grace" is a word to note in Shakespeare's later plays'; and R. Speaight, *Nature in Shakespearian Tragedy*, p. 188: 'The key-word of "grace" – one of the ideas that we have been tracing thoughout this study.'

25 Cf. discussion of *Cymbeline* by Sir. A. Quiller-Couch, *Shakespeare's Workmanship*.

26 Both M. M. Mahood, *Shakespeare's Wordplay*, p. 150, and M. D. Parker, *The Slave of Life*, p. 183, speak of 'grace' as a keyword of *The Winter's Tale;* cf. my article, 'A Theology of Grace in *The Winter's Tale*', *English Literature and Language* (Tokyo) 1964, pp. 27–50.

27 Antony himself is addressed as 'thou Arabian bird!' (iii. 2). On the other hand, in *The Phoenix and the Turtle* Shakespeare speaks of the two birds as 'twain' and praises their 'mutual flame' – as it were anticipating 'such a mutual pair and such a twain' (*Antony and Cleopatra* i. 1).

28 Cf. W. K. Wimsatt, 'Poetry and Morals', *Thought*, June, 1948, p. 295.

29 Cf. G. Wilson Knight, *Byron and Shakespeare*, p. 234, and E. M. Waith, *The Herculean Hero*, pp. 113–21.

30 Cf. *A Midsummer Night's Dream* i. 1: 'Quick bright things come to confusion'; and *Richard II* ii. 1: 'Violent fires soon burn out themselves'.

31 Cf. J. D. Wilson, *op. cit.* pp. 70–3.

32 Cf. T. Spencer, *Shakespeare and the Nature of Man*, pp. 109–21; also my *Introduction to Shakespeare's Plays*, pp. 89–95.

33 Cf. *ibid.* p. 128.

34 Richard is defended by John Masefield: 'It is part of his tragedy that it is not intellect that triumphs in this world, but a stupid thought righteous something, incapable of understanding intellect'. Falstaff, in Bradley's opinion, enables us to take a moral holiday from 'old father antic the law and the categorical imperative' ('The Rejection of Falstaff', *Oxford Lectures on Poetry*, p. 262). Macbeth is defended by G. Wilson Knight: 'He has established an honest relationship with the community. He knows what he has done, and knows that other people know it' ('The Avenging Mind', *Shakespeare and Religion*, p. 190).

35 The question of Othello's damnation is discussed by S. L. Bethell, 'Shakespeare's Imagery: the Diabolical Images in *Othello*', *Shakespeare Survey* 1952, pp. 78–9; P. N. Siegel, 'The Damnation of Othello', *PMLA*, 1953, pp. 1068–78, and *Shakespearean Tragedy and the Elizabethan Compromise*, pp. 128–31; I. Ribner, *Patterns in Shakespearian Tragedy*, pp. 112–15; and R. H. West, *Shakespeare and the Outer Mystery*, pp. 111–26. On the reading of 'base Judean', cf. note 17 to Ch. V.

36 W. M. Merchant, *op. cit.* p. 77, speaks of Kent's 'stoic acceptance of suicide'.

37 G. Wilson Knight, *The Sovereign Flower*, p. 249, insists that for Shakespeare salvation comes about 'not through repentance, but by recognition and acceptance'; cf. also his *Shakespeare and Religion*, pp. 13, 18, 186, 224, 232, 296.

38 Cf. O. J. Campbell, 'The Salvation of Lear', *ELH*, 1948, pp. 93–109.

XII Theology

1 Cf. I. Brown, *How Shakespeare Spent the Day*, p. 10: 'Obviously his mind ranged widely, but he was not a consistent or committed man with a clear-cut philosophy. Amid a life of such various activities, his thinking was quick impulsive and intermittent.'

2 W. C. Curry, *Shakespeare's Philosophical Patterns*, p. xii, acknowledges 'only Shakespeare's individual dramas, each one of which is a unique world unto itself, governed by its proper laws, peopled by its special characters, and integrated by a philosophical pattern separate and distinct from all others'. In particular, he discerns a scholastic pattern in *Macbeth* and a Neo-Platonic pattern in *The Tempest*. For him Shakespeare is the great dilettante.

3 R. M. Frye, *Shakespeare and Christian Doctrine*, p. 94, denies that the dramatist embodied in his plays 'an exclusively Christian theology'; and p. 133, emphasizes that 'he was primarily concerned with the life of man within the secular order'.

4 Cf. G. Wilson Knight, *Principles of Shakespearian Production*, p. 231: 'Orthodox Christianity and Shakespeare confront each other with a contrast and a similarity that challenge our attention'; also *passim* in *Shakespeare and Religion*.

5 Cf. R. M. Frye, *op. cit.* pp. 275–93: 'The Roman Catholic Censorship of Shakespeare, 1641–1651'.

6 Cf. J. Vyvyan, *The Shakespearean Ethic*, p. 89: 'His debt to the Middle Ages is very great, and it includes their respect for logic. This is fortunate for us; because it means that he develops his ideas, though often veiled in allegory, with a consistency that we discover we can trust'; also my article, 'Shakespeare's Medieval Inheritance', *Shakespeare Studies* (Tokyo) 1963, pp. 49–62.

7 The term is derived from the text of *Ecclesiasticus* vii. 40: 'Remember the last things.' Sir Thomas More, *The Four Last Things* (1522), follows Denis the Carthusian, in defining them as 'death, doom, pain and joy'. Cf. my *Christian Themes in English Literature*, pp. 97–103.

8 R. M. Frye, *op. cit.* p. 134, dismisses such expressions as 'essentially commonplaces, varied from immemorial usage only enough to make poetic what might otherwise have been a mere cliché or platitude'. He does not explain why they recur so often in the plays.

9 Cf. John Donne, *Holy Sonnets* VII: 'At the round earth's imagin'd corners, blow/Your trumpets, Angels, and arise, arise/From death, you numberless infinities/Of souls, and to your scattered bodies go.'

10 R. M. Frye, *op. cit.* p. 134, says: 'References to heaven are not only rare but exceedingly brief'; though a glance at the *Concordance* reveals more than 600 such references. Discussions of Shakespeare's imagery, from C. Spurgeon onwards, mostly overlook the important imagery of heaven and hell.

11 Cf. J. Vyvyan, *Shakespeare and the Rose of Love*, p. 175: 'There are depths of reason below this surface of emotion.'

12 Cf. J. D. Wilson, *What Happens in Hamlet*, pp. 52–60; I. J. Semper, *Hamlet Without Tears*, pp. 14–40, and 'The Ghost in *Hamlet*, Pagan or Christian?' *The Month*, April 1953, pp. 222–34; and L. B. Campbell, *Shakespeare's Tragic Heroes*, pp. 121–8.

13 Cf. discussion on p. 29, with note 9 to Ch. II.

14 I. Brown, *Shakespeare*, p. 330, asks: 'Was it ever Christian doctrine that spirits are imprisoned at the North Pole or are blown round about the pendent world?' It was never indeed Christian doctrine, but it was the Christian imagination of the Middle Ages, which fed upon the apocryphal *Visio Pauli* and *Gospel of Nicodemus*. Cf. R. Farmer, *On the Learning of Shakespeare* (1767).

15 K. Muir, New Arden edition of *King Lear*, p. 190, cites the medieval *Prick of Conscience*, lines 6576 and 7124.

16 Cf. E. M. W. Tillyard, *Shakespeare's Last Plays*, p. 84; R. Speaight, *Nature in Shakespearian Tragedy*, p. 121; J. Vyvyan, *The Shakespearean Ethic*, p. 168; M. Lings, *Shakespeare in the Light of Sacred Art*, p. 20; and my own *Introduction to Shakespeare's Plays*, pp. 147, 153–4.

17 Cf. R. M. Frye, *op. cit.* p. 165. In Bartlett's *Concordance* there are twelve columns of references to God.

18 Cf. note 15 to Ch. XI.

19 Cf. R. G. Hunter, *Shakespeare and the Comedy of Forgiveness*, pp. 106–31.

20 Cf. J. F. Danby's study of 'The Two Natures', *Shakespeare's Doctrine of Nature*, pp. 15–23.

21 Cf. D. G. James, *The Dream of Prospero*, pp. 16–19; and my *Christian Themes in English Literature*, p. 75.

22 Cf. my article, 'A Theology of Grace in *The Winter's Tale*', *English Literature and Language* (Tokyo) 1964, pp. 27–50; and the discussion on pp. 234–5.

23 Cf. discussion on pp. 26, 93–4.

24 Cf. G. R. Elliott, *Dramatic Providence in Macbeth*, sub-titled 'A Study of Shakespeare's Tragic Theme of Humanity and Grace.'

General Index

Bibliographical Index

to books mentioned in the notes

Acheson, A. *Shakespeare and the Rival Poet* (1903), x.16

Albright, E. 'Shakespeare's *Richard II* and the Essex Conspiracy', *PMLA* 1927, ix.28

Anderson, M. D. *Drama and Imagery in English Churches* (1963), ii.12, 13, 19, 20

Baker, O. *In Shakespeare's Warwickshire and the Unknown Years* (1937), ii.29

Baldwin, T. W. *On the Compositional Genetics of the Comedy of Errors*, iii.19; iv.2 15; vi.9, 12

— *Shakespeare Adapts a Hanging* (1931), iv.2

— *William Shakespere's Petty School* (1943), ii.23; vi.1

— *William Shakespere's Small Latine & Lesse Greeke* (1944), ii.24; v.29

Bartlett, J. *Complete Concordance to Shakespeare's Dramatic Works and Poems* (1894), xii.10, 17

Barton, J. *The Wars of the Roses* (1970), x.8

Battenhouse, R. *Marlowe's Tamburlaine* (1941), x.18, 19, 22, 28

— *'Measure for Measure* and the Christian Doctrine of the Atonement', *PMLA* 1946, xi.22

— *Shakespearean Tragedy its Art and its Christian Premises* (1969), xi.15

— 'Shakespearean Tragedy, a Christian Approach', in *Approaches to Shakespeare* (1964), v.17, 19; xi.16

Bayne, R. 'Religion', in *Shakespeare's England* (1917), viii.10

Bethell, S. L. 'Shakespeare's Imagery: the Diabolic Images in *Othello*', *Shakespeare Survey* No. 5 (1952), x.31; xi.35

Birch, W. J. *An Inquiry into the Philosophy and Religion of Shakspere* (1848), v.9; x.4; xi.1

Blench, J. W. *Preaching in England in the Late Fifteenth and Sixteenth Centuries* (1964), vi.7, 14

Bowden, H. S. *The Religion of Shakespeare* (1899), ii.2, 4, 7; viii.9, 15; ix.8

Bradbrook, M. C. *The School of Night* (1936), x.16

Bradley, A. C. 'The Rejection of Falstaff', in *Oxford Lectures on Poetry* (1909), x.11; xi.34

Brandes, G. *William Shakespeare, a Critical Study* (1896), x.15

Brooke, C. Tucker *The Life of Marlowe* (1930), x.18

Brown, I. *Shakespeare* (1949), vi.1; vii.10; xi.2; xii.1, 14

— *How Shakespeare Spent the Day* (1963), xi.2

Brownlow, F. W. Doctorate thesis on S. Harsnet's *Declaration of Egregious Popish Impostures*, Univ. of Birmingham (1963), iii.21

Buckley, G. T. *Atheism in the English Renaissance* (1932), x.7, 17, 18, 19, 25

Camm, B. *Forgotten Shrines* (1936), i.4; iii.3

Vyvyan, J. *The Shakespearean Ethic* (1959), ii.12; v.16; xi.13, 15; xii.6, 16
— *Shakespeare and Platonic Beauty* (1961), v.14; x.13; xi.13
— *Shakespeare and the Rose of Love* (1960), v.5; x.10; xi.17; xii.11
Waith, E. M. *The Herculean Hero* (1962), xi.29
West, R. H. *Shakespeare and the Outer Mystery* (1968), xi.35
Whitaker, V. 'Philosophy and Romance in Shakespeare's "Problem
    Comedies"', in *The Seventeenth Century* (1951), vii.7
— *Shakespeare's Use of Learning* (1953), v.18; vi.11; vii.7, 11, 13; x.21
Wilson, E. *Shaw on Shakespeare* (1962), xi.3
Wilson, J. Dover *The Essential Shakespeare* (1932), iv.18
— *The Fortunes of Falstaff* (1943), ii.17; v.11; x.11; xi.19, 31
— 'Malone and the Upstart Crow', *Shakespeare Survey* No. 4 (1951), iv.18
— New Cambridge edition of *Hamlet* (1934), iii.32; ix.18
— New Cambridge edition of *Henry VI* Part I (1952), iv.18
— *What Happens in Hamlet* (1935), ii.10; ix.18, 37; xii.12
Williamson, H. Ross *The Day Shakespeare Died* (1962), iii.4
Wimsatt, W. K. 'Poetry and Morals', *Thought* 1948, x.8; xi.28
Wordsworth, C. *Shakespeare's Knowledge and Use of the Bible* (1864), v.2
Wright, L. B. *Middle-Class Culture in Elizabethan England* (1965), vii.8
Yates, F. A. *Giordano Bruno and the Hermetic Tradition* (1964), x.14, 15
— *A Study of Love's Labour's Lost* (1936), iii.17; vii.3; viii.2, 16; x.15, 16, 20